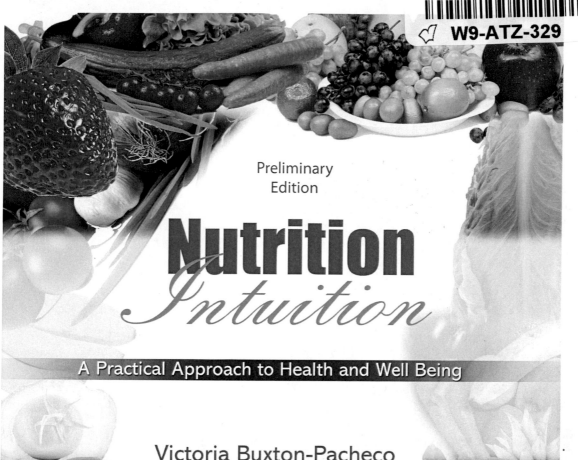

Preliminary
Edition

# Nutrition
## *Intuition*

### A Practical Approach to Health and Well Being

## Victoria Buxton-Pacheco

# Kendall Hunt
publishing company

Food in Focus: © Shutterstock, Inc.
Nutrition Nerd Alert: © Shutterstock, Inc.
Cover image © Shutterstock, Inc.

# Kendall Hunt
publishing company

www.kendallhunt.com
*Send all inquiries to:*
4050 Westmark Drive
Dubuque, IA  52004-1840

Printed in the United States of America
10  9  8  7  6  5  4  3  2  1

# ACKNOWLEDGMENTS

This book is dedicated to my friends and family who always support and encourage me. To my husband Tim for his unconditional love, patience, kindness, and ongoing encouragement that gave me the push to complete this project. To my students who have always been a joy to me at Pasadena City College, thank you for your kind words and appreciation. I would also like to thank Jennifer Jackson and Andrea Chang Bortnik for their contributions to this book. Thank you so much to Shelly and Angela from Kendall Hunt Publishing for your patience and determination to help make this dream become a reality for me.

# BRIEF CONTENTS

# CONTENTS

# ABOUT THE AUTHOR

Victoria Buxton-Pacheco is professor of nutrition at Pasadena City College in the Health Sciences Division. She is also a professor at California State University, Los Angeles in the Kinesiology and Nutritional Sciences Department. She earned her bachelors and masters degree in Nutritional Sciences at California State University, Los Angeles. She also completed her internship program to become a Registered Dietitian at California State University, Los Angeles in the Coordinated Dietetic Program.

Victoria also divides her time between working as an outpatient dietitian for a hospital and working as a consultant dietitian for a physician. Victoria is an active member in the American Academy of Dietetics and Nutrition.

Victoria has been teaching for 10 years for both non-nutrition and nutrition majors. She has a strong appreciation for the goals and objectives in her nutrition courses and understands the needs of the students. This teaching experience, along with her clinical experience, has helped her to create an exciting and refreshing textbook for the introductory nutrition course.

# Nutrition Intuition: A Common Sense Approach

# CHAPTER 1

© 2012, Shutterstock, Inc.

## Learning Objectives

- Learn how nutrition has evolved throughout the years
- Define a calorie
- List the macronutrients and their calories
- Identify water and fat soluble vitamins
- Outline the USDA Dietary Guidelines
- Understand the Dietary Reference Intakes
- Describe who is a nutrition expert

*Intuition* (noun) the power of knowing or understanding something immediately without reasoning or being taught:

Welcome to *Nutrition Intuition: A Practical Approach to Health and Well Being.* I truly believe that many of us possess a basic understanding of nutrition. With so much conflicting information coming from various sources, however, we often lose sight of what is really important. I am very excited to introduce you to the many aspects of nutrition and I hope to dispel many myths and misinformation. In this class you will be taught practical applications which you can start to apply right away. Often I have students who go home after a lecture and want to share this information with their family members. Taking a nutrition class becomes a very personal experience because we eat every day to survive. Have you ever thought of what happens to the foods we eat? Or do you just chew it up, swallow it, and hope for the best? This course will help you understand that nutrition is about the choices we make and how those choices affect us now as well as later in life.

## Functional Food Facts

What exactly is a functional food? A **functional food** is one that has health benefits built right into the food; this can be a whole food, a fortified or enriched food, or a food that has added ingredients to make the food healthier. Certain foods will contain phytochemicals, especially plant-based foods, which provide protective benefits. When we eat the plants, we also get the health benefits which make them good for us. Throughout this textbook you will find functional food facts at the beginning of each chapter. I hope this will encourage you to include a variety of functional foods in your diet.

## The Basics of Nutrition

In order to understand nutrition it is important to cover some key terms and principles that will help you to learn the basics. Every day we make decisions about what to eat, how much to eat, and why we enjoy eating certain foods. We base our decisions on what to eat on certain physiological as well as psychological needs we have as human beings. Our culture and upbringing also have influences on why we choose certain foods. We eat when we are happy, we eat when we are sad, we eat when we are bored, and we eat because there is a special celebration. My point is that we have many different reasons to eat and we do not always think of eating only when we are hungry.

## Nutrition Is a Science?

When we think of science, we usually think of topics such as chemistry, anatomy, and physiology, we do not always think of nutrition as being a science. Of course, compared to other sciences, nutrition is a relatively newer science. **Nutrition** is a science that combines many other sciences such as chemistry, anatomy, and physiology to help us to understand what is happening to the foods we eat and how the body is using important nutrients for energy.

In the early 1900s there was a disease later named pellagra spreading throughout the United States that was characterized by four major symptoms. These symptoms were later labeled the four D's. The symptoms that developed were diarrhea, dermatitis (a skin condition), dementia, and finally death. Most of the cases of pellagra were seen in southern states in the United States. Many people were dying, and in 1914 the U.S. surgeon general asked a physician by the name of Joseph Goldberger to take a closer look at this disease and try to find out how to stop it from spreading. Initial observations made by Dr. Goldberger were that this disease did not appear to be contagious. He noticed that those affected usually lived in poor conditions. In one case Dr. Goldberger had observed that inmates in a prison suffering from these symptoms were in close contact with the prison guards. The guards did not exhibit the same symptoms as the inmates which led Dr. Goldberger to believe that this was not a contagious disease.

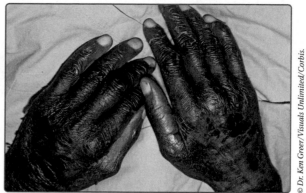

**Figure 1.1**  Man with pellagra

Dr. Goldberger suspected that this disease was caused by something in the diet. The diet consisted of mostly corn, hominy, and grits (a corn product) which were typical staple foods in the South. If you were poor in the South you did not consume very much meat because meat was more expensive.

Several experiments done by Dr. Goldberger proved just that, but critics and other doctors were not convinced. Frustrated with the lack of support from the medical community, Dr. Goldberger took matters into his own hands and formed what he later called a "filth party." He proceeded to inject himself and his assistant with blood from patients who had these symptoms. He even swabbed secretions from patients' eyes and noses and rubbed them into his and his assistant's own eyes and noses. They also ingested scabs from those patients who had dermatitis. As expected, neither Dr. Goldberger nor his assistant got pellagra.[1] I do not think many doctors today would go to such extremes to prove a point. Because of Dr. Goldberger it was later determined that a deficiency of niacin (a B vitamin) was the reason for the development of pellagra. Niacin can stay bound (cannot be used properly) by the body when there is a low protein intake such was the case with those who were too poor to have meat with their meals on a regular basis.

**Figure 1.2**  Dr. Goldberger

[1] Kraut, A: Joseph Goldberger and the war on Pellagra. National Institutes of Health. history.nih.gov/exhibits/Goldberger/docs/pellagra_5.htm. Accessed 6-24-10.

## We Get Energy from Food

When we eat food we obtain energy in the form of calories. A **kilocalorie** (kcal or cal) is a unit of energy needed to raise the temperature of 1 liter of water 1 degree Celsius. Energy in the form of calories is obtained from food. Have you ever wondered how they figure out the calories for all of our foods? The United States and Canada joined in an effort to come up with caloric values for food. The instrument used is called a **bomb calorimeter**. A bomb calorimeter is a device that can measure the energy content of foods in kilojoules (kj). **Kilojoules** are a measurement of how much heat a food gives off when burned in the bomb calorimeter. For example, if we take a medium-size apple and place it in the bomb calorimeter, the apple will be burned to completion. What is leftover is ash and some minerals since most minerals are heat resistant. When we eat the same medium apple, the apple is not burned to completion. There is going to be some fiber that is not digestible as well as other elements to consider, such as the energy requirements of the processes of digestion and absorption. Adjustments are made in the amount of energy that the apple gives off during the burning process which will translate to calories; therefore, when we eat the apple the amount of calories provided will equal about 60.

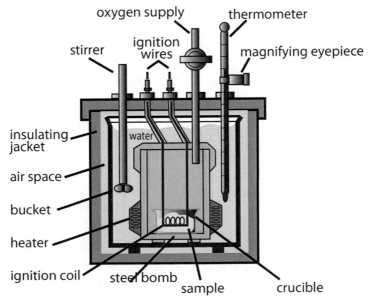

**Figure 1.3** A bomb calorimeter

## Nutrients

The foods that we eat contain nutrients. Food itself gives us calories but the content of the food gives us the nutrients. **Nutrients** are substances important for growth and development. Nutrients are often divided into macronutrients and micronutrients. **Macronutrients** are those nutrients which we need more of to support growth and development in the body; they also provide calories. Examples of macronutrients include carbohydrates, proteins, and fats. **Micronutrients** are those nutrients which are needed in smaller amounts and do not provide any calories. Examples of micronutrients would include vitamins and minerals. When comparing macronutrients to micronutrients, it is important to note that we are referring only to the amounts that are needed in the body. Would you say that any of these macro or micronutrients is more important to our body than others? I would say that all of them are important and play specific roles which we will explore more in later chapters.

### NUTRITION NERD ALERT

Nutrients are nourishing, but even too much of them can be a bad thing. Too much zinc (think supplements) makes your body leach other important minerals, such as copper.

### Essential vs. Nonessential

To say that a nutrient is **essential** means that it is necessary for the body. An essential nutrient is one that cannot be made by the body, so we have to eat it. "If you can't make it, you will have to take it." We often take in essential nutrients by including them in our diets and obtaining them from food sources. Some of these nutrients are needed more often than others. We will look at some essential amino acids (proteins) and a few essential fatty acids (fats) that are necessary for the body and find out from which foods to get them. **Nonessential** then means that our body does make it and therefore we do not have to obtain these particular nutrients from our diets as often.

### Organic vs. Inorganic

When we think of the word *organic* we often think of foods that are grown without pesticides. In nutrition science, however, we when we say organic, we are not talking about organic foods. Instead, we are referring to the chemical composition of nutrients. **Organic** refers to a carbon-containing nutrient such as carbohydrates, proteins, and lipids (fats). Vitamins also contain carbon but do not provide any

calories. Inorganic structures therefore do not contain carbon. Examples of inorganic nutrients include minerals and water. Other important elements that make up the chemical structures of our nutrients include nitrogen (exclusive to protein), oxygen, and hydrogen.

---

### Elements in the Six Classes of Nutrients

Inorganic Nutrients - do not contain carbon

- Minerals
- Water

Organic Nutrients - contain carbon

- Carbohydrates
- Lipids (fats)
- Proteins
- Vitamins

---

## Standards of Nutrition

Standards of nutrition are necessary to help people maintain a healthy balance of all of the nutrients. Committees of scientists and other health professionals use research and statistics to evaluate the needs of a population. Most countries have adopted standards and made recommendations as to how much of these important nutrients we should have on a daily basis. When defining the needs of a population we must first define our population. We will define our population as "all healthy people"; this means that the person is in general good health and not in the hospital. When people are in the hospital or suffering from certain chronic diseases, these conditions can change the needs for that person. In the United States we have the **Dietary Guidelines for Americans**, created and updated by the United States Department of Agriculture and the Department of Health and Human Services.

NUTRITION NERD ALERT

Did you know? Many daily values on nutrition labels are from the 1980s and 1990s. Some are even as old as 1968!

## Dietary Guidelines for Americans, 2010

The 2010 Dietary Guidelines for Americans (the 7th edition of these guidelines) are meant to help the average American make healthy choices and combat the obesity epidemic. Twenty-three Key Recommendations are included in the Guidelines, included under four categories:

- Balancing Calories to Manage Weight
- Foods and Food Components to Reduce
- Foods and Nutrients to Increase
- Building Healthy Eating Patterns[2]

A detailed summary of the Dietary Guidelines is available on the National Dairy Council website at http://www.nationaldairycouncil.org/SiteCollectionDocuments/ education_materials/dietary_guidance/Evolution_of_the_Dietary_Guidelines_for_ Americans_2005-2010.pdf

## Dietary Reference Intakes

In the United States we have Dietary Reference Intakes (DRI) developed by the Institute of Medicine of the National Academies. The following categories are subcategories of the DRI:

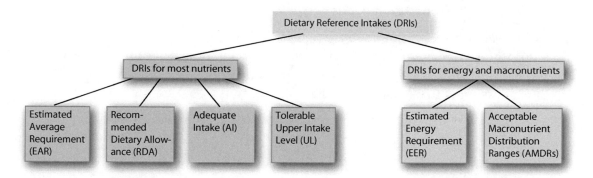

**Figure 1.4** The Dietary Reference Intakes (DRIs) for all nutrients. Note that the Estimated Energy Requirement (EER) only applies to energy (kilocalories), and the Acceptable Macronutrient Distribution Ranges (AMDRs) only applies to the macronutrients and alcohol.

---

[2] http://www.cnpp.usda.gov/Publications/DietaryGuidelines/2010/PolicyDoc/ExecSumm.pdf. Accessed 7-23-11.

### Estimated Average Requirement (EAR)

- The EAR is the median daily intake value that is estimated to meet the requirement of half the healthy individuals in a life-stage and gender group. At this level of intake, the other half of the individuals in the specified group would not have their needs met.

- The EAR is based on a specific criterion of adequacy, derived from a careful review of the literature. Reduction of disease risk is considered along with many other health parameters in the selection of that criterion.

- The EAR is used to calculate the RDA. It is also used to assess the adequacy of nutrient intakes, and can be used to plan the intake of groups.

### Recommended Dietary Allowance (RDA)

- The RDA is the average daily dietary intake level that is sufficient to meet the nutrient requirement of nearly all (97 to 98 percent) healthy individuals in a particular life-stage and gender group.

- The RDA is the goal for usual intake by an individual.

### Adequate Intake (AI)

- If sufficient scientific evidence is not available to establish an EAR on which to base an RDA, an AI is derived instead.

- The AI is the recommended average daily nutrient intake level based on observed or experimentally determined approximations or estimates of nutrient intake by a group (or groups) of apparently healthy people who are assumed to be maintaining an adequate nutritional state.

- The AI is expected to meet or exceed the needs of most individuals in a specific life-stage and gender group.

- When an RDA is not available for a nutrient, the AI can be used as the goal for usual intake by an individual. The AI is not equivalent to an RDA.

### Tolerable Upper Intake Level (UL)

- The UL is the highest average daily nutrient intake level likely to pose no risk of adverse health effects to almost all individuals in a given life-stage and gender group.

- The UL is not a recommended level of intake

- As intake increases above the UL, the potential risk of adverse effects increases.

### Estimated Energy Requirement (EER)

- An EER is defined as the average dietary energy intake that is predicted to maintain energy balance in healthy, normal weight individuals of a defined age, gender, weight, height, and level of physical activity consistent with good health. In children and pregnant and lactating women, the EER includes the needs associated with growth or secretion of milk at rates consistent with good health.

- Relative body weight (i.e., loss, stable, gain) is the preferred indicator of energy adequacy.

### Acceptable Macronutrient Distribution Range (AMDR)

- The AMDR is a range of intake for a particular energy source (protein, fat, or carbohydrate), expressed as a percentage of total energy (kcal), that is associated with reduced risk of chronic disease while providing adequate intakes of essential nutrients.[3]

**NUTRITION NERD ALERT**

Know your food laws. The Food and Drug Administration (FDA) has not finalized the rules for levels of certain ingredients in foods, including some that people may be allergic to at certain levels. This means that there is no guarantee of the honesty of claims such as "gluten free."

---

[3] dsp-psd.pwgsc.gc.ca/collection/H44-87-2005E.pdf. Accessed 6-27-10.

# An Introduction to the Nutrients

## Carbohydrates

**Carbohydrates** are the preferred source of energy for the brain. When we think of carbohydrates, foods like bread, rice, grains, and cereals often come to mind; but did you know that fruit and milk are also good sources of carbohydrates? Carbohydrates provide 4 calories per gram. Carbohydrates can be **simple** and **complex**. In the chapter on carbohydrates we will look at the chemical structure of carbohydrates, which are composed of carbons, hydrogen, and oxygen.

© 2012, Shutterstock, Inc.

## Fats

**Fats** are an important component of energy that we store for future use. Fats are the most energy dense because they provide 9 calories per gram. The chemical structure of fats also contains carbon, hydrogen, and oxygen, and fats are often referred to as **fatty acids**. The length of the fatty acids vary depending on their function.

## Proteins

**Proteins** are critical to the building up and breaking down of structures in the body. Many of the important functions of proteins will be discussed in further detail in a later chapter. Protein provides 4 calories per gram but, unlike fat and carbohydrates, protein is unique because it contains nitrogen in its chemical structure. I often ask if protein is responsible for building muscle, and most people agree; however, protein does not build muscle, muscle builds muscle. Protein helps to repair muscle among many other structures.

© 2012, Shutterstock, Inc.

| Calorie Values | |
| --- | --- |
| **Nutrients** | **KCalories (per gram)** |
| Carbohydrates | 4 cal/gm |
| Protein | 4 cal/gm |
| Fat | 9 cal/gm |
| *alcohol contributes 7 cal/gm but is not considered a nutrient | |

## Water

**Water** is not usually thought of as a nutrient, but water is definitely essential to life. The average human being usually cannot go more than a few days without water. Water is essential in supporting many body functions. Adequate water intake helps to ensure proper cell function, regulation of electrolyte balances, muscle contraction and relaxation, nutrient transport, and excretion of waste products. We will be taking a closer look at the many functions of water in Chapter 9.

© 2012, Shutterstock, Inc.

## Vitamins

**Vitamins** play an important role in energy metabolism of protein, carbohydrates, and fats. Vitamins are organic, which means that they contain carbon in their structure, but they do not provide the body with any calories. Vitamins are divided into two categories, water and fat soluble. The **water soluble vitamins** include all of the B-vitamins and vitamin C. Water soluble vitamins are easily dissolved in water and we store them for a relatively short period of time, which means that we need to intake them more often. The **fat soluble vitamins** dissolve easily in fat and we store them longer in the body. Because we store them for a longer period of time, there is an increased chance that we can intake toxic levels of the fat soluble vitamins (usually in the form of supplements). The fat soluble vitamins include vitamins A, D, E, and K. Both the water and fat soluble vitamins will be discussed further in a future chapter.

**EVERY DAY**
## SUPERFOODS

Broccoli is a nutrient powerhouse. High in vitamin C (a full day's worth can be found in the stalk), beta carotene (especially in dark green/purple flowers), and sulforaphane (a potent cancer fighter).

**Table 1.1** Overview of Vitamins

| Type | Names | Characteristics |
|------|-------|-----------------|
| Fat soluble | A, D, E, and K | Soluble in fat<br>Stored in the human body<br>Toxicity can occur from consuming excess amounts, which accumulate in the body |
| Water soluble | C, B vitamins (thiamin, riboflavin, niacin, vitamin B6, vitamin B12, pantothenic acid, biotin, and folate) | Soluble in water<br>Not stored to any extent in the human body<br>Excess excreted in urine<br>Toxicity generally only occurs as a result of vitamin supplementation |

## Minerals

Minerals are inorganic, meaning their structure does not contain any carbon. There are two different categories of minerals; they are **major minerals** and **trace minerals**. Major minerals include calcium, phosphorus, sodium, potassium, chloride, sulfur, and magnesium. These major minerals are usually needed in amounts greater than 100 mg/day. Trace minerals include iron, zinc, copper, manganese, fluoride, chromium, molybdenum, selenium, and iodine. These trace minerals are needed in amounts usually less than 100 mg/day. Most of these minerals are obtained in adequate amounts from the diet. When using the words major or trace to define these minerals, it is important to understand that they refer to the amounts needed. All of the minerals are going to play important roles in the body (to be discussed in the following chapters).

## Nutrition and Our Health

### How Has Our Food Changed?

Our food has gone through some dramatic changes in the last ten years. The way that food is grown, handled, and processed has evolved due to advances in technology. Our ancestors would not recognize many of the foods that are

*Nutrition Intuition*

**Table 1.2** Overview of Minerals

| Type | Names | Characteristics |
|---|---|---|
| Major minerals | Calcium, phosphorus, sodium, potassium, chloride, magnesium, sulfur | Needed in amounts greater than 100 mg/day in our diets<br>Amount present in the human body is greater than 5 grams (or 5,000 mg) |
| Trace minerals | Iron, zinc, copper, manganese, fluoride, chromium, molybdenum, selenium, iodine | Needed in amounts less than 100 mg/day in our diets<br>Amount present in the human body is less than 5 grams (or 5,000 mg) |

offered today in many grocery markets. The food industry has come up with methods to increase the yield in many products such as meat and dairy. There are numerous preservatives, additives, and colorings that are added to our foods to increase freshness, taste, or eye appeal. The Food and Drug Administration has a list on their website called the GRAS list which stands for generally recognized as safe. This list contains the names of these above-mentioned items and we will take a closer look at this list in a later chapter in which we discuss food safety and sanitation. As consumers it is important to know where our food is coming from. There are many ways in which we can increase awareness about our food choices and how they impact our environment.

## A "Westernized" Diet

A "Westernized diet" is a diet that often refers to foods that are high in fat, simple carbohydrates, and—usually—processed foods. In the United States we have an abundance of food that is available every day, 24 hours per day. Many experts believe that we live in a toxic food environment. This diet is often adopted especially by those who come to the United States from other countries. Traditional diets from other countries usually consist of fruits, vegetables, and lean sources of protein. Adopting a Westernized diet could have detrimental effects on those who are not used to eating that way.

## Healthy People 2020

The Office of Disease Prevention and Health Promotion along with the U.S. Department of Health and Human Services revises and releases goals every 10 years to address public health needs. Since 1979, Healthy People has set and monitored national health objectives to meet a broad range of health needs, encourage collaborations, and guide individuals toward making informed health decisions. The mission of Healthy People 2020 (HP 2020) is to:

- Identify nationwide health improvement priorities;

- Increase public awareness and understanding of the determinants of health, disease, and disability, and opportunities for progress;

- Provide measurable objectives and goals that are applicable at the national, state, and local levels;

## FOOD IN FOCUS  Dietary Guidelines for Americans

Here are some suggestions on how to make the Dietary Guidelines useful. Find the focus area in which you are interested and read the key recommendations. Take steps to make small changes to adopt a healthier lifestyle.

### 2010 Dietary Guidelines for Americans

| Focus Area | Key Recommendation | Examples in Action – First Steps |
|---|---|---|
| Balancing Calories to Manage Weight | • Improved eating and physical activity behaviors<br>• Control total calorie intake (if overweight or obese, consume fewer calories from foods and beverages)<br>• Increase physical activity and reduce sedentary time<br>• Maintain appropriate calorie balance during each stage of life | • Take the stairs instead of the elevator<br>• 1 less soda or other sugary beverage per day<br>• Do chores around the house (or garden!) instead of watching television |
| Foods and Food Components to Reduce | • Reduce daily sodium intake to less than 2300 mg (age 50 and younger) or less than 1500mg (age 51 and older)<br>• Consume less than 10% calories from saturated fats<br>• Consume less than 300 mg cholesterol per day<br>• Aim to consume no trans fatty acids<br>• Reduce calories from solid (saturated, trans) fats and added sugars<br>• Limit consumption of refined grains<br>• Consume alcohol in moderation | • Choose fresh or frozen fruits and vegetables over the canned varieties<br>• Limit eggs to 1 per day, a few days a week<br>• Eat less processed foods and more whole foods<br>• Eat whole-grain products |

| Foods and Nutrients to Increase | • Increase fruits and vegetables<br>• Eat a variety of vegetables from a rainbow of colors, especially dark green, red and orange<br>• Consume half of grains as whole grains<br>• Increase intake of fat-free and low-fat milk<br>• Choose a variety of lean protein sources<br>• Replace some meat and poultry with seafood<br>• Replace solid fats with oils<br>• Choose foods with higher potassium, fiber, calcium, and Vitamin D content | • Choose lean protein sources, such as plant-based foods<br>• Eat fresh fiber first, meaning that a whole fruit or vegetable should be the first thing eaten at meals or snacks throughout the day |
|---|---|---|
| Building Healthy Eating Patterns | • Select an eating pattern that meets nutrient needs over time at an appropriate calorie level<br>• Account for all foods (and beverages!) consumed and assess how they fit within a total healthy eating pattern<br>• Follow food safety recommendations when preparing and eating foods to reduce the risk of foodborne illness | • Choose 5 small meals per day every few hours, instead of 3 large meals<br>• Keep a log of sugary beverages and snacks to gain an accurate feeling for calories consumed<br>• Wash hands (the number one way to prevent foodborne illness) and exercise proper food handling to reduce cross-contamination risk |

Adapted from:  http://health.gov/dietaryguidelines/dga2010/DietaryGuidelines2010.pdf

- Engage multiple sectors to take actions to strengthen policies and improve practices that are driven by available evidence and knowledge;

- Identify critical research, evaluation, and data collection needs.[4]

These are important goals and objectives because they help to establish guidelines for health professionals and the general public. For example, some of the new HP 2020 objectives focus on achieving and maintaining a healthy weight for children much in line with First Lady Michelle Obama's initiative against childhood obesity called "Let's Move." In addition, The Partnership for a Healthier America works alongside this campaign and tracks data that can help make sure these objectives are met.[5]

---

[4] www.healthypeople.gov. Accessed 6-24-10.
[5] http://www.letsmove.gov/partnership-healthier-america. Accessed 7-23-11.

## Risk Factors

A **risk factor** is a lifestyle habit that may increase your risk for getting certain diseases. For example, smoking can increase your risk for getting lung cancer. Lack of physical activity can be a risk factor for obesity and many diseases are related to obesity. Risk factors can also be related to your family history. For example, if your mother has diabetes, there is a risk that you may also get diabetes. Modifications in our lifestyles and adopting better habits may significantly decrease our risk for getting certain diseases.

## Improving Our Health

Most people agree that a healthy diet plays an important role in decreasing our risk for many chronic diseases. The table below is the top ten leading causes of death in the United States; those that are highlighted represent the diseases that are most closely related to our lifestyles. When looking at this list it becomes evident that much of what we eat and our lifestyles we choose can lead to some of the diseases listed. Making better choices and leading healthier lifestyles can prevent or delay chronic diseases. Improving our health requires good education and implementation. Good education is important and it needs to begin early in life. Nutrition education should be more of a priority in our school systems. Teaching nutrition to our children is a big responsibility. Parents need to be involved in the education as well so they can set a good example. Taking a nutrition class can help you learn about the steps you need to take to better health and well being. By taking this class you will learn about the importance of nutrition and how you can improve your life and the lives of your families. In each chapter there will be tear-out sheets that you can use to take what you have learned in each chapter and apply it right away. Implementation of what you have learned is also important. Change is not always easy; taking small steps will help you to succeed.

## Top Ten Leading Causes of Death in the United States

According to the Centers for Disease Control and Prevention (CDC) the top ten leading causes of death in the United States are as follows: [6]

- Heart disease
- Cancer
- Stroke (cerebrovascular diseases)
- Chronic lower respiratory diseases
- Accidents (unintentional injuries)

---

[6] www.cdc.gov/nchs/pressroom/data/state_mortality_rank_06.htm. Accessed 6-27-10.

- Diabetes
- Alzheimer's disease
- Influenza and pneumonia
- Nephritis, nephrotic syndrome, and nephrosis
- Septicemia (blood poisoning)

## Summary

The choices we make and the lifestyles we choose to live have an impact on our health and well being. Poor eating habits and lack of physical activity can lead to many chronic diseases, including heart disease, diabetes, cancer, and obesity.

Nutrition is a science. Although comparatively a newer science, nutrition has made many discoveries about the importance of nutrients and the roles they play in our health. The brave act that Dr. Goldberger took to prove that pellagra was not a contagious disease proves that his commitment to finding a solution was important in saving the lives of many. The science of nutrition is constantly evolving and improving the way that we live. Nutrition education and prevention of disease is the key to living a long healthy life.

We get energy from our food. The use of the bomb calorimeter has helped us to figure out how many calories we get from each food item. Calories are a source of fuel for the body and calories are obtained from the foods that we eat. A calorie is the heat energy needed to raise the temperature of 1 liter of water 1° Celcius. Carbohydrates provide 4 calories per gram, proteins provide 4 calories per gram, and lipids provide 9 calories per gram. Carbohydrates, proteins, and lipids are organic which means that they contain carbon in their chemical structure. Vitamins are also organic; however, minerals and water are not. There are nutrients that are essential and nonessential to intake daily for our health. The essential nutrients are important because the body cannot make them. We consume these nutrients through our dietary intake. The nonessential nutrients are those which we do not need to consume because the body already makes them. Organic nutrients contain carbon. Those include carbohydrates, lipids, protein, and vitamins. Inorganic nutrients include minerals and water.

There are six major classes of nutrients: carbohydrates, lipids, proteins, vitamins, minerals, and water. The body needs all of these nutrients to maintain optimal health. These nutrients help us to maintain our energy levels, rebuild muscle, and regulate many important processes.

Standards of nutrition guide us to intake the proper amounts of the nutrients. Guidelines and recommendations are made to ensure that we do not develop deficiencies or toxicities. The Dietary Reference Intakes (DRI) include the Estimated Average Requirement (EAR), which is the amount needed to meet 50% of the populations needs for all healthy people. Recommended Dietary Allowances (RDA) are determined to meet 97–98% of the needs for all healthy people. Adequate Intake (AI) is used for those nutrients in which an RDA has not been established. Tolerable Upper Intake Level (UL) is used to indicate the highest amount that can be taken that may not cause harm. The Acceptable Macronutrient Distribution Ranges (AMDR) are those guidelines to indicate what percentage of total energy intake of the macronutrients to include in our diet. Carbohydrates should comprise 45–65%, proteins should comprise 10–35%, and lipids should be 20–35% (to include the essential fatty acids) of our daily caloric intake.

Improving our health plays an important role in decreasing our risk for chronic diseases. The top ten leading causes of death shows us that many chronic diseases could be preventable if we make better choices with our health and lifestyle habits. Good education about health and nutrition is important and should be a priority in our school systems. Good nutrition begins at home; taking this class will give you the tools you need to improve your own health and well being. Remember that changing bad habits into good takes time.

# HOW MANY CALORIES DO YOU NEED?

Have you ever wondered how many calories you need on a daily basis? There are several equations that can help to estimate your calorie needs. The Institute of Medicine (IOM) sets the Dietary Reference Intakes for energy as the Estimated Energy Requirement (EER). Establishing the EER was intended to increase awareness of obesity and its relationship to taking in excess calories. The EER is a set of equations and factors that account for an individuals energy intake, energy expenditure, age, sex, weight, height, and physical activity level.

© 2012, Shutterstock, Inc.

The following equations are commonly used to assess your basal energy needs or basal metabolic rate (BMR). Basal energy needs will only reflect the number of calories that are needed to do important things like breathe in and out and digest and absorb your nutrients.

Here are examples of 2 equations:

- Mifflin-St. Jeor Equation:
  Male: 10W+6.25H-5Age+5
  Female: 10W+6.25H-5Age-161

- Harris Benedict:
  Male: 66.5+13.8W+5.0H-6.8A
  Female: 655.1+9.6W+1.9H-4.7A

\*Weight is measured in kilograms. To convert your weight to kilograms, take your weight in pounds and divide by 2.2. For example, if someone weighs 176 pounds, they would weigh 80 kilograms.

\*Height is measured in centimeters. To convert your height to centimeters, take you height in inches and multiply by 2.54. For example, if someone is 63 inches, their height in centimeters is 160 centimeters.

In addition to this number, you will need to add physical activity factors as indicated in the chart below:

| Activity Level | Description | Formula |
| --- | --- | --- |
| Low | You get little to no exercise | Calories Burned a Day = BMR x 1.2 |
| Light | You exercise lightly (1-3 days per week) | Calories Burned a Day = BMR x 1.375 |
| Moderate | You exercise moderately (3-5 days per week) | Calories Burned a Day = BMR x 1.55 |
| High | You exercise heavily (6-7 days per week) | Calories Burned a Day = BMR x 1.725 |
| Very High | You exercise very heavily (i.e. 2x per day, extra heavy workouts) | Calories Burned a Day = BMR x 1.9 |

http://www.bmrcalculator.org/

# CHAPTER 2

# The "Un-Diet" Approach to Healthy Eating

## Learning Objectives

- Understand why we make certain food choices
- Learn principles of a healthy meal plan
- Outline a meal plan
- Describe the parts of a food label
- Identify food groupings using Choose My Plate
- List reliable sources of nutrition information

*Health* (noun) the state of being well and free from illness:

> In this chapter we will explore what it means to be healthy and how health is defined by more than just being free from disease or illness. Wellness is a word that is used to describe multiple facets in our lives that make up good health and wellbeing. We will also look at reasons why we make certain food choices and how these choices influence our overall health and wellbeing. The "un-diet" approach in this chapter will help you to take a different look at what it means to eat healthy, and we do not need to "diet" to achieve it.

### Functional Food Fact   Tomato

Tomatoes contain an important caroteniod called lycopene. Lycopene is best known for studies that have shown that men who consume higher amounts of lycopene have a lower risk of prostate cancer. Tomato sauce is a great source of lycopene because it is more concentrated. Other fruits that contain lycopene include pink grapefruits, guava, watermelon, and papaya.

## The "Un-Diet" Approach

The "un-diet" approach to nutrition is something I am very passionate about as a professor and a Registered Dietitian. It is important to educate patients and students that eating healthily should not include adopting some kind of diet. Think of what images you might conjure up when you hear the word diet. We often feel deprived and we often think about favorite foods that we have to give up. I always say that diet is die with a "t" on the end and that is the way we feel when we are on a diet.

I like to approach healthy eating by using the acronym **HEALTHY** to help us understand important components of healthy eating and meal planning.

**H** is for **habit.** It is important that we adopt healthy habits that will last a lifetime. Change is difficult for us as humans and adopting good habits are not always easy. It is much easier to keep our bad habits, but making healthy choices and adopting good habits (for example eating breakfast every morning instead of skipping meals) can help us to achieve better health.

**E** is for **eating.** Eating three fruits and three vegetables every day can provide tremendous health benefits along with many important vitamins and minerals. Current recommendations based on the food guide pyramid state that we should have at least five servings of fruits and vegetables every day.

**EVERY DAY
SUPERFOODS**

Calcium, potassium, and magnesium all work together to help bone density and lower blood pressure. Yogurt, milk, boiled beans, cooked greens, nuts and baked potatoes contain all three!

**A** is for **adequate.** That means that we should have adequate amounts of nutrients every day. Protein, carbohydrates, and fat are all important nutrients in our meal plan. Moderation is the key when it comes to getting enough of these important nutrients on a daily basis.

**L** is for **limit.** Limit your intake of processed foods, canned goods, and high-fat foods. These food choices can increase your risk for heart attack or stroke. The number one killer of Americans in the United States is heart disease. Limiting these foods can help you to be "heart smart."

**T** is for **try.** Trying new foods is important to ensure that you are getting enough variety in your diet. We are so fortunate to have many different ethnicities and cultural diversity that can offer a world of different varieties of foods—so take advantage and try something new.

**H** is for **healing.** There are many promising studies and research being done in the area of antioxidants and phytochemicals that come from many of our plant-based foods. Antioxidants have been shown to play an important role in our health and well being and may offer healing properties when we eat them regularly.

**Y** is for **years.** Adopting all of these principles may help us to add years to our lives. Healthy eating habits have long been studied and shown to reduce our risk for cancer, heart disease, and many other diseases.

# Healthy Habits Can Last a Lifetime

You should not be surprised to find out that healthy habits can help us to live longer and stronger healthier lives. Habits can be both good and bad. It seems much easier to keep our bad habits than it is to adopt new ones. Changing habits takes time. Research about what it takes to change our bad habits to good ones has long been the interest of many scientists in the study of human behavior.

Readiness to change has a lot to do with the success of changing a behavior. Here are some tips to see if you are really ready to make a commitment to adopt a good healthy habit. Find your stage of change; the following will help you to determine if you are ready to make a change for the better.

- **The Contemplation Stage** "It has crossed your mind that you need to make a change." In this stage you have been considering change but are not quite ready to start. You believe that your health, energy level, and overall well being will improve if you develop these new habits. You may need to seek some support from friends or family members to get going and you are unsure if you can overcome any roadblocks that may stand in your way.

- **The Preparation Stage** "You have made up your mind that it is time to change." In this stage you begin planning and figuring out what specific things you need to do to start your journey to better habits. You are ready to take action and you set some specific goals to meet. You have thought about ways to achieve these goals and you are ready to put your plan into action.

- **The Action Stage** "You are going to go for it." In this stage you have been making eating or physical activity changes in the last 6 months. You are noticing that you feel better when you eat healthier and maintain your physical activity regimen. You have figured out how to overcome obstacles and you are always thinking of new ways to keep yourself motivated.

© 2012, Shutterstock, Inc.

- **The Maintenance Stage** "You are in the zone." You are in the maintenance stage when your changes have become a habit, something you do not have to think much about, you just do it! You have

© 2012, Shutterstock, Inc.

adopted these good habits and you can see that you are setting a good example for your friends and family. You may have some setbacks but you always bounce back with a plan and get right back on top of things.[1]

## Science Fiction vs. Reality

Can you imagine being asked for a DNA sample to get a job promotion? Could a company ask for a DNA sample to determine if you were the right person for that job? Sounds like science fiction, right? The reality is that the International Human Genome Sequencing Consortium published the finished version of the human genome in 2003. Our DNA is what makes us different from each other. This knowledge of the complete DNA of the human genome comes with great responsibility to do the right thing with this kind of information. Due to the implications of these findings there is already legislation put in place to protect people from having to give DNA samples for jobs, promotions, etc.

A current study being done by the National Human Genome Research Institute is conducting research to find out how young people (aged 25–45 years old) view the role genetics plays in improving health. Almost 2,000 participants were involved in the study in which the researchers obtained blood samples for "multiplex genetic testing." A key focus of this research was to see how participants in the study viewed health behaviors and genetic makeup in the cause of a disease. The study indicated that knowing your family history was an effective motivator of health behavior change. Those participants who knew their family history and their risk for developing certain diseases placed more value on pursuing genetic information.[2]

**Nutrigenomics** is an emerging field in nutrition that can use this information about the human genome and determine what nutrients or other food-derived substances may

[1]win.nikkd.nih.gov/publications/changinghabits.htm..Accessed 7-5-10.
[2]www.genome.gov/27539652. Accessed 7-5-10.

interact with your genes. Imagine specialized diets just for your own genetic makeup. Nutrigenomics is not quite ready for application to the general population just yet. This field requires a special knowledge in genetics and genomics concepts, but the future looks bright for those who are willing to take on the challenge.

## Food Choices

Every day we make choices on what we eat and how much we eat. These choices we make are shaped by our parents or caregivers, culture, habits, economics, and food preferences. We do not always eat just because we are hungry.

© 2012, Shutterstock, Inc.

**Food choices are shaped by our parents or caregivers.** Parents and caregivers have the potential to positively or negatively influence the choices that we make as children. Studies with young children have found that children's intake of certain foods is strongly correlated with the intake of the parents. Parents and caregivers have many opportunities when children are young to influence their food choices and be positive role models. This influence, however, is decreased when children reach adolescence as the influence of the media, friends, and the need for independence increase.[3] Whether you consider yourself a "picky eater" is often due to the influences that your parents or caregivers had on your food selections.

**Food choices are shaped by our culture.** Your culture defines some of your food choices. Special dishes will have special meaning to you and you continue to choose these foods for a lifetime. The foods that you have grown up with have special meaning to you.

**Food choices are shaped by our habits.** We have discussed good habits and bad ones. Good habits can help you to make better food choices. A habit may be a something like you eat oatmeal every day for breakfast.

**EVERY DAY**
### SUPERFOODS

Some potatoes have amounts of flavenoids (cancer-fighting phyto-chemicals) that rival broccoli! Aside from providing important carbohydrates, they also contain Vitamin C, folic acid, and even kukoamines (the blood pressure lowering molecules found in gogi berries). I don't know about you, but I'm hungry for some fall vegetable stew!

---

[3] Chrisa Arcan and others: Parental eating behaviours, home food environment and adolescent intake of fruits, vegetables and dairy foods: longitudinal findings from project EAT. *Public Health Nutrition* 2007: 10(11), 1257-1265.

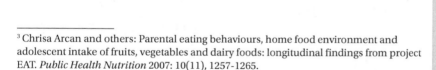

Food can be addicting just like drugs and alcohol. We eat when we are happy and we eat when we are sad. Research about depression and eating has shown that those with depression could be "self-medicating" with foods, even chocolate. A study done by the University of California, San Diego looked at the relationship between chocolate and mood. The participants were asked how much chocolate they ate and their level of depression was measured on a standard depression scale. Those who were diagnosed with depression ate an average of 8.4 servings of chocolate each month, while those who were not depressed ate an average of 5.4 servings of chocolate each month. Those who were considered to be most depressed ate an average of 11.8 servings of chocolate per month.[4]

## Nutrient Density vs. Caloric Density

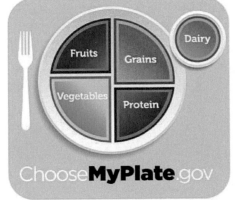

**Nutrient Density** is a measurement of the nutrients compared to the calories the food provides. A good example is choosing a medium-sized apple that provides only 60 calories but also provides important vitamins and minerals. The more nutrients and lower calories the food provides, the greater the nutrient density. Choosing more foods that are nutrient dense can help you to plan a healthier diet.

**Caloric Density** is a term used to describe a food that provides more calories and fewer nutrients per serving. Today, many of the fast-food chains offer very caloric dense foods that are relatively low in many vitamins and minerals but provide many calories. A cupcake would be a caloric dense food, but remember health is also about moderation in our choices.

## A Practical Approach to Meal Planning

### My Plate

My Plate can be a practical tool to use when learning how to plan meals and make

[4] Beatrice A. Golomb, M.D. and others: Chocolate a Sweet Pick-Me-Up for the Depressed. www.nlm.nih.gov/medlineplus/print/fullstory_98039.html. Accessed June 27, 2010.

healthier food choices. Choose My Plate was developed by the United States Department of Agriculture (USDA) to help consumers apply the 2010 Dietary Guidelines for Americans and remind them to eat healthfully.[5] The Plate was developed to replace the traditional Food Guide Pyramid. In June 2011, the Plate was updated to provide a more familiar, visual, and understandable approach to meal times for most Americans.

You can access the choosemyplate.gov website to access updated information about the Plate. Interactive tools include:

- **Daily Food Plan** - provides a quick estimate of how much food you should eat on a daily basis. You simply provide your age, gender, and activity level.[6]

- **MyFoodapedia** - provides quick access to information about the calories and food group location of various foods. It also provides an option to compare two foods for calorie and nutrient density.[7]

- **Food Tracker** - in this section you can track your foods and activity to see if you are on the right track when it comes to following a healthy meal plan. You can input your foods and activities to see if you are meeting or exceeding your daily calorie allowances. You have access to over 8000 foods and 600 activities and the list is always being updated. Research shows that keeping track of your foods can be a great way to get enough variety in your foods as well as help those who are trying to lose weight.

- **Food Groups (under The Basics on the main page)** - provides an in depth look at every food group and includes recommendations for each group. The amount (and type) of each food group is also highlighted. Common measurements are explained in more detail with examples included. The individual nutrients found within each food group and their health benefits are detailed. Tips for eating the right types of foods (and recipes!) are also included under each food group. Discretionary calories have been taken out of the recommendations and are now included under Foods to Decrease.[8]

Despite all the benefits the website provides, there are still people who may not use it. Those who do not have computers or Internet access, which can include older adults, or those may not be familiar with how to use a computer are potentially left out. Additionally, the Plate is currently available only in the English language—which

---

[5] http://www.cnpp.usda.gov/MyPlate.htm Accessed 7-23-11

[6] http://www.choosemyplate.gov/myplate/index.aspx Accessed 7-23-11

[7] http://www.myfoodapedia.gov/ Accessed 7-23-11

[8] http://www.choosemyplate.gov/foodgroups/index.html Accessed 7-23-11.

may be a barrier to those for whom English is not their first language. Choose My Plate can also provide insight into a serving size, but may not include enough information about combination foods such as pizza, casserole dishes, and sandwiches. Other research into the previous MyPyramid has shown that despite the familiar image of the food guide pyramid people do not use it. Some insight into the lack of use of MyPyramid has been studied using focus groups. Health professionals have concluded that the public finds the Pyramid confusing at times because of the expectations in the knowledge of the serving sizes. It appears that to understand the serving sizes better, one must carry around measuring cups and spoons and most people feel that this is unrealistic.

**NUTRITION NERD ALERT**

Extra calories are extra calories (i.e., excess of food if eaten in addition to a diet that is already sufficient in calories), even if they are from fruits and vegetables.

## Food Labels: Friend or Foe?

Food labels are required on most food items that are found in the grocery markets. Food labels are regulated by the Food and Drug Administration (FDA) and were established to assist consumers with making better choices when trying to choose healthier foods.

© 2012, Shutterstock, Inc.

### What Is Required on the Food Label?

There are basic requirements for the food label as established by the FDA. The food label must provide:

- A statement of identity: the name of the product or an appropriate identification must be displayed clearly so the consumer knows what the product is.

- The net contents of the package: accurate quantities of the food should be displayed on the package. The manufacturer may express these contents using measurements such as grams, fluid ounces, or provide the number of items per package.

- Ingredient list: the ingredients must be called by their common name and listed in descending order. The first ingredient listed is the predominant ingredient in that food item.

- The name and address of the food manufacturer, distributor, or packer. This information can be used to contact the company if you would like to compliment or complain about a product.

- Nutrition Facts Panel: This is the primary tool to assist the consumer in choosing healthy food items. This facts panel will provide detailed information about the product as listed below.

**Nutrition Facts**

Serving Size 1/4 Cup (30g)
Servings Per Container About 38

**Amount Per Serving**

**Calories** 200  Calories from Fat 150

| | % Daily Value* |
|---|---|
| **Total Fat** 17g | **26%** |
| Saturated Fat 2.5g | **13%** |
| Trans Fat 0g | |
| **Cholesterol** 0mg | **0%** |
| **Sodium** 120mg | **5%** |
| **Total Carbohydrate** 7g | **2%** |
| Dietary Fiber 2g | **8%** |
| Sugars 1g | |
| **Protein** 5g | |

| | | |
|---|---|---|
| Vitamin A 0% | • | Vitamin C 0% |
| Calcium 4% | • | Iron 8% |

*Percent Daily Values are based on a 2,000 calorie diet.

© 2012, Shutterstock, Inc.

## What to Look for on the Food Label

### Serving size and servings per container:

What do you look for on a food label? What part of the food label do you find informative or confusing? The best place to start when reading a food label is to look at the serving size and servings per container. The serving sizes represent the amount that people would typically eat for that food item. With thousands of food items in the grocery markets today, there is much confusion about the standardization of serving sizes. The serving size is predominantly determined by the food manufacturer and that can be misleading to consumers. For example, you purchase a blueberry muffin. You notice that this blueberry muffin contains 120 calories. You look closely at the serving size and it says that 1/3 of the muffin is the portion that is typically eaten. That means that if you decide to eat the whole muffin you have consumed 360 calories! The FDA has defined serving sizes for selected items, but most are determined by the food manufacturers. The serving sizes are supposed to represent the estimated amount someone would typically eat. Often the serving sizes are not good estimates of how much someone would typically eat, so you need to pay attention to how many servings you are having and make sure to calculate the calories so you are aware how many you are actually eating.

## FOOD IN FOCUS  Add More Color to Your Life!

by Andrea Chang Bortnik

Who says college students have to gain the freshman 15? Nobody wants to gain weight, but somehow in college, the pounds decide to add themselves onto our bodies. And… without our consent! How rude! Or, could this be the result of our lifestyle choices? According to a study conducted at Indiana University in Bloomington, 67% of female college students gained an average of 10 pounds and 86% of men, a whooping 14 pounds from their freshman to senior year.[4] Do we have to be victims of this obesity epidemic? Or, should we make a few life-style choices that will rejuvenate our bodies? After all, college is about our newfound freedom. No longer do we have to adhere to the lifestyle choices of our past, especially if it includes dinners at fast food restaurants or late night snacks of salty and hydrogenated fat-laden chips. So, join me in making a few simple decisions that will change the way you feel and look.

**Simply put: More Fruits and Vegetables.** Most of us have heard of the carbohydrate star-vation diet (Atkin's) or maybe even of the boring Cabbage Soup diet, but does starving our body of one kind of ingredient or overindulging our body of another type really work? There are so many different fad diets from the Slim-fast diet to the protein diet, to even, the cookie diet! Wow! The cookie diet? I'm suspicious. We are bombarded with too many diets with creative regulations. So, what is the secret? More colorful fruits and vegetables! Next time you are in class, instead of eating a Twinkie that has a lifespan of probably 100 years, or munching on a high salt, high fat chip, how about a crispy, juicy and fresh apple? Or a yellow banana on-the-go? Or, maybe a few orange baby carrot sticks, slivers of yellow peppers, and crisp green snow peas? Every day, you can make simple choices of incorporating maybe just one new vegetable into your diet. What will it be today?

**References:**
Hellmich, Nanci. "Beer, bad habits fuel college weight gain." *USA Today* 29, October 2008.
USAToday.com. accessed 15 March 2010: < http://www.usatoday.com/news/health/weightloss/2008-10-28-college-weight_N.htm>

## Total calories and calories from fat per serving:

Take a look at this section of the label and determine if the food is high in fat. The label will display the number of calories from fat based on the number of fat grams per serving. Heart disease is still the number one killer of people in the United States, and many consumers must be aware of their fat intake and how many calo-ries are coming from fat per serving. The important point again is that you must look at the serving size first. If you are planning on eating more than one serving, you must adjust the number of calories accordingly.

## List of nutrients:

The nutrients that are listed at the top of the label are chosen because they play significant roles in our health. Total fat, saturated fat, cholesterol, and sodium are listed here so that the consumer can tell if the product is high or low in these nutrients. Limiting these nutrients can help someone live a healthier life. The nutrients that are listed at the bottom are those that we should consume more. Nutrients such as fiber, vitamins A and C, calcium, and iron are chosen because they also play significant roles in our health. When we consume more of these nutrients, we can live a healthier life. We will take a closer look at all of these nutrients and their impact on our health in future chapters.

## The percent daily values (%DV):

The **percent daily values** can tell you how much of a nutrient meets your overall daily intake. Remember in Chapter 1 when we discussed the RDA's and AI values that are determined for many of our nutrients. These RDA's and AI values are used here and the percent is based on a predetermined amount of calories. The percent daily values are based on a 2000-calorie diet as set by the FDA. If you are not sure if you are consuming 2000 calories, the percent daily values may not be that useful for you. They are useful if you use them to determine if one or more nutrients are high or low in a food item. For example, if you are looking at a food label and you see that the %DV is 30% for fat, then that means that this food item will provide 30% of your daily value for fat. This food item would be significantly high in fat and should be avoided by someone who needs to watch their total intake of fat.

## Health claims:

What health claims do you find on a label? Health claims are used by the manufacturers as a marketing tool to inform consumers of potential health benefits they may get by purchasing certain food items. The FDA has guidelines about health claims and how they can be used on the food label. The FDA adopted the use of scientific evidence to back up the claims presented on the food labels. In 2003, a Health Claims Report Card was developed so that consumers can better understand the value of a claim listed on the food label. The grading system is listed below:

- An "A" indicates that the claim is supported by scientific research.
- A "B" indicates that the claim has some evidence base but is inconclusive.
- A "C" indicates that evidence for this claim is limited and is inconclusive.
- A "D" indicates that the claim has little evidence.

For more information about these health claims visit the FDA website at www.fda.gov.

## Tips on How to Make the Most of the Food Label

Remember that the food label is just one way to make better choices in healthy eating. Here are some tips on how to make the most of the food label so that you can understand what you are reading.

- Look at the serving size first; if you are going to have more than one serving then you need to make sure to take a closer look at the calories and adjust accordingly.

- Use the percent daily values to determine if the item has a large amount of sodium, fat, or cholesterol.

## Summary

The "un-diet" approach is a way that I like to teach nutrition. If you are constantly dieting to keep up with current trends or fads, these behaviors can easily lead to unhealthy eating habits. By using the HEALTHY approach, you can apply the principles of healthy eating and meal planning.

**H** is for habit, when we adopt healthy habits, these can last a lifetime. **E** is for eating and I have challenged you to try to eat at least three fruits and three vegetables per day. **A** is for adequate, take a closer look at the amounts of nutrients that you eat every day to make sure you include enough of each one. Carbohydrates, proteins, and fats all play an important role in our health and we need adequate amounts on a daily basis. **L** is for limit. Limit the amount of processed and high-fat foods that you include in your daily intake. **T** is for try, try new foods and challenge your taste buds. Trying new foods can add more variety to your diet to ensure that you are getting enough of the nutrients, vitamins, and minerals you need. **H** is for healing. There is so much research being developed about the importance of a healthy diet and how foods have the potential to heal our bodies by providing us with phytochemicals and antioxidants. **Y** is for years. Adopting all of these healthy habits may add years to your life. Living longer is good, but living longer and living stronger is even better.

Changing habits takes time. Stages of change include the contemplation stage where the person is thinking of making a change but has not quite made up his/her mind. In this stage you may seek help or support from family and friends in the early stages. The next stage is the preparation stage. In this stage you have made up your mind that it is time for a change and you begin planning and figuring out what specific things you will have to do to put your plan into action. The action stage is where you are "going for it." You are seeing the positive aspects of your change;

others around you are also noticing and commending you on a job well done. The maintenance stage is when you are "in the zone" and your changes have now become a habit. When you have a setback you always bounce back and get back on top of things.

What we once thought of as science fiction has now become a reality. The discovery and completion of the human genome project has given us an inside view of the human DNA. With this knowledge comes a great responsibility to use the information wisely. Legislation has already been put in place to protect us from the misuse of DNA against us as individuals. Imagine if you were asked to submit DNA for a new job or a promotion? The emerging field of nutrigenomics is quickly growing and will continue to grow as we discover more connections with our health and the foods that we eat. Specialized diets to treat different diseases are used today, but specialized diets that target your specific DNA may be here sooner than we think. The field of nutrigenomics will be a challenging one, but the future looks bright for those who are willing to increase their knowledge of genetics and genomics.

Every day we make choices on what types and how much food we eat. These choices are shaped by many factors in our lives. For example, we make food choices based on our upbringing. The foods that our parents or caregivers introduced to us when we were young have a lasting impact on us. Food choices are also shaped by our culture. Foods will have special meaning to you depending on the occasion or celebration. We also make food choices according to our habits. We discussed the steps we need to take to make bad habits into good ones. Good food habits can help you to make better choices and maintain your health. Food can also be addicting like alcohol or drugs. Several studies have shown that when we eat our favorite foods, the pleasure centers of the brain are stimulated and we remember the good feelings that we got from eating that food. Similar things happen with alcohol and drugs. The good feelings that are produced in the brain will cause the person to want that feeling again and again, thus causing an addiction.

Nutrient dense versus caloric dense foods will have varying impacts on our healthy eating habits. Nutrient dense foods will be those that are lower in calories and provide more nutrients. The example used was a medium apple that contains about 60 calories and provides important nutrients such as vitamins and minerals. A caloric dense food is one that will give us too many calories and not provide much in the way of nutrients. Most of our processed foods and fast foods are categorized as caloric dense foods.

Practical approaches to meal planning include the ability to understand how to use the new My Plate. In this section we discussed the evolution of the food guide pyramid and the development of the new My Plate. The My Plate plan allows the user to get a quick estimate of how much food he/she should eat on a daily basis. Inside My Plate allows the user to take an in depth look at the different food groups. Common measurements help explain in more detail the proper portion sizes. Discretionary calories are also discussed in this section; portion sizes allow the user to include foods higher in fat or sugar as well as alcohol. The various tracking methods discussed are excellent online tools that allow the user to track food items and get analysis and feedback on the choices they make. The downside to this online tool is that not everyone has Internet access and these tools are not widely used in populations that are not familiar with the use of computers.

Another tool that can help in making healthier food choices is the ability to read and understand a food label. The food label is regulated by the FDA. The FDA has requirements as to what is required on a food label. The statement of identity helps the consumer to clearly identify what the food item is. The net contents displays the accurate quantities of the food item. The ingredient list lists the ingredients in descending order, which means that the highest quantity nutrient is listed first. The name and address of the manufacturer is required so a consumer can contact the company for additional questions or concerns regarding the product. Finally, the nutrition facts panel gives the specific nutrient composition of the product based on the serving size listed.

Most serving sizes are decided by the manufacturer of that product, which is supposed to be consistent with what portion someone would usually eat. If more than one serving of the item is going to be consumed, then you must calculate the totals accordingly. Total calories and total calories from fat are also listed per serving. As a consumer you can quickly assess the food item to see if it is high in calories or fat. People with certain diseases, especially heart disease, have to pay attention to their total fat intake. The lists of nutrients on the nutrition facts panel are chosen because of the significant role they play in our health. The recommendations for each of these nutrients are based on the RDA's or DRI levels as discussed in chapter one. The percent daily values can be used to determine if a nutrient is high or low in a product. These values are based on a 2000-calorie daily intake. The footnotes are usually located on the bottom of the food label if they fit; footnotes are not required. The footnote information can tell the consumer some specific guidelines and recommendations about their daily intakes based on 2000- and 2500-calorie levels. Health claims on labels are indicated by a grading system that was developed by the FDA. This system is based on grades ranging from A to D to indicate whether or not the claim on the label is backed up by scientific evidence or research.

# How To Visualize the Serving Size

Think of food amounts in terms that are easy for you to visualize so you can accurately estimate the serving size.

Meat - 3 oz.  **think of** Size of a deck of cards

Apple/Peach  **think of** Tennis ball

Cheese - 1 oz.  **think of** 4 dice

Broccoli - 1 cup  **think of** Your fist

Peanut butter or butter - 1 tsp.  **think of** Tip of thumb

Nuts/Candy - 1 oz.  **think of** A handful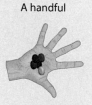

For a nutritious diet, you need daily:
- Vegetables: 3-5 servings
- Fruits: 2-4 servings
- Grains: 6-11 servings
- Meat: 2-3 servings
- Dairy: 2-4 servings

# CHAPTER 3

# Digestion and Absorption: The Human Body at its Best

© 2012, Shutterstock, Inc.

## Learning Objectives

- Define the role of the hypothalamus in the regulation of hunger
- Outline the roles that the mouth, stomach, small intestine, large intestine, as well as the liver, gallbladder, and pancreas play in digestion and absorption
- List major nutrition-related gastrointestinal health problems and their treatments
- Understand the importance that hormones play in the regulation of digestion and absorption
- Explain the difference between the lymphatic and the vascular systems and the role they play in nutrient transport

*Nutrient* (adj) a nutritive substance or ingredient

Nutrients are provided by our foods. The digestion and absorption of nutrients in our body is a carefully orchestrated event. We often take for granted how efficient our bodies are.

## Functional Food Fact  Garlic

Garlic is an herb that has long been known for its healing properties. Used for many years in folk medicine as an antibiotic, antihypertensive, and cholesterol lowering medication. Garlic has been shown to inhibit tumorigenesis (to prevent development of tumors) in some animal studies. Watch out, vampires!

## Brain Power

Many people would believe that hunger is controlled by our stomach. Animal studies have been done in which the researcher removed the stomach from the animal and the animal would still exhibit hunger. Such studies led researchers to take a closer look at the brain and the role the brain plays in hunger. It was discovered later that the hypothalamus along with several hormones play an important part in hunger and satiety. The **hypothalamus** is a collection of specialized cells located in the lower central part of the brain and is the control center for hunger and satiety. When we are hungry, these specialized cells send a series of messages via hormones to the cells of the stomach and small intestines to find out whether or not there is any food present. If you have not eaten for several hours, the signal that the hypothalamus will receive is that it is time to eat. The hypothalamus also plays a role in regulation of thirst.

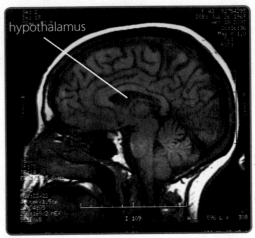
hypothalamus

© 2012, Shutterstock, Inc.

### Hunger vs. Satiety

As mentioned above, hunger is sensed when the stomach is empty. The hypothalamus is also a control center for satiety. **Satiety** is the state of fullness which signals a feeling of being satisfied. Hunger and satiety work in opposite ways in the body. Hunger tells the person to start eating; satiety tells the person to stop eating. The problem is that we do not always "listen" to the signal that is telling us to stop eating. It would be beneficial if there were a bell or whistle that went off to stop excessive intake of food, but there is not.

## Using Our Senses

There is a saying that goes "we eat with our eyes and not with our stomach." As human beings we are very visual, and we use our sense of vision in the selection of foods. Imagine a plate in front of you that has cauliflower (a white-colored vegetable) and a piece of chicken with some type of white sauce or gravy with a side of white pasta. This dish would look very bland and un-appetizing to most. Restaurants, grocery markets, and other places where food is served make sure that your meals are not only enjoyable by taste but also by color. Taste and smell are other senses that we use when selecting foods. Taste and smell are also very intimately connected—meaning one will usually not function if the other is not working properly. For example, you have a cold and you are congested which affects your sense of smell. You eat and you notice that your food lacks taste (or the taste can sometimes be altered).

**NUTRITION NERD ALERT**

Vitamin D is well-known to facilitate the absorption of calcium. It also facilitates the absorption of other equally important bone-healthy minerals: magnesium and phosphorous.

## We Get Energy from Food

### Digestion and Absorption

Have you ever wondered what happens to the food you eat? Or do you just chew it up and hope for the best? The process of digestion and absorption is often taken for granted. Most of the digestion and absorption processes are not under our control. Once you have chewed and swallowed your food, your body will take over the rest. The autonomic control of the nervous system will control the processes of digestion and absorption. Think of *autonomic* as being similar to the word *automatic*, meaning your body will automatically know what to do. Sometimes there can be problems that arise in the digestion and absorption of our foods; some of them are discussed later in this chapter.

In order to obtain energy from our food, our food has to go through many changes. Digestion and absorption of our nutrients is the way that we get fuel for our bodies. Like a car needs fuel to run, our bodies need food for fuel. Digestion is the way by which food is broken down into smaller components. **Digestion** is divided up into two parts: mechanical and chemical. **Mechanical digestion** involves the salivary enzymes that are needed to begin the digestion of some carbohydrates. Mechanical digestion is also the action of the mouth in which we chew our food to break it down into smaller pieces. **Chemical digestion** is all the enzymes that are used to break down the food into smaller components for absorption. **Peristalsis** is the muscular action of digestion. The gastrointestinal tract (GI tract) is lined with ringed muscles that contract and relax in response to food entering the esophagus. The purpose of peristalsis is to keep food moving in one direction. The contractions and relaxations of the muscles occur at varying rates and speeds depending on which part of the GI tract the food is in. **Enzymes** are complex proteins that are produced to speed up chemical reactions which are necessary for the breakdown of the nutrients. Throughout this book we will discuss several enzymes and the important roles that they play. **Absorption** is the way by which the nutrients are used by the body after being broken down in the small intestine. The absorption of nutrients goes either into the blood for immediate use or takes another route via the lymphatic system to be discussed later.

## Mouth

The mouth performs many functions other than just chewing our food and reducing it to smaller components. The mouth is also responsible for the secretion of some important enzymes that are needed to begin digestion; that is why we say that digestion begins in the mouth. Salivary glands in the mouth secrete **salivary amylase** which begins the digestion of carbohydrates. (See Chapter 4 for additional information on carbohydrate digesting enzymes.)

## Esophagus

The **esophagus** is a long tube that connects the **pharynx** to the stomach. The pharynx is located at the back of the throat. During the swallowing phase, the **bolus** of food is directed toward the esophagus. The trachea (also known as the windpipe) is the passageway to the lungs and is also close to the back of the throat. To prevent the bolus of food from going into the trachea and down the lungs a small flap of tissue called the **epiglottis** folds down over the trachea to protect the airway. A bolus of food going into the trachea instead of the esophagus would result in choking. If choking does occur the victim will not be able to speak or breathe. A technique called the Heimlich maneuver is performed by trained individuals to dislodge the object from the victim's airway. For more information on the Heimlich maneuver and the proper way to handle a choking victim visit www.heimlichinstitute.org for details. The bolus of food that travels down the esophagus is moved in coordination with muscular contractions and relaxations called **peristalsis**. Peristalsis allows the whole length of the gastrointestinal tract (GI tract) to keep food moving in one direction. Each section of the GI tract is separated by **sphincters**. At the end of the esophagus is the **lower esophageal sphincter (LES)** that separates the esophagus from the stomach, to be discussed in the next section.

## Stomach

The stomach is made up of mostly muscle. When empty, the stomach is about six ounces which is a little less than a cup. When full, the stomach can expand to almost thirty-two ounces which is about four cups.

When food enters the stomach from the esophagus, the bolus of food passes the LES. This separation allows the bolus of food to enter the stomach in small amounts.

Sometimes there can be a malfunction of the LES. The LES is a small muscle structure that opens and closes in response to a bolus of food. The muscle can weaken and the LES may not close completely, which can allow some of the stomach contents to back up into the lower part of the esophagus, causing a burning feeling. Patients who experience heartburn complain of a burning sensation near the heart, but it is not the heart that is affected. Frequent heartburn can lead to a condition called gastroesophageal reflux disease (GERD). This condition should be treated appropriately by your doctor. Frequent heartburn has been linked to esophageal ulcers and even esophageal cancer when left untreated.

When food enters the stomach, it activates cells within the stomach lining that produce hydrochloric acid (HCl). This acid allows the food contents to be broken down further for proper absorption in the small intestine. The pH of the acid is approximately about a 2 on the pH scale which is equivalent to about the acidity of car battery acid. The lining of the stomach is protected by a layer of mucus that brings the pH to a more tolerable level of about 7 which is more neutral. Bacteria called *Helicobacter pylori* or *H pylori* can become active in the stomach and cause erosion of the stomach lining which can cause an ulcer to develop. As we age, we sometimes lose the ability to produce adequate amounts of acid which can lead to a condition called atrophic gastritis which will be discussed in a later chapter on aging and nutrition.

The muscles of the stomach allow the stomach to mix and churn the food that has just been eaten. There is no digestion that takes place in the stomach. The acidity assists the stomach in mixing and churning the food and eventually it will become chyme. **Chyme** is the mixture of acid and partially digested nutrients that goes to the small intestine to prepare for absorption.

NUTRITION NERD ALERT

Blood lipid (triglycerides) and cholesterol levels are a hot topic in health and nutrition. There is only one healthy habit that has been shown to lower the lousy, or LDL, cholesterol. Exercise! It's the best free drug you will find.

## Absorption

The absorption of nutrients occurs so that we can use the food that we just ate as energy. The nutrients are absorbed across the cell membrane in the small intestine via three different ways. The first one we will discuss is **simple diffusion**. Simple diffusion allows the nutrient to be absorbed across the cell membrane and does not require any transport proteins (proteins that allow nutrients to cross the cell membrane) or energy (in the form of ATP) in order to get the nutrient from one side of the cell membrane to the other. The second way the nutrients can be absorbed is **facilitated diffusion**. Facilitated diffusion requires protein transport. The nutrient attaches to the specific carrier protein and then passes to the other side of the cell membrane. Facilitated diffusion does not require energy. The third way that nutrients can pass the cell membrane is called **active transport**. Active transport also requires a protein carrier to cross the cell membrane and then energy is required to move the nutrient from one side to the other. Different nutrients require different ways to be absorbed.

## Small Intestine

The *small intestine* is the primary site of absorption for the nutrients and is segmented into three parts, the **duodenum**, **jejunum**, and **ileum**. The small intestine is about 10 feet in length, is somewhat tubular shaped, and is about an inch in diameter.

The small intestine appears to be smooth on the surface, but a closer look in the microscope reveals that there are many small folds that make up the structure. The inner walls of the small intestine contain thousands of fingerlike projections called villi. A closer look at the villi in the microscope exposes even smaller projections called microvilli which are made up of highly specialized cells that trap nutrients and absorb them across the cell membrane.

Once these fresh nutrients have been absorbed, they travel to the liver via the portal vein. The liver, which is the body's major metabolic organ, will then act as the "food police." The liver is set up to protect us from substances that might harm the heart or brain. The liver can withstand much damage before it actually gives out. The liver is the only organ in the body that can regenerate itself. Imagine the possibilities if all of our organs could do this. We will discuss more important functions of the liver later in this chapter.

Once the liver has completed its duties as the "food police," the nutrients are then released in the body for use. Protein and carbohydrates are released into the vascular system. Vascular means "blood"; this system transports carbohydrate and protein for immediate use. Fats, however, take another route and will be transported into the lymphatic system. We will further explore fat digestion and absorption in the chapter on fats. The lymphatic system is largely made up of our immune system. The "lymph" is a clear yellowish fluid that contains our white blood cells which are important for the immune system for fighting off bacteria and viruses.

## Large Intestine

The contents of the small intestine pass another sphincter called the **ileocecal valve**. The foods you have eaten no longer bear a resemblance to food at this stage. Some carbohydrates, fats, and protein do reach the large intestines, but only a small amount.

The large intestine has the largest bacterial population compared to the other parts of the GI tract. These bacteria help the final remnants of digestion and prepare the food for evacuation from the body. The bacteria located in the large intestine are present to protect our health. These bacteria have been shown to protect us from other disease-causing bacteria. The fecal bulk will remain in the last segment of the large intestine called the **rectum** until elimination occurs.

We also produce vitamin K, which is a fat-soluble vitamin, in the large intestine. The important functions of vitamin K will be discussed in the chapter on vitamins.

NUTRITION NERD ALERT

Did you know? If you are deficient in a micronutrient (e.g. iron, folate), you will absorb a higher percentage of it from food and supplements. For example, if someone has iron-deficiency anemia, they will absorb more iron than someone who is not deficient.

## Accessory Organs

The accessory organs include the liver, the gallbladder, and the pancreas. These organs are part of the process of digestion but are not part of the GI tract. Each organ performs specialized functions to aid in digestion and absorption of nutrients.

The **gallbladder** is a small organ located right underneath the liver. The gallbladder serves as a small compartment that can hold a substance called **bile**. The bile is made by the liver and sent to the gallbladder. Did you know that you could survive without your gallbladder? Sometimes people must have their gallbladders removed because of gallstones or some other disease that has affected the function of the gallbladder. Bile aids in the digestion of fats in the small intestine.

When fat is sensed in the small intestine by way of some hormone messengers, the gallbladder contracts and releases the bile to help emulsify the fats and break them into smaller droplets to prepare for absorption across the cell membrane walls. Think of emulsification action as similar to that of laundry detergent. When we wash our clothes, we add laundry detergent to the water to break up the oils and dirt left on our clothes.

The **pancreas** is a spongy-shaped organ that secretes important enzymes that are necessary for the complete breakdown of carbohydrates, proteins, and fats into smaller components in preparation for absorption. Even more important is the ability of the pancreas to secrete bicarbonate into the small intestine when the food contents (chyme) come from the stomach, passing by the **pyloric sphincter**. The acidic contents of the stomach must be neutralized to bring the pH of the stomach acids into a more tolerable range. The pancreas also secrets two important hormones called insulin and glucagon which help to regulate your blood sugar. These hormones and their connection to diabetes will be discussed in Chapter 4.

The **liver** is an amazing organ that does thousands of different functions in the body. The liver processes and stores many nutrients. This organ is also responsible for making cholesterol in the body. When we eat carbohydrates, the liver stores some of them in the form of glycogen for later use. This storage of glycogen will play an important role later when we discuss how the blood sugar is maintained.

## Common Problems with Digestion

### Heartburn

**Heartburn** is a condition that stems from a malfunction in the lower esophageal (LES) sphincter, which is a small ring-shaped muscle that opens and closes in response to a bolus of food coming from the esophagus to the stomach. Sometimes the muscle of the LES becomes weak and the stomach contents—which are very acidic—will flush back into the esophagus. Many Americans suffer from heartburn; some of the symptoms of heartburn include a burning sensation near the breastbone or slight pain in the upper chest. Here are some contributing factors to heartburn:

- obesity
- smoking

- alcohol
- consumption of acidic foods such as coffee, citrus, carbonated beverages, peppermint, greasy foods, and spicy foods.

## GERD

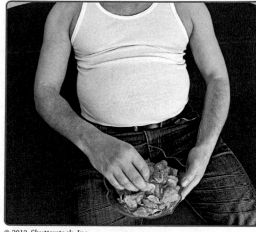
© 2012, Shutterstock, Inc.

**Gastroesophageal reflux disease (GERD)** is a condition in which heartburn becomes more frequent and includes symptoms of nausea, gagging, and coughing. This is a serious disease that should be treated by a doctor. There are many over-the-counter medications that are available to treat this condition, but you should consult with your doctor before using them. These medications can help to neutralize the acid and decrease the burning sensation. There are other drugs that also help to decrease acid in the stomach by signaling the stomach to make less acid.

Those who suffer from GERD should seek treatment right away. Symptoms that are not treated properly could lead to esophageal ulcers which can be very painful. The back flow of acids from the stomach can sometime erode the surface of the esophagus causing the ulcers to develop. An ulcer that begins to bleed can be very dangerous and lead to iron-deficiency anemia. Signs of a bleeding esophagus include coughing up of blood and blood in the stool (stool will become very dark and tarry looking). Patients with GERD also have a higher chance of developing esophageal cancer. Here are some foods to avoid for patients with GERD; these foods are known to contribute to the relaxation of the LES:

- chili powder, onions, and garlic

- peppermint

- caffeine, alcohol, and chocolate

The treatment for GERD includes eating small frequent meals and avoiding high fat and greasy foods. It is also advised that you wait about 2 hours after a meal before lying down.

## Ulcers

A **peptic ulcer** is a sore that develops on the surface of the lining of the stomach or in the lining of the small intestine. Peptic ulcers can develop in the stomach and these are referred to as **gastric ulcers**. The other place that peptic ulcers can develop is in the first part of the small intestine called the duodenum; these are referred to as **duodenal ulcers**.

A doctor can detect an ulcer by performing a procedure called an upper endoscopy. The procedure requires medication to relax the patient, then the doctor will insert a flexible scope into the mouth and lead the scope down the esophagus and into the stomach so the ulcer can be viewed on a monitor. The following factors may increase the risk of developing an ulcer:

- excess acid production

- emotional stress

- over-use of non-steroidal anti-inflammatory drugs (NSAIDS)

- alcohol consumption

- genetics

- infection with *H pylori*

- smoking[1]

## Diarrhea/Constipation

**Diarrhea** is a condition defined as having frequent, loose bowel movements. In the large intestine the patient can absorb more water than usual and cause diarrhea to occur. Diarrhea most often occurs because of a disturbance to the GI tract such as a bacterial or viral infection. Occasional diarrhea can be treated with non-prescription medication.

A patient with frequent bouts of diarrhea can become dehydrated very quickly. The elderly and children are at especially high risk for dehydration associated with diarrhea and must be treated properly. Fluids that contain important electrolytes are often used for patients who have lost an excess amount of fluids. Diarrhea that lasts longer than a few days could be an indication of a serious intestinal disease and should be monitored by a doctor.

**Constipation** is a condition characterized by having infrequent and sometimes painful bowel movements. The feces can become impacted and make it difficult to pass the stools. Constipation could be caused by a lack of dietary fiber intake or the intake of too much fiber if the body is not used to it. Drinking plenty of water is recommended when adding more fiber to the diet which can help to prevent constipation.

## IBS

**Irritable bowel syndrome (IBS)** is a condition characterized by abdominal pain, intestinal cramps, and abnormal bowel function with alternating periods of diarrhea

---

[1] http:/digestive.niddk.nih.gov/ddiseases/pubs/pepticulcers_ez

and constipation. It is estimated that 20% of adult Americans suffer from IBS and it is more common in women than men.[2]

The exact cause of IBS is not clear. Some research suggests that IBS might be related to stress or sensitivity to certain foods. It is also difficult to diagnose IBS because there is no blood test that can confirm a diagnosis. IBS is diagnosed based on the patient's having symptoms for at least 12 weeks; the 12 weeks do not have to be consecutive.[3]

The following have been reported to worsen symptoms of IBS:

- Large meals
- Bloating from gas in the colon
- Certain medications
- Wheat, rye, barley, chocolate, milk or dairy products, alcohol
- Caffeinated drinks
- Stress or emotional upsets

The treatment for IBS varies depending on the severity of the symptoms. Some patients are prescribed medications for severe symptoms, other patients will have to make dietary and lifestyle changes. The following suggestions may be beneficial in the treatment of IBS:

- Relaxation and meditation
- Regular exercise and yoga
- Decrease stress
- Adequate sleep
- Increase fiber in the diet
- Increase consumption of fruits and vegetables
- Decrease caffeine and carbonated drinks
- Drink 8–10 glasses of water per day

**EVERY DAY**
**SUPERFOODS**

Did you know? There was a study done about the inclusion of particular foods in the diet (almonds, barley, flax, oats, psyllium, tofu/edamame) that can have the same cholesterol-lowering effect as statin drugs. Plus it helps improve blood pressure and triglyceride numbers!

---

[2] http://digestive.niddk.nih.gov/ddiseases/pubs/ibs/
[3] same as above

## Summary

Digestion and absorption require the body to work at its best. The hypothalamus is the control center of hunger. Hunger is sensed when a series of hormones and messages are received from the hypothalamus to the stomach and vice versa. Satiety, which is a feeling of fullness, is also controlled by the hypothalamus which tells the person to stop eating.

We eat with our senses, especially our eyes. Color, texture, and smell of foods are intimately connected to our food choices. Food choices are also based on preferences, culture, and special occasions.

Digesting and absorbing our foods involves a synchronization of different processes in the body. Our body is all about being efficient; digestion and absorption of foods are no exception. Digestion begins in the mouth and requires chemical and mechanical actions to break down foods.

The mouth and teeth crush and break the food into smaller pieces. A bolus of food enters the esophagus which serves as a connection to the stomach. Peristalsis occurs all along the GI tract to help move the food. The stomach functions to mix and churn the foods and mix gastric juices to form chyme. Chyme enters the small intestine and starts the process of absorption. The small intestine is made up three parts, the duodenum, jejunum, and ileum. Absorption of nutrients occurs by simple diffusion, facilitated diffusion, and active transport. Fresh nutrients leave the small intestine by way of the portal vein and go to the liver. The liver evaluates all nutrients and attempts to detoxify any substances that might be harmful to the body. The liver and muscles stores extra monosaccharides (a type of carbohydrate) as glycogen for future use if needed. The large intestine serves as a holding tank for waste products until elimination occurs.

Accessory organs, such as the gallbladder which produces bile, help with fat digestion in the small intestine. The pancreas produces bicarbonate to neutralize the acid coming from the stomach. The pancreas also secretes many important enzymes that help to break down carbohydrates, fats, and proteins into smaller components for absorption. The GI tract is separated into different sections by the lower esophageal sphincter and the pyloric sphincter.

Heartburn is a condition in which the lower esophageal sphincter is not functioning properly, which allows the acidic stomach contents to back-up into the esophagus causing a burning sensation. Gastroesophageal reflux disease (GERD) is a condition in which heartburn becomes more frequent and sometimes serious. Medications can be used to treat GERD. It is recommended that patients with GERD make changes in their food choices and lifestyle habits in order to decrease the symptoms.

Ulcers are caused by the *Helicobacter pylori* bacteria. Ulcers can be found in the stomach and the duodenum. Ulcers can be treated with some medications and also require that the patient make dietary and lifestyle changes.

Diarrhea is a disturbance of the GI tract which may occur due to bacterial or viral infection. Diarrhea can lead to severe dehydration especially in children and elderly. Constipation is a common health problem which can cause abdominal discomfort. Straining to pass hard stools can sometimes cause hemorrhoids or diverticulosis in some patients. In both cases patients are encouraged to eat healthily and include plenty of fiber and water in their diets.

Occasional constipation is a common health problem. Constipation can be caused by a lack of dietary fiber or excess intake of fiber in the diet, both of which can result in decreased bowel movements (constipation) which can cause abdominal pain and bloating. Drinking plenty of water can help to relieve constipation.

Irritable bowel syndrome (IBS) is a condition characterized by abdominal cramping, bloating, and pain. A patient with IBS will have alternating periods of diarrhea and constipation. The exact cause of IBS is unknown and it is more common in women than men. Treatment for IBS depends on the severity of the symptoms.

# PROBIOTICS: GOOD FOR DIGESTIVE HEALTH OR HYPE?

Bacteria are usually thought of as bad because of their disease causing reputation. It is important to note that there is a "good" bacterium that exists in the body, especially in the large intestine. Current research suggests that taking in foods that contain certain live bacteria can be good for us. Fermented foods and drinks are becoming increasingly popular with people who are trying to take care of their digestive health.

© 2012, Shutterstock, Inc.

Some doctors may even suggest that patients with Irritable Bowel Syndrome (IBS) may benefit from taking a probiotic supplement.* Healthy bacteria in the large intestine can also be beneficial for the immune system.

Below is a list of common probiotic containing foods:

• Yogurt - available in many flavors or plain (choose the lower sugar variety)

• Kefir - sold as a drink in most stores (choose the lower sugar version)

• Sauerkraut - a German form of pickled cabbage

• Dark chocolate - the more pure, the more probiotics

• Microalgea - spirulena

• Miso soup - a Japanese soup

• Pickles - pickled cucumbers

• Tempeh - a fermented soy product

• Kimchi - an Asian form of pickled cabbage

• Kombucha tea- a fermented tea

Probiotics are generally considered to be safe. Make sure to read the label on all products that claim to have probiotics. Also be aware of supplements that are sold in the United States. Remember that supplements are not tested and approved in the same way as drugs according to FDA regulations. Health benefits of probiotics are still being studied.

*Check with your doctor or other medical provider to discuss which probiotics may be beneficial to your health.

# Carbohydrates: "The Good, The Bad, and The Better"

# CHAPTER 4

© 2012, Shutterstock, Inc.

## Learning Objectives

- Explain the importance of carbohydrates in the body and why we need carbohydrates to prevent ketosis
- Define the different types of carbohydrates and the food sources for each one
- Outline the health effects and accusations against sugars in our diet
- List the different types of non-nutritive sweeteners and their actions in the body
- Understand the importance of getting adequate amounts of fiber in the body
- Explain the difference between type 1 and type 2 diabetes
- Describe a "Westernized diet" and its health implications

*Energize* (noun) to give energy to:

We get energy from the foods that we eat. Carbohydrates are the brain's preferred source of energy and it is important that we intake carbohydrates on a daily basis.

---

**Functional Food Fact** \ Oats

Oats have been widely studied for their cholesterol-lowering properties. Marketing of cereals that lower your cholesterol have proven to be a profitable business for food manufacturers. There is favorable evidence that consuming oats may reduce total cholesterol and low density lipoprotein (LDL) which is also known as the "bad cholesterol." Eating oatmeal for breakfast is a great way to include oats in your diet. Here's to a healthy heart!

# Carbohydrates

## Introduction to Carbohydrates

It is often said that carbohydrates are the enemy when it comes to losing weight—the so-called "bad carbohydrates." Popular diet fads such as the Atkins diet took this similar approach to carbohydrates by eliminating all carbohydrates from the diet for an extended period of time to help jump-start weight loss. In theory this does work for some people, but what happens when carbohydrates are

© 2012, Shutterstock, Inc.

added back into the diet? Which types of foods come to mind when you think of carbohydrates? Most people name the common foods such as bread, pastas, rice, grains, and cereals. In this chapter on carbohydrates we will find that there are carbohydrate sources that can be beneficial to our health and may even promote weight loss. Categorizing foods as "good" and "bad" can set us up for failure when we are trying to adopt healthier eating habits.

When we think of **carbohydrates** we often think of foods such as bread, rice, pastas, and cereals. We also tend to blame carbohydrates for excess weight gain—which could not be further from the truth. As you will learn in this chapter, carbohydrates fuel the brain for many important functions. Even as you read this book, your brain is carefully calculating the amount of available carbohydrates in your body to keep you focused on what you are doing. The main form of carbohydrate that supplies the brain is glucose. We do not eat glucose directly, but instead rely on food sources to provide a sufficient amount daily. A lack of carbohydrates can decrease your concentration. The brain is a very complex and sophisticated organ. When carbohydrates are lacking in the diet, the brain will know how to modify other nutrients to get the glucose needed to sustain energy.

# The Chemistry Behind the Carbohydrates

## Structures of Carbohydrates

These structures consist of a single unit of a sugar molecule called a **monosaccharide**, or they consist of two units of sugar called a **disaccharide**. The monosaccharides that are most important to us in nutrition are in the shape of 6-carbon hexoses. To better understand the chemical structures of these monosaccharides and disaccharides, let's look at some basic concepts about chemistry.

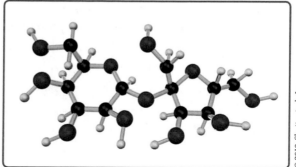

© 2012, Shutterstock, Inc.

Each atom can form a certain number of chemical bonds with other atoms. In nutrition we will deal mostly with carbon, nitrogen, hydrogen, and oxygen. The following bonds are required for each of these atoms:

- **Carbon** atoms form four bonds.
- **Nitrogen** (which is unique to protein structures) forms three bonds.
- **Oxygen** forms two bonds.
- **Hydrogen** forms one bond.

### Monosaccharides

The **simple carbohydrates** are the most important sugars. Our bodies use these simple sugars to build larger sugar molecules that have many different functions. The word *mono* means one and *saccharide* means sugar.

The three monosaccharides are as follows:

- Glucose
- Fructose
- Galactose

**Glucose** is commonly referred to as our blood sugar. When we eat, food is broken down to provide an adequate glucose supply. The cells in the body uptake glucose, which is a source of energy. The red blood cells and the brain depend on glucose for a quick source of energy. The human body can carefully calculate how much available glucose there is available for the brain to function properly. Later in the chapter we will look at the hormones involved in the regulation of glucose which will lead us to a discussion about diabetes.

**Fructose** is commonly found in fruit, honey, and some vegetables. Fructose tastes much sweeter than glucose. **High fructose corn syrup (HFCS)** is made from corn and is widely used by food manufacturers because it is a cheaper form of sugar and they only have to use a small amount to get the desired sweetness.

**Galactose** is not commonly found in foods. A glucose molecule and a galactose molecule combine to form lactose which is the sugar found in milk and dairy products. See Figure 4.1.

**Figure 4.1** Monosaccharides

## Disaccharides

To better understand the formation of the disaccharides we must first take a look at a few chemical reactions that bond these sugar molecules together. The first chemical reaction that takes place to bond two molecules together is called **condensation**. Condensation requires a molecule of water to complete the reaction. A simple way to illustrate condensation is to think about a window in the classroom. If the classroom is warm and it is cold outside sometimes condensation (water molecules) will collect on the window. Unless someone has intentionally wet the window, the molecules of water are pulled from the air and collect on the window. The second reaction is called **hydrolysis**. This reaction breaks the bond apart. We will look at hydrolysis later when we discuss digestion and absorption of carbohydrates.

The three disaccharides are as follows:

- Maltose

- Sucrose

- Lactose

**Maltose** consists of two glucose molecules; maltose is a product of the fermentation process. **Sucrose** consists of glucose and a fructose molecule. Sucrose is also known as table sugar and is refined from sugarcane and sugar beets. **Lactose** consists of glucose and a fructose molecule and is also known as milk sugar.

As previously mentioned, Americans have an obsession with sugar. Brown sugar, honey, raw sugar, and table sugar are treated the same in the body. There are not significant nutritional differences in any of these sugars and all sugar should be consumed in moderation.

Sucrose is made from sugar cane or sugar beets which are crushed and ground up in a factory. The mixture is then heated up until sugar crystals form and then the sugar is processed on a large round device that is used to "spin" the sugar to separate out any impurities. Molasses is one of these impurities which is a dark sticky substance that is produced when sugar is refined; it is usually added back to make brown sugar. Molasses is sold in the market and is sometimes used in cooking. To make white sugar, the molasses is removed.

How much sugar should we have on a daily basis? There is no RDA for sugar at this time, but most health professionals agree that the best way to watch our sugar intake of all sugar is to read the food labels. As you have already learned, looking at the serving size first is important when reading a food label. If your food item contains 10 grams or more of sugar per serving, you should look for another product that is lower. See Figure 4.2.

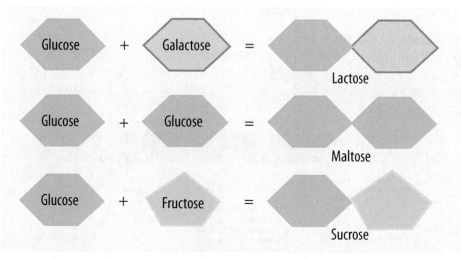

**Figure 4.2** Disaccharides

## Polysaccharides

The simple carbohydrates are the monosaccharides and disaccharides previously mentioned. The polysaccharides are also referred to as the complex carbohydrates.

They are referred to as complex because of their chemical structure. The three polysaccharides are as follows:

- Glycogen
- Starches
- Fiber

**Glycogen** is the stored form of glucose. After a meal, the liver receives all the fresh nutrients from the small intestine, including glucose. The liver tightly packs the glucose molecules and stores them away for use later if needed. Glycogen is also stored in the muscles. Why would we need to store glycogen for later use? The storage of glycogen acts as a "back-up" system and a way for the brain to get glucose for energy when you have not eaten for several hours. Under normal circumstances, our regular food intake would supply adequate amounts of glucose to the brain; but if you have not eaten for awhile, this is the brain's way of having a secondary source of energy.

**Starches** are plant-based polysaccharides contained in foods. These polysaccharides are long chains that are linked together in complex looking arrangements which are how they got the name complex carbohydrates. Starches are found in various seeds, some vegetables and tubers (potatoes), as well as breads, grains, and cereals.

**Fiber** is found in the structural parts of plants—these structures have strong bonds between them. These strong bonds cannot be broken down by the body; therefore the fiber will remain intact until excretion with the bowel movements. Dietary fiber is important to the body. Fiber is divided into two types, soluble fiber and insoluble fiber. See Figure 4.3.

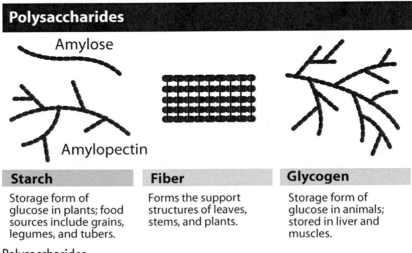

**Polysaccharides**

Amylose

Amylopectin

| Starch | Fiber | Glycogen |
|---|---|---|
| Storage form of glucose in plants; food sources include grains, legumes, and tubers. | Forms the support structures of leaves, stems, and plants. | Storage form of glucose in animals; stored in liver and muscles. |

**Figure 4.3** Polysaccharides

## Carbohydrate Digestion

As the saying goes, digestion begins in the mouth. The reason behind this saying is the fact that when you take a bite of food, an enzyme called **salivary amylase** goes to work on the polysaccharides to break them down into shorter disaccharides and monosaccharides. When the bolus of food reaches the stomach, the salivary amylase enzyme action is no longer active due to the acids in the stomach. The ultimate goal of digestion is to break all of the carbohydrates down into monosaccharides to cross the cell membrane. Remember in the chapter on digestion and absorption, we discussed the different ways in which the nutrients are absorbed. When the carbohydrates reach the small intestine, the pancreas releases additional enzymes that aid in the breakdown of the disaccharides.

**EVERY DAY SUPERFOODS**

Grapes are a great source of carbohydrates. We often think of breads, grains, and cereals as carbohydrates, but fruits are carbohydrates too. Grapes contain phenolic compounds which are said to be protective against heart disease. Red wine is also an excellent source of phenolic compounds but should be consumed in moderation.

© 2012, Shutterstock, Inc.

These enzymes are:

- Maltase - breaks down maltose into two glucose molecules

- Sucrase - breaks down sucrose into one glucose and one fructose molecule

- Lactase - breaks down lactose into one glucose and one galactose molecule

Within a few hours, all of the sugars and starches have been digested. Only the fiber remains in the digestive tract. Some fibers will be broken down and some fibers will remain intact. Later in this chapter we will discuss the different types of fiber and the health benefits associated with proper fiber intake.

## Carbohydrate Absorption

Carbohydrates are often misunderstood for being the culprit for weight gain. Most people tend to think that eating carbohydrates can make us gain weight. The truth is that our body has to take extra steps to store carbohydrates as fat and this is considered to be an inefficient process.

Carbohydrate absorption requires specialized protein carriers that follow facilitated and active transport absorption. Remember from Chapter 3 that we have three different ways in which the nutrients are absorbed, they are: simple diffusion, facilitated diffusion (a form of passive diffusion), and active transport.

Once all of the disaccharides are hydrolyzed back into the monosaccharides glucose, fructose, and galactose; all of these monosaccharides are transported to the liver via the portal vein. The liver tightly packs some of these monosaccharides to form **glycogen** which is a stored form of glucose that we can depend on for later use. We store glycogen in the liver as well as the muscles.

Why would we need the glycogen for later use? When energy or glucose levels are low in the bloodstream, this is our back-up plan to get sugar into the bloodstream quickly. The brain can signal the liver to release glycogen from the liver and muscle for a quick source of energy. There are limits to how much glycogen can be stored in the liver and the muscle tissue. Once the liver and the muscles have reached their storage limit, excess glucose, fructose, and galactose are released directly into the bloodstream for use by the brain. The brain's preferred source of energy is carbohydrates in the form of glucose. Other organs that use the monosaccharides are the muscles, kidneys, and adipose tissue.

It is true that carbohydrates that are consumed in excess can be stored in the adipose tissue, but this is mostly due to excessive intake of carbohydrates at mealtimes. Your body can only store and process so much. When intake of all nutrients exceeds the amount of calories you burn, the usual result is weight gain.

### NUTRITION NERD ALERT

The glycemic index measures the ability of a food to raise blood sugar levels. The glycemic load takes into account that the amount of food consumed at one time also affects this blood sugar increase. What is the best way to lower the glycemic index/load of a food? Eat it with a protein!

## Lactose Intolerance

Lactose intolerance is a condition in which your body does not produce enough of the lactase enzyme. Remember that an enzyme is needed to help speed up reactions or help to break things down. Lactose is a disaccharide that requires the lactase enzyme to break it down into glucose and galactose for absorption.

When we are born we have the highest amounts of the lactase enzyme available in the body. Our primary food source when we are born is breast milk or formula. It is very rare for babies to be born without adequate amounts of the lactase enzyme. By the time we reach adolescence, the activity of the lactase enzyme dramatically decreases. Statistics say that only about 30% of the adult population is able to tolerate milk and milk products.

## The Role of Glucose in the Body

Cells in the body use glucose for energy. Most of the glucose in the body is used by the brain, red blood cells, and the nervous system. During fat metabolism in the body, the cells require glucose to metabolize fats completely. If there is not any glucose available for fat metabolism, a ketone body is formed. A **ketone body** is a byproduct of incomplete fat metabolism. Ketone bodies are made up of different components of acids. No or low carbohydrate diets can force the body into ketosis which will burn fat for fuel. Burning fat sounds appealing to someone who is trying to lose weight, but ketosis is not a usual state for the body. Ketosis can disrupt the body's ability to maintain balance in the normal blood chemistry, especially acid-base balance. If ketosis develops in people with diabetes, this condition could be very dangerous and even cause death.

## Carbohydrate Metabolism and Diabetes

### Does Eating Sugar Cause Diabetes?

As a health professional I often encounter this question. Many people believe that eating sugar is a cause of diabetes. It is a myth that eating sugar is the cause of diabetes. In this section we will discuss the different types of diabetes, the complications, and the best ways to possibly prevent diabetes.

© 2012, Shutterstock, Inc.

## The Facts about Diabetes

Diabetes is a group of diseases characterized by high levels of blood glucose that is a result of defects in insulin production, the action of insulin, or both. It is estimated that almost 26 million people in the United States have diabetes. It is also estimated that another 79 million people have pre-diabetes, which is a condition in which the blood glucose levels are higher than normal but not high enough to be diagnosed with diabetes.

© 2012, Shutterstock, Inc.

Here are some other facts about diabetes:

- Type 1 diabetes accounts for approximately 5% of all diagnosed diabetics in the United States

- Type 2 diabetes accounts for 90–95% of all diagnosed diabetics in the United States

# FOOD IN FOCUS Secret Sugars

by Jennifer Jackson

We hear a lot about sugar-sweetened beverages (sodas, sports drinks, etc) and beverages (like fruit juice) which are naturally sweetened with sugar in the form of fructose. Any which way you look at it, sugar is sugar, is sugar. Efforts to try and keep our total grams of sugar at the recommended levels between 12-36 grams (according to the American Heart Association) may be difficult if you don't consider other foods that have added sugar.

Below is a list of some foods that may contain added sugar:

- Sauces (condiments and entrée sauces)
- Flavored yogurts
- Instant flavored oatmeal
- Low-fat processed foods
- Pasta sauce
- Frozen dinners
- Baked beans
- Whole grain cereals

On the food label, it may not be easy to identify sugar. There are many other names for sugar listed below, see if you recognize any of these:

- Brown/white/raw sugar
- Dextrin/maltodextrin
- Corn syrup solids
- Invert sugar
- Maple/rice/sorghum gum
- Evaporated cane juice
- Malt
- Molasses
- Agave nectar
- Honey
- Dextrose, fructose, glucose, lactose, maltose, saccharose, sucrose, xylose
- treacle

Diabetes is a condition that is brought on by the inability of the body to use glucose adequately. Insulin is a hormone that is produced by the pancreas. A human cannot live more than a few days without adequate insulin. The action of insulin is compared to that of a lock and key system. When you eat a meal, your blood sugar goes up, which signals insulin to come in and open up the cells to allow the glucose to enter.

## What Are the Differences between Type 1 and Type 2 Diabetes?

### Type 1 Diabetes

Type 1 diabetics are usually diagnosed in childhood, between birth and about 18 years old. Type 1 diabetes is an autoimmune disease that causes total destruction of the beta cells in the pancreas, which are responsible for secreting insulin. A person with type 1 diabetes will rely on exogenous insulin for the rest of his/her life. Insulin is administered by injection. Some patients use an insulin pump which will be further discussed in class. This type of diabetes has a very quick onset, meaning that the symptoms present quickly. The cause of type 1 diabetes is not completely understood. The following are some possible causes of type 1 diabetes:

- Early exposure to cow's milk before the age of 1
- Certain viruses that occurred during childhood
- Ethnicity

Symptoms of type 1 diabetes include:

- Frequent urination
- Unusual thirst
- Extreme hunger
- Unusual weight loss
- Extreme fatigue and irritability

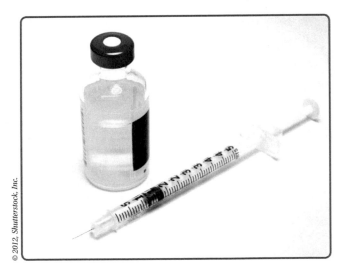

© 2012, Shutterstock, Inc.

## Type 2 Diabetes

Type 2 diabetes is the most common type of diabetes. Type 2 diabetes used to be referred to as adult onset diabetes. Today this is not the case as we are seeing an increase in the number of overweight or obese children who are being diagnosed with type 2 diabetes. Type 2 diabetes has reached epidemic proportions in the United States.

The following are some common causes of type 2 diabetes:

© 2012 Shutterstock, Inc.

- Genetics

- Obesity

- Ethnicity

- History of gestational diabetes

Certain ethnicities are at higher risk for developing type 2 diabetes than others. Americans who have Hispanic, Asian, Native American, African American, or Pacific Islander ancestry are at an increased risk. Unlike type 1 diabetes, the onset for type 2 diabetes is much slower. The onset of symptoms may take longer to manifest. Many people with diabetes go undiagnosed until they go to the doctor or have their blood sugar tested. Many people without medical insurance have type 2 diabetes and are not receiving proper care as a result. The complications of diabetes when uncontrolled are devastating.

Symptoms of type 2 diabetes include:

- Any of the above type 1 symptoms

- Frequent infections

- Blurred vision

- Cuts or bruises that are slow to heal

- Tingling or numbness in the hands or feet

- Frequent bladder infections, bleeding gums

If any of the symptoms above occur, it is recommended that you see a doctor immediately. The sooner you get help, the better chance you have to decrease the risk of long-term complications.

**Gestational diabetes** is a type of diabetes that occurs during pregnancy. Mothers who have a history of gestational diabetes are also at risk for developing type 2 diabetes. Gestational diabetes will be discussed in more detail in a later chapter.

## Complications of Diabetes

Complications of diabetes can be very costly to the healthcare system and decrease a patient's quality of life. Diabetes is a serious disease, but it can be treated effectively when the patient is empowered and educated. Diabetes is a complicated disease to learn about; but education is the key to preventing complications associated with both types of diabetes. The following complications are seen in people with diabetes:

- Blindness
- Neuropathy which causes nerve damage
- Nephropathy which causes kidney damage
- Skin breakdown, wounds that do not heal
- Heart attack or stroke
- High blood pressure

Most health professionals agree that when a patient takes control of their diabetes, their quality of life increases. Uncontrolled blood glucose can lead to the complications discussed above. High blood glucose levels are perceived as toxic by the body and complications will soon follow. Teaching patients how to take care of their diabetes is a fulfilling role as a health professional. Doctors and other specialists who are trained in diabetes care can assist a patient in choosing the right treatment options. Some patients will be able to control diabetes with diet and exercise. Other patients will require medications or even insulin.

## How to Prevent Diabetes

Knowing your family history is a great first step to preventing or decreasing your risk for diabetes. Being physically active and eating healthier can also play a role in decreasing your risk. The following recommendations may help to prevent or delay the onset of diabetes:

- Get regular check-ups with your doctor
- Know your family history
- Exercise and eat healthily
- Lose weight or maintain a healthy weight

## Health Effects of Sugar Intake

According to the USDA, Americans consume approximately 136 lbs of sugar each year. This includes table sugar, honey, high fructose corn syrup, and other added sugars. Moderation is the key for all of our favorite foods, and sugar is not any different. Most of our sources of sugar come in the form of empty calorie foods. Foods that are high in sugar are often low in vitamins and minerals. Even foods that are marketed as "healthy" can contain too much sugar; for example, cereals and cereal bars. Cereal is a commonly eaten breakfast food here in the United States; but if you look closely, many cereals contain sugar and are very low in fiber. You can make better choices for cereal if you take a closer look at the label. For example, choosing a cereal that has no more than 10 grams of sugar and at least 5–6 grams of fiber per serving can be a healthy addition to your breakfast. Cereal bars are marketed to offer a quick breakfast item in the morning, but be aware of these too. These cereal bars can contain as much sugar as some candy bars.

© 2012, Shutterstock, Inc.

### NUTRITION NERD ALERT

Whole fruit is preferred to fruit juice for many reasons. Consider that it takes approximately 13 oranges to make one 8 ounce glass of orange juice. Juice will have all the sugar and not enough fiber. It is better to eat the fruit than drink the juice!

## Alternative Sweeteners

Alternative sweeteners are often referred to as artificial sweeteners. The most common ones used today include saccharin, sucralose, and aspartame. The subject of cancer often comes up when discussing the use of artificial sweeteners. Early animal studies conducted in the 1970s using saccharin had shown it to cause bladder cancer in rats. Recent research has not provided clear evidence of an association with cancer in humans. Moderation is important when it comes to consuming artificial sweeteners.

**Saccharin** has been around since 1879. Saccharin is the oldest of the artificial sweeteners and is used in over 90 countries. The most common name for saccharin that is marketed in North America is Sweet N Low® which is most recognizable as being packaged in the pink packets. Saccharin was originally listed as a carcinogen (a cancer causing agent) by the Food and Drug Administration (FDA). Since animal studies on rats were conducted in the 1970s resulting in the development of bladder cancer, the FDA required special labeling on items containing saccharin to warn consumers of the possible carcinogenic effects. After further research was conducted, there was not enough evidence to prove that saccharin was in fact a carcinogen so in the year 2000, FDA removed saccharin from the carcinogen list.[1]

**Sucralose** is marketed here in the United States as Splenda® and is commonly found in the yellow packets. Sucralose is about 600 times sweeter than sugar and is made by adding three chlorines to sugar. Sucralose is approved for use in many different food items such as frozen items, dairy, ice cream, jams, fruit juices, and as a table sugar. Sucralose is also stable in high heat so you can bake with it.

**Aspartame** is commonly marketed as Equal® and is commonly found in the blue packets. Aspartame has received some negative complaints posted on the FDA website. Common complaints include headaches, dizziness, nausea, seizures, and other side effects. Compared to the population as a whole, it seems that only a small part of the population has these complaints according to the FDA. Aspartame is made from the amino acid phenylalanine and aspartic acid. In the chapter on protein, we will discuss how amino acids are the building blocks for many different structures in the body. Phenylalanine is an amino acid that is considered to be "conditionally essential." There is

© 2012, Shutterstock, Inc.

a small percentage of people who cannot consume products or foods with phenylalanine. This condition is called phenylketonuria. Phenylketonuria is characterized by the inability to break down phenylalanine correctly in the body due to a lack of an enzyme. This condition will be discussed further in the chapter on protein.

### Does sugar cause hyperactivity in children?

Sugar has often been blamed for misbehavior in children. The truth is that many studies have been done to show that sugar is not the cause of hyperactivity in children. Hyperactivity refers to increased movement, impulsiveness, being easily distracted and having a shorter attention span.[2]

[1] www.cancer.gov/cancertopics/factsheet/Risk/artificial-sweeteners
[2] www.nlm.nih.gov/medlineplus/ency/article/002426.htm. Accessed October 6, 2010.

# Health Effects of Fiber and Starch Intake

## Choose Healthier Carbohydrates

Fiber is a class of polysaccharides. There are different groups of fiber that can play a beneficial role in our health. There are two different types of fiber, soluble and insoluble. Both provide benefits to our health.

Below is a list of different classes of fibers:

- Cellulose (insoluble)
- Hemicellulose (insoluble)
- Pectin (soluble)
- Mucilages (soluble)
- Lignins (soluble)

**Cellulose** and **hemicellulose** are both non-fermentable fibers. Non-fermentable also means insoluble, meaning they cannot be broken down in the GI tract. Pectin, mucilages, and lignins are soluble fibers, which means they are soluble in water. **Pectin** is a fiber that is found in between the cell walls of plants. **Mucilages** are commonly found in seaweed, and **lignins** (considered non-carbohydrates) are part of an alcohol structure.

It has long been known that fiber has numerous health benefits. Fiber comes from breads, grains, cereals, fruits, and vegetables. Whole wheat products are also a great source of fiber. Reading the food label can help you to choose better carbohydrates. Be aware that just because a product says whole grain, it does not mean that the product has more fiber. There is a common misunderstanding amongst consumers that whole grain products contain more fiber. The fiber listed on the label does not always distinguish between soluble and insoluble fibers. The current recommendation for fiber intake on a daily basis is about 25–30 grams. Most Americans get only half of the recommended amount of fiber daily. Low fiber intake has been blamed on numerous health problems such as diverticulosis.

## Diverticulosis

Fiber is important for good health. Adequate fiber can help to decrease the risk of diseases such as obesity, heart disease, and certain intestinal tract diseases. Diverticulosis is a disease found in the large intestine. Small pockets or tiny sacs called diverticula develop in the large intestine possibly due to a diet that is low in fiber. What causes diverticular disease?

Although not proven, the dominant theory is that a low-fiber diet causes diverticular disease. The disease was first noticed in the United States in the early 1900s, around the time processed foods were introduced into the American diet. Consumption of processed foods greatly reduced Americans' fiber intake.

© 2012, Shutterstock, Inc.

Diverticular disease is common in developed or industrialized countries—particularly the United States, England, and Australia—where low-fiber diets are consumed. The disease is rare in Asia and Africa, where most people eat high-fiber diets.

Fiber is the part of fruits, vegetables, and grains that the body cannot digest. Some fiber, called soluble fiber, dissolves easily in water. It takes on a soft, jelly-like texture in the intestines. Insoluble fiber passes almost unchanged through the intestines. Both kinds of fiber help prevent constipation by making stools soft and easy to pass. Constipation or hard stool may cause people to strain when passing stool during a bowel movement. Straining may cause increased pressure in the colon, which may cause the colon lining to bulge out through weak spots in the colon wall. These bulges are diverticula. See Figure 4.4 below.

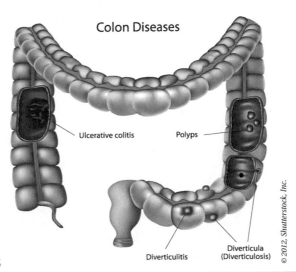

**Figure 4.4** Diverticulitis

Lack of exercise also may be associated with a greater risk of forming diverticula, although the reasons for this are not well understood.

Doctors are not certain what causes diverticula to become inflamed. The inflammation may begin when bacteria, seeds, or stool are caught in the diverticula. An attack of diverticulitis can develop suddenly and without warning. Diverticulitis often results in a visit to the hospital due to the pain and discomfort that the patient experiences. Treatment for diverticulitis includes medications to decrease inflammation and a low-fiber diet that allows the bowel to rest. Once the patient has recovered, a high-fiber diet is recommended.

## Summary

Americans have a love affair with sugar. Carbohydrates are often blamed for weight gain and un-healthy eating. Popular diets often decrease or eliminate carbohydrates from their meal plans. Carbohydrates can come from different foods such as breads, grains, cereals, fruits, vegetables, and dairy. Choosing better carbohydrates can improve your health and well being. The brain prefers carbohydrates because they can turn into sugar quickly in the body. The brain carefully calculates the available amount of glucose and can signal other organs when levels begin to fall below desirable levels.

Monosaccharides consist of a single sugar molecule. Glucose, fructose, and galactose are all monosaccharides. Disaccharides consist of two sugar molecules joined together by a molecule of water. Maltose, sucrose, and lactose are all disaccharides. Monosaccharides and disaccharides are considered simple carbohydrates.

Polysaccharides are considered complex carbohydrates. The polysaccharides are complex looking chemical structures and are made up of numerous sugar molecules. Glycogen, starches, and fiber are polysaccharides.

Carbohydrate digestion begins in the mouth. Salivary amylase works on the long chains of polysaccharides to break them down into shorter disaccharide and monosaccharide chains. The stomach works to mix and churn the contents in preparation for the small intestine. In the small intestine, carbohydrate-digesting enzymes such as maltase, sucrase, and lactase are secreted from the pancreas to break down the disaccharides into monosaccharides.

Absorption of the monosaccharides occurs when they pass the cell membrane and go to the vascular system to be utilized by the body for many important functions. The brain's preferred source of energy is carbohydrates.

Lactose intolerance occurs when the body does not make sufficient lactase enzyme. Symptoms of lactose intolerance include bloating, gas, and diarrhea.

The role of glucose in the body includes the necessity of carbohydrates in the metabolism of fat. Without proper carbohydrate intake, incomplete fat metabolism will result in the formation of a ketone body. Ketones are made up of different types of acids. Ketosis can lead to chemical imbalances in the blood and can be very dangerous or even deadly.

Diabetes is a group of diseases characterized by high levels of glucose in the bloodstream that is a result of a defect in insulin production, the action of insulin, or both. It is estimated that 26 million Americans have diabetes. Of those 26 million, 5 to 10% of them are type 1 diabetics and 90 to 95% are type 2 diabetics. Gestational diabetes is a condition that occurs in pregnant women. Type 1 diabetics are usually diagnosed before the age of 18 and do not produce insulin; therefore insulin must be injected. Complications of diabetes occur largely because of uncontrolled blood glucose levels. Complications of diabetes are similar for type 1 and type 2 diabetics. Complications can be slowed down or prevented when the patient is taking proper measures to control blood sugar. Education is the key to helping patients take control of their diabetes and improve their quality of life. Prevention of diabetes begins with getting regular check-ups with the doctor, knowing your family history, and understanding your risk. Healthy habits can last a lifetime and help to prevent the onset of diabetes.

All sugar should be consumed in moderation. Those who are trying to control their sugar intake may resort to using alternative sweeteners. Currently there is not any proven evidence that artificial sweeteners cause cancer. Common artificial sweeteners that are on the market include aspartame, sucralose, and saccharin.

Fiber should be included in a healthy diet. Current recommendations suggest that we consume 25–30 grams of fiber per day. Fiber is divided into two categories, soluble and insoluble. Both types of fiber have health benefits. Low-fiber diets can lead to a condition called diverticulosis. Diverticulosis is characterized by pockets that form in the large intestine. If inflammation occurs, the condition is referred to as diverticulitis and usually requires hospitalization for treatment. The initial dietary treatment of diverticulitis during the inflammation period is a low-fiber diet to allow the bowel to rest. Once the patient has recovered, a high-fiber diet is recommended to prevent a reoccurrence.

# DIABETES FACT SHEET

According to the American Diabetes Association over 25 million people in the United States have diabetes (including children and adults). Approximately 18 million are diagnosed and 7 million are undiagnosed. There are also an additional 79 million people that have pre-diabetes. With these frightening statistics, how can you protect yourself from getting diabetes? Of course your chances of getting diabetes depend on your family history and pre-existing health conditions.

© 2012, Shutterstock, Inc.

**Here are some suggestions that may be helpful in preventing diabetes:**

- If you are overweight, studies show that as little as a 5–7% weight loss decreased a person's chance of getting diabetes by over 50%
- Exercise at least 30 minutes per day most days of the week
- Follow a heart healthy diet (see tip sheet in chapter 5)
- Get regular check-ups with your doctor

**Here is a list of possible signs and symptoms associated with diabetes:***

- Extreme thirst followed by frequent urination
- Always hungry
- Weight loss
- Blurry vision
- Tingling in the hands or feet
- Feeling tired all the time

*if you experience one or more of the symptoms listed above, you should see your doctor right away

# Lipids: Be Good to Your Heart

## Learning Objectives

- Distinguish between the different classes of lipids
- Learn the difference between monounsaturated and polyunsaturated fats and their sources
- List the various functions of lipids
- Explain how lipids are digested and absorbed in the body
- Discuss the various fats and their impact on the development and prevention of cardiovascular disease

© 2012, Shutterstock, Inc.

## Functional Food Fact \ Flaxseed Oil

Fats and oils can be heart healthy. Oils that come from plants and seeds can be beneficial to our health. Linolenic acid is an essential fatty acid which means that we have to consume it from a food source. Linolenic acid is also known as the omega-3 fatty acid. Most people think of fish when they think of an omega-3 fatty acid. Flaxseed oil is composed of at least half omega-3 fatty acids. Regular consumption of flaxseed oil is an excellent way to keep your heart healthy. The omega-3 fatty acid is involved in decreasing inflammation in the body which may be beneficial to people with heart disease.

## Introduction to Lipids, Fats, and Oils

When adopting healthier eating habits most people understand that cutting down on fat in the diet is important. Providing 9 calories per gram, fats contain more than twice as many calories per gram as carbohydrates and protein. High-fat diets are often blamed when a person experiences a heart attack or stroke, but did you know that some fats are actually considered "heart healthy"? Fat is often misunderstood when it comes to health. Most people think that only inactive, overweight, or obese people get heart disease, but did you know that even the healthiest of athletes can have heart disease? In this chapter we will discuss the different types of fats and the function of fats. We will take a look at the digestion and absorption of fats and the impact that fats have in the development of heart disease.

## Lipids: Basic Components

Like carbohydrates, lipids contain carbon (C), hydrogen (H), and oxygen (O) in their structure. Lipid structures contain more hydrogen and carbon than oxygen. Lipids are slightly more than twice as energy dense and will give us 9 calories per gram as compared to carbohydrates and protein which give us 4 calories per gram. Lipids are not soluble in water. If you pour oil into a glass of water, the oil will float to the top of the glass. Mixing oil and water requires emulsification or the use of an emulsifying agent which will be discussed further in the section on digestion and absorption of fat. There are three classifications of fats, triglycerides, phospholipids, and sterols. Each one of these fats has a different function in the body.

### Fatty Acids

Fatty acids have one end that contains an oxygen-containing carboxyl group and the other end is composed of a hydrogen-containing methyl group. Fatty acid chains vary in length; a unique feature of the fatty acid chain is that the number of carbons along the chain exist in even numbers. The number of carbons can be anywhere from 4 to 24 carbons long. The 18-carbon containing fatty acids are the most common in our foods.

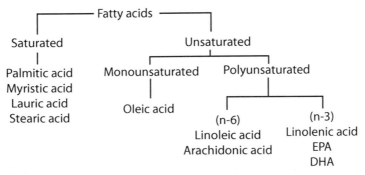

**Figure 5.1** Fatty acids

## Triglycerides

Most of the fats and oils that are consumed in the diet are in the form of triglycerides. The structure of triglycerides comprises a glycerol molecule attached to three fatty acid chains. See Figure 5.2 below.

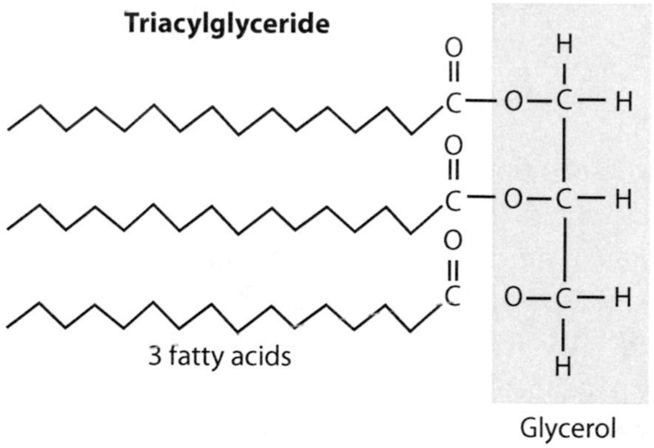

**Triacylglyceride**

3 fatty acids

Glycerol

**Figure 5.2** The chemical structure of triglycerides

## Saturated vs. Unsaturated Fats

The fats in our foods are made up of different types of fatty acids. These fats can be categorized further as being saturated or unsaturated.

A **saturated fat** is a fatty acid that is completely filled up or "saturated" with hydrogen bonds on each carbon. The strength of the structure of this fatty acid is strong enough to retain its shape at room temperature. The alternate definition of a saturated fat is that it can retain its shape at room temperature. Think of a stick of butter or lard. Both of these fats can retain their shape even when they are not refrigerated. When you add heat, this will cause the structure to fall apart. See Figure 5.3 below.

Saturated fats are found in:

- Whole milk, cream, butter, and cheese
- Coconut, palm oils, and palm kernels
- Fatty cuts of beef and pork

An **unsaturated fat** is a fatty acid chain that contains at least one carbon-carbon double bond. Recall from the chemistry snapshot above that a carbon will always need to make four bonds. If another connection to another element cannot be made, carbon will make another bond with another carbon in the fatty acid chain. This is referred to as a degree of un-saturation. This double bond formation weakens the structure of the fatty acid and causes the structure to fall apart.

Unsaturated fats are found in:

- Vegetable-based oils

- Nuts and seeds

- Fatty fish

Think of oils that you can pour out of a bottle. When there is one double bond formation on the fatty acid chain, this is referred to as a **monounsaturated fat**, *mono* means *one*. Good examples of monounsaturated fats are canola and olive oils. When there is more than one double bond formation on the fatty acid chain, this is referred to as a **polyunsaturated fatty acid**, *poly* means *many*. Examples of the polyunsaturated fatty acids are corn, soybean, safflower, and sunflower oils. The monounsaturated and polyunsaturated fats are considered to be more "heart healthy" because they do not clog the arteries like the saturated fats do. Remember that, although these fats are more heart healthy, fat still contains 9 calories per gram. See Figure 5.3.

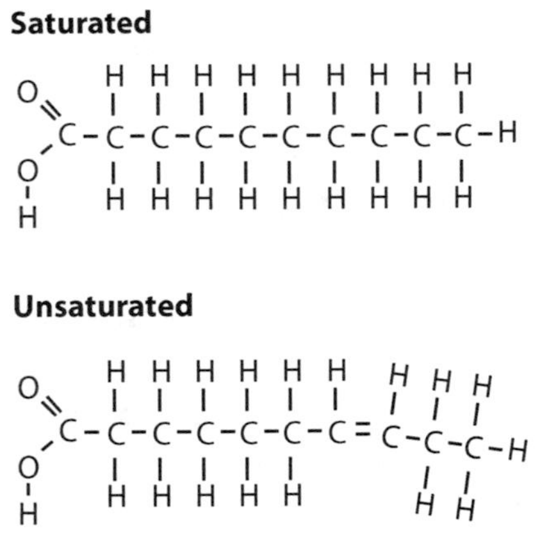

**Saturated**

$$O=C-C-C-C-C-C-C-C-C-C-H$$

**Unsaturated**

$$O=C-C-C-C-C-C-C=C-C-C-H$$

**Figure 5.3** Chemical structures of saturated and unsaturated fats

## Trans Fats

As with all fat intake, moderation is key. Most health professionals agree that trans fatty acid intake should be kept to a minimum. Studies have shown that high intake of trans fat and saturated fat is closely linked to the development of cardiovascular disease. Trans fats behave similar to saturated fats in the body.

There are some naturally occurring trans fats that come from some meat and milk products. However, it is estimated that 80% of the trans fat that we consume in our diet comes from processed and packaged food items.[1] The development of a trans fats is a chemical process by which hydrogens are forced onto an otherwise unsaturated fatty acid to make it solid again. This process changes the chemical properties of the structure of the fat and causes the hydrogen atoms to switch from one side of the structure to the other. The structure starts off in a cis formation and changes into a trans formation.

Common food items that contain trans fats include:

- Deep fat fried foods (using shortening)

- Snack foods, baked goods, crackers, and chips

- Margarine

- Imitation cheese

- Meat and dairy products (contain naturally occurring trans fats in small amounts)

Trans fats can help prolong shelf life of some of these items because they can slow down oxidation which can cause a product to spoil. Studies about the use of trans fats in our foods has led to concerns about the increased risk of atherosclerosis (defined later in this chapter) and the development of heart disease. Growing concern over the use of trans fats by food manufacturers led to the requirement that trans fats be listed on the food labels as of January 2006. The Food and Drug Administration require food labels to list trans fats on the label, but there are some apparent loopholes. For example, if there is less than .5g per serving, the manufacturer is allowed to list the amount of trans fats as zero on the label. If you have more than one serving, chances are you are consuming small amounts of trans fats in that food item. Growing concerns about trans fats and the development of heart disease has also led to some cities banning the use of trans fats in fast food chains and restaurants.

NUTRITION NERD ALERT

Trans fats can be less than 0.5 g per serving and still say 0% daily value on the nutrition facts label. Check the ingredients section of the food label for words like: "partially hydrogenated" and "shortening" to help keep trans fats as close to 0 g as possible.

---

[1] U.S. Department of Agriculture and Health and Human Services: Dietary Guidelines for Americans 2005.

### Phospholipids

The second group of lipids to be discussed is the phospholipids, which are important components of cell membranes. Phospholipids help to move fat inside and outside of the cell membrane. As indicated in the name, a phospholipid contains phosphorus as part of its chemical structure. The phosphorus in the structure helps to allow the fat to be soluble in water.

© 2012, Shutterstock, Inc.

**Figure 5.4** Phospholipids are emulsifiers used in olive oils and salad dressings to keep them from separating.

In the food industry phospholipids are used as emulsifiers. An **emulsifier** helps to keep products that contain oil and water stay mixed together. Mayonnaise is a good example, as well as some salad dressings. **Lecithin** is the most common phospholipid in the body. Lecithin is often marketed as a supplement. Marketing of lecithin often includes claims such as "helps to maintain cell membrane integrity." This sounds like an important function, and it is true; but the truth about lecithin is we already make it in the body via the liver. The other reason we do not need a lecithin supplement is that we make an enzyme called lecithinase to break down excess lecithin. Thus, a lecithin supplement would be a waste of time and money. Why would we take a supplement of something that is already made in the body and that our body will just break down if we have more than we need?

**NUTRITION NERD ALERT**

Not all omega-3s are created equal. ALA omega-3s may actually raise the risk of prostate cancer. These can be found in soybean oil (the major ingredient in mayonnaise) and flax seeds. DHA and EPA omega-3s may lower the risk of heart disease, cancer, Alzheimer's, eye disorders, and other conditions. The best sources are fish and fish oils.

## Sterols

The third group of lipids to be discussed is the **sterol** group. The most common sterol that most people recognize is cholesterol. Cholesterol comes only from animal sources. Egg yolks, meat, liver, poultry, milk, and dairy are all sources of cholesterol. The structure of sterols is commonly described as multiple ringed structures, which makes them different from other lipid structures. Below is a comparison of the cholesterol structure and a triglyceride structure (Figure 5.5).

**The Structures of Cholesterol and Triglycerides**

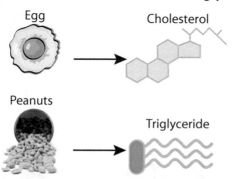

**Figure 5.5** The structures of cholesterol and triglycerides

## Different Types of Cholesterol

There are two different types of cholesterol; we have endogenous cholesterol which is made by the liver and exogenous cholesterol which comes from the diet. The cholesterol which is made by the liver is really all the cholesterol we need in the body. It is important to note how each of these sources of cholesterol plays a role in the body. According to the American Heart Association (AHA), saturated fatty acids and trans fatty acids consumed in the diet tend to be the biggest contributor to our overall cholesterol levels. It is recommended that we consume no more than 300 milligrams of cholesterol per day. If you have heart disease, the AHA recommends that you consume no more than 200 milligrams of dietary cholesterol per day.[2] Just to give you a frame of reference, an egg with the yolk contains 210 milligrams of cholesterol. Of course, if you discard the yolk you do not get any of the cholesterol.

---

[2] www.americanheart.org, AHA Scientific Position Statement.

When you have your cholesterol levels checked by your doctor, the lab value that you see is representing the amount of cholesterol in your blood (exogenous). Later in this chapter we will discuss what components make up your total cholesterol levels and how to read lab values.

Foods that contain cholesterol include:

- Eggs
- Dairy
- Meat, poultry, and shellfish

## Functions of Cholesterol

Cholesterol plays a role in bile acids, sex hormones such as testosterone, stress hormones such as cortisol, and assists us in changing vitamin D from the sun into its active form in the body. Most of the cholesterol in our body is inside the cells. Cholesterol is a waxy-like substance that can form deposits in the arterial walls which can lead to a condition known as **atherosclerosis**. Atherosclerosis can cause blockages to occur in the arteries and can lead to a heart attack or stroke. We will discuss cardiovascular disease at the end of this chapter.

### NUTRITION NERD ALERT

Saturated fats should be limited in the diet but a unique type, called medium chain triglycerides, may actually help with weight loss and nutrient absorption issues. They can be found in coconut and palm oils.

## Digestion and Absorption of Fats

As mentioned earlier, most of the fats that we consume in the diet are in the form of triglycerides. In digestion and absorption of fats the goal is to break down the triglycerides into monoglycerides for transportation across the cell membrane.

Fat digestion begins slowly in the mouth; your body temperature warms up and melts the fat and mixes it with **lingual lipase**. Lingual lipase is an enzyme found in the mouth and plays a small role in the digestion of fats in adults but plays a bigger role in digestion of fats in infants. Lingual lipase helps infants to break down longer chain fatty acids (found in milk) into shorter ones so it is easier for them to digest. Once the lingual lipase gets to the stomach, the enzyme becomes inactivated by the

*Nutrition Intuition*

hydrochloric acid in the stomach. Remember that the stomach's job is to mix and churn everything up. If you mix oil and water in a glass, the oil floats to the top of the glass. The muscle contractions of the stomach do not allow the fat to float to the top; instead the fat is mixed in with the other nutrients to form chyme. **Chyme** is a semi-liquid mixture of the stomach contents which is ready to enter the small intestine

**Gastric lipase** is another enzyme produced by the stomach that will further break down the fat molecules into smaller droplets in preparation for the small intestine. There is little absorption of fat in the stomach.

When fat arrives in the small intestine, a series of hormones aids in its absorption. **Cholecystokinin (CCK)** is the hormone that signals the pancreas to release digestive enzymes. **Pancreatic lipase** is one of the enzymes released from the pancreas and it assists in the digestion of the triglycerides. Pancreatic lipase reduces the triglycerides down to monoglycerides.

CCK also stimulates the gallbladder to release **bile** into the duodenum. Bile acts as an emulsifier which keeps the fats dispersed into smaller particles and aids in the mixing of fat with water. Remember that bile is made by the liver and stored in the gallbladder until needed.

The monoglycerides are the smallest component of the fatty acids. The monoglycerides can pass the cell membrane and go into the bloodstream. Some of the short and medium chained fatty acids can go directly into the bloodstream for immediate use by the body. Other fragments of fats then get re-packaged into a transport lipid called a lipoprotein.

A type of lipoprotein that is used in the body is called a **chylomicron**. These chylomicrons are large molecules and therefore do not fit directly into the vascular system. Chylomicrons serve as the transport vehicle for the lipids through the lymphatic system until it finally reaches the vascular system near the heart.

Once the chylomicron reaches the vascular system, the fats are ready for use. An enzyme called **lipoprotein lipase** begins breaking down the chylomicron into smaller components. Lipoprotein lipase is a gender-specific enzyme that signals the body and tells it where to deposit the fat. Females tend to deposit more fat on the hips and thighs area and males tend to deposit more fat on the abdominal area.

Some of the fats are used for energy and some are deposited in the **adipose cells**. Adipose cells serve as the storage site for fat. Fat storage in the adipose cells is virtually unlimited. Excessive storage of fats in the adipose cells is what leads to obesity. Other parts of fats are reduced down to cholesterol-rich components which then go to the liver to be utilized for other lipid-containing compounds.

Lowering cholesterol in the diet can lead to better heart health. Food manufacturers are making claims on labels that are trying to promote heart health and promise lower cholesterol. Products like cereals and juices are putting claims on their labels that consuming these products can help you to lower cholesterol. How can they do this? These products contain soluble fiber. Soluble means that it can dissolve easily in water. Soluble fiber is also in foods such as some fruits, vegetables, and oats.

Plant sterols may also be added to foods and can provide an additional heart health benefits. Plant sterols may be able to lower your LDL or "bad" cholesterol. Plant sterols are found in products such as margarines and some yogurts.

Lowering cholesterol in the diet means that you might have to make some changes to the amount of protein and fat that you consume in the diet. Consuming lean proteins such as chicken and fish are beneficial. Choosing non-animal proteins such as tofu and beans can offer more variety in the diet. Replace saturated and trans fats in the diet with more mono and polyunsaturated fats. Research has shown that polyunsaturated fats are able to lower LDL a little bit more than monounsaturated fats. Good sources of polyunsaturated fats include soybean, corn, and sunflower oils.

Lowering simple carbohydrates in the diet can also be heart healthy. Research has shown that high intakes of simple carbohydrates such as white pasta and white rice can raise triglyceride levels in the blood. The higher the triglyceride levels, the "thicker" the blood can get. Higher triglyceride levels are associated with increased risk for heart attack or stroke.

Including plenty of fiber in the diet can also help to lower cholesterol. Soluble fibers were discussed above. Insoluble fiber comes from whole wheat, fruits, and vegetables and can help to lower cholesterol by binding with extra cholesterol in the body. We can remove this extra cholesterol via the bowel movements. It is recommended that we consume at least 25-30 grams of fiber per day.

## Fat Consumption in the United States

### The Westernized Diet

In many cultures traditional foods have significant meanings and often tell us a lot about the culture's people. Traditional foods associated with different ethnicities are usually rich in fruits, vegetables, and grains, with small amounts of red meat. A great example of this is the Mediterranean diet. A Mediterranean diet is primarily composed of fruits, vegetables, grains, olive oil, nuts, and lean meats such as chicken and fish. Dairy products and red meats are consumed less often. The adoption of the Mediterranean diet has been shown to improve insulin sensitivity, lower levels of total cholesterol, and lower blood pressure in overweight and obese people.[3]

A Westernized diet is also known as the standard American diet (SAD). The Westernized diet or SAD is one that is made up of many processed foods and is high in saturated fat and refined carbohydrates.[4] A Westernized diet is often adopted by individuals who migrate to the United States and it can negatively impact their health and well being. The adoption of more convenient and processed foods in the diet has been shown to increase the incidence of obesity, high blood pressure, heart disease, and diabetes amongst these individuals.

## Recommendations for Fat Intake—Dietary Guidelines for Americans, 2010

According to the Dietary Guidelines for Americans, the following recommendations are important to note when it comes to fat consumption:

- Consume less than 10 percent of calories from saturated fatty acids by replacing them with monounsaturated and polyunsaturated fatty acids.

- Consume less than 300 mg per day of dietary cholesterol.

- Keep trans fatty acid consumption as low as possible by limiting foods that contain synthetic sources of trans fats, such as partially hydrogenated oils, and by limiting other solid fats.

- Reduce the intake of calories from solid fats and added sugars.

**EVERY DAY**
**SUPERFOODS**

A 2011 study conducted by the USDA's Agricultural Research Service found that fat from pistachios is not as readily absorbable as once thought and could create less calories than indicated on the nutrition facts label. The fat that is absorbable helps lower LDL (lousy) cholesterol and improve lipid profiles.

## Cardiovascular Disease

**Cardiovascular disease** is a general term that describes various diseases of the heart and blood vessels. Cardiovascular disease is the number one killer of Americans. Coronary heart disease (CHD), or coronary artery disease (CAD), is a condition

---

[3] Lipids in Health and Disease, http://www.lipidworld.com/content/6/1/22
[4] The Standard American Diet and its Relationship to the Health Status of Americans, http||ncp.sagepub.com/content/25/6/603

associated with the build-up of plaque in the arterial walls which can eventually lead to a heart attack or stroke. Most people believe that plaque build-up occurs only during our adulthood years. The truth is that we begin to build-up plaque in the arterial walls when we begin to consume solid foods as infants. See Figure 5.6 below that compares a normal artery to an artery that has plaque which causes a narrowing of the artery.

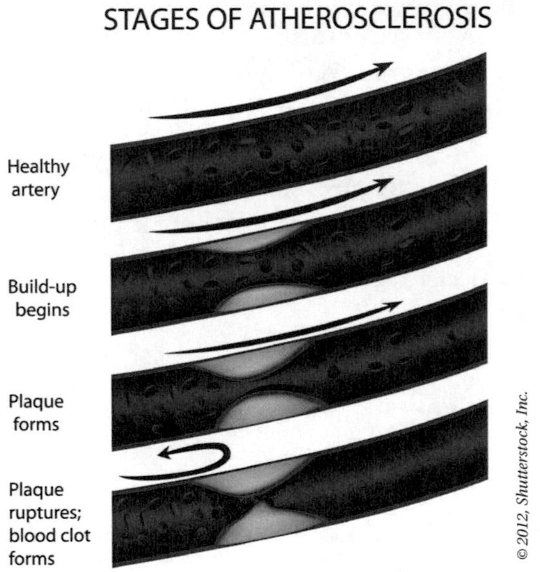

STAGES OF ATHEROSCLEROSIS

Healthy artery

Build-up begins

Plaque forms

Plaque ruptures; blood clot forms

© 2012, Shutterstock, Inc.

**Figure 5.6** Comparison of a normal artery and an artery that has been narrowed by plaque.[4]

## How You Can Be Heart Healthy

Because heart disease is the number one killer in the United States it is very important that we take steps to keep our hearts healthy. Heart disease was originally thought of as a "man's disease," meaning more men than women died of heart disease. Today, heart disease is the number one killer of women in the United States. Heart attacks and strokes are largely preventable diseases. Our lifestyles, poor eating habits, and lack of exercise put us at risk for a heart attack or stroke. Is it only "couch potatoes" who get heart disease? The answer is no. A family history of heart attack or stroke can also put us at risk. Regular physical examinations by a medical doctor are important for your overall health and well being. The doctor can check your lab values to see if they are in the desirable ranges.

---

[4] The Standard American Diet and its Relationship to the Health Status of Americans, http||ncp.sagepub.com/content/25/6/603

Below is a list of desirable lab value ranges for a healthy heart:

- Total Cholesterol: < 200mg/dL

- LDL Cholesterol: < 100mg/dL

- HDL Cholesterol: > 60mg/dL

- Triglycerides: < 150mg/dL

Cholesterol as mentioned above is a waxy substance that is found among the lipids in the bloodstream and in the cells of the body. Remember that the transport of fats around the body depends on lipoproteins. **Low-density lipoprotein (LDL)** is also known as the "bad cholesterol." LDL cholesterol is increased in the body by consuming diets that are higher in saturated and trans fats. LDL cholesterol circulates in the bloodstream and carries cholesterol to the arteries, which contributes to plaque formation. The best way that we can reduce our LDL level in the body is to decrease our consumption of saturated and trans fats in the diet.

**High-density lipoprotein (HDL)** is also known as the "good cholesterol." HDL cholesterol carries cholesterol away from the heart and back to the liver where it will be made into other components or excreted from the body. The best way to increase HDL in the body is to exercise. Originally it was thought that we could increase our HDL levels in the body by choosing more heart healthy fats. Current research has suggested that HDL levels are increasing in response to the amount of exercise a person does. The mechanism is not exactly clear at this time as to how the HDL levels are increased.

Other factors that can influence cholesterol in the body are smoking and alcohol intake. Smoking has been shown to lower HDL levels in the body and is a definite contributor to heart disease as a whole. Moderation of alcohol intake has been shown to perhaps increase HDL levels, but the risks outweigh the benefits in this case. Moderation in alcohol consumption is one drink per day for women and two drinks per day for men. Consulting with a physician about alcohol intake and heart disease is recommended.

## Summary

Fat is often misunderstood when it comes to health. High-fat diets are blamed when someone is overweight or obese or experiences a heart attack or stroke. In this chapter we have looked at the different types of fats and determined that there are heart healthy fats. In all, fats must be consumed in moderation.

Fats are the most energy dense of all of our nutrients. Fat provides 9 calories per gram which is twice as much as carbohydrates or proteins. In nutrition we see fatty acid structures that vary in length. What makes these fatty acid structures unique is the fact that they have an even number of carbons in the length of their chains.

Triglycerides are the most common types of fats consumed in our diet. Triglycerides are composed of three fatty acids bonded to an alcohol group. Approximately 95% of the fats that we eat in the diet are in the form of triglycerides.

Saturated fats are completely filled up with hydrogen molecules along the fatty acid chain. The hydrogen molecules allow the fatty acid structure to stack up and give it strength. A saturated fat is able to retain its shape at room temperature. Examples of saturated fats include butter, lard, margarine, coconut and palm oils, and fatty cuts of beef and pork.

Unsaturated fats include monounsaturated and polyunsaturated fats. These fats contain double bond formations in their structures. This does not allow the fatty acid to stack well together and therefore the structure falls apart. Unsaturated fats are considered to be more heart healthy. Examples of unsaturated fats include vegetable oils, nuts, seeds, and fatty fish.

Trans fatty acids are produced by forcing hydrogen molecules onto an unsaturated fatty acid. There are very little amounts of naturally occurring trans fatty acids in meat and dairy products. All other sources of trans fats are made by the hydrogenation process. Consuming trans fats in the diet should be kept to a minimum. Trans fats have been shown to increase atherosclerosis in the arteries and increase LDL levels (the bad cholesterol). Sources of trans fats include fried foods, snack foods, baked goods, margarine, and some imitation cheese food products.

Phospholipids provide support for the cell membrane structures. Phospholipids allow fats to be soluble in water for absorption.

Sterols are a group of compounds that can come from both plant and animal sources. The most common sterol that we deal with in nutrition is cholesterol. Cholesterol is made by the liver and serves many functions in the body. It is recommended that we consume no more than 300 mg of cholesterol per day. Cholesterol is found in foods of animal origin. Cholesterol is a waxy-like substance that can form deposits in the arterial walls and lead to atherosclerosis.

Digestion of fats begins with lingual lipase, an enzyme that is found in the mouth and begins the breakdown of longer chain fatty acids. In the stomach, gastric lipase further breaks down the fat molecules into smaller droplets. CCK is the hormone that signals the pancreas to release digestive enzymes. Bile is made by the liver and held in

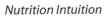

the gallbladder. CCK signals bile to be released in response to fat released in the duodenum from the stomach. Pancreatic lipase assists in the digestion of triglycerides, which will eventually be reduced to monoglycerides.

Absorption of fats begins when fat arrives in the small intestine. A series of hormone messages helps the absorption process. Bile is released in response to fat being sensed in the small intestine. Bile helps to emulsify the fat and disperse the fat molecules into smaller particles. The triglycerides and other fatty acids are eventually broken down into monoglycerides in order to pass the cell membrane. Once the monoglycerides have passed the cell membrane, they are re-packaged into triglycerides and put into a transport vehicle that is made of lipoprotein. This lipoprotein is called a chylomicron. Chylomicrons serve as the transport vehicles for fats in the lymphatic system. Once the chylomicrons reach the vascular system, lipoprotein lipase (LPL) begins to break down the chylomicron and utilize the fats in the body. Some of the fats will be put into storage and some of the fats will be used immediately for energy.

The Westernized diet or the Standard American Diet (SAD) is a diet that is high in saturated fats, processed foods, and simple sugars. Traditional food practices around the world tend to be much healthier in comparison. Many cultures have fruits, vegetables, and grains as a foundation for their food intake. After migrating to the United States, many cultures adopt Westernized diets, which can lead to numerous health problems such as obesity, heart disease, and diabetes.

Cardiovascular disease (CVD) is the number one killer of Americans. CVD is a general term that describes various diseases of the heart, including CAD and atherosclerosis. Heart disease can lead to heart attack or stroke.

You can be heart healthy by making positive lifestyle changes. Eating healthily and exercising regularly are a great way to get started. It is true that even healthy people can get heart disease due to a genetic pre-disposition. Knowing and understanding your lab values is a great start to becoming heart healthy.

# SHOP HEART SMART

Everybody should be heart smart. Whether young or old, heart disease can affect us all. Shopping heart smart means that you choose foods that are lower in fat and focus on the good fats in the diet. Always shop with a list and do not go to the store hungry. Current recommendations suggest that 20–35% of calories come from fat. If you are trying to be heart healthy, stay on the lower end of the recommendation.

© 2012, Shutterstock, Inc.

**Here are some tips on how to shop heart smart:**

- Buy fresh fruits and vegetables
- Choose fat-free or reduced fat cheese
- Avoid products with trans fats
- Choose lean meats and low fat dairy
- Use only 100% whole wheat breads and pastas
- Buy olive, canola, or grape seed oil

**Here are some tips to replace fat in recipes to lower the overall fat in the recipe.**

- Replace heavy cream in a recipe with fat-free evaporated milk
- Trade cream cheese for reduced fat cream cheese
- Smashed white beans or black beans can replace some of the butter or oil in a recipe, great when baking brownies
- Prune puree can replace butter or oil in a recipe
- Use tofu
- If a recipe calls for an egg, use the white only to lower cholesterol

# Proteins: Building Blocks to Health and Well Being

# CHAPTER 6

© 2012, Shutterstock, Inc.

## Learning Objectives

- Describe the difference between essential and nonessential amino acids
- List the primary functions of proteins in the body
- Distinguish between high and low qualities of protein and give examples of each
- Understand how protein is digested and absorbed in the body
- Calculate protein needs based on the RDA recommendations
- Define a variety of vegetarian diets
- Discuss how protein-energy malnutrition affects overall health status

## Functional Food Fact    Fish

Omega-3 fatty acids have been shown to have protective benefits against heart disease. Studies done in the early 1970s on Eskimos in Alaska showed that these people have little to no incidence of heart disease. A closer look at their diet had shown that high intakes of fatty fish rich in omega-3 played a protective role against heart disease. In a Westernized diet, the consumption of omega-3 fatty acids is usually low.

## Introduction to Proteins

Protein plays numerous important roles in our health. When students are asked to identify which of our nutrients such as carbohydrates, fats, and proteins is the most important most students will say protein. When asked why protein is considered to be the most important, most will reply "because protein builds muscle." You will be surprised to find that this statement is false. All of our nutrients are important to the body and, although protein is an exceptional nutrient, it does not "build muscle"; it repairs muscle. Muscle builds muscle—meaning you have to challenge and work the muscle to increase its size. Eating protein, taking in protein shakes and bars alone will not build muscle; but it can increase your weight if you are not exercising regularly.

## Proteins: Basic Components

Protein is the major structural component of all of our cells. Proteins are large complex molecules made up of long chains of amino acids. Amino acids are the building blocks of protein structures. In this book, we will take a look at 20 different amino acids. To better understand the chemical structure of an amino acid, take a look at Figure 6.1 below. As you can see in this picture, the basic chemical structure of all amino acids is similar. Protein is unique from carbohydrates and fats because it contains a nitrogen group. What makes each amino acid different from each other is its side group. Each side group gives that amino acid its unique function.

### Amino Acid Structure

Hydrogen

Amino

Carboxyl

R-group
(variant)

**Figure 6.1** The chemical structure of an amino acid

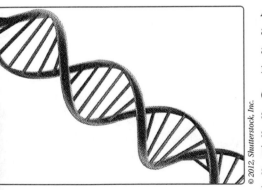

© 2012, Shutterstock, Inc.

Amino acids are linked together by **peptide bonds**. Two amino acids linked together form a **dipeptide**; three amino acids linked together form a **tripeptide**. Ten or more amino acids linked together form a **polypeptide**.

One of the most famous protein structures you typically see is DNA. DNA is usually depicted as a double helix structure. The double helix structure is shaped that way because some of the amino acids are **hydrophobic** and some are **hydrophilic**. This results in a structure that twists and turns because the amino acids are attracting and repelling water at the same time. A DNA picture is shown here.

*Nutrition Intuition*

## Classification of Amino Acids

Amino acids are classified as being either **essential** which means needed or necessary or **nonessential** which means that the body can produce them. Out of the 20 amino acids, 11 are considered to be nonessential because the body makes them and 9 are essential which means we must obtain these through the diet. A few amino acids are considered to be "conditionally essential" which means that an amino acid may be missing. In the case of a patient with phenylketonuria, a patient is missing a certain amino acid called phenylalanine. This condition is known as an inborn error of metabolism. See the Food in Focus section featuring phenylketonuria. Below is a list of the essential and nonessential amino acids.

**Essential—Must be obtained from the diet**

- Histidine
- Isoleucine
- Leucine
- Lysine
- Methionine
- Phenylalanine
- Threonine
- Tryptophan
- Valine

**Nonessential—Made by the body**

- Alanine
- Arginine
- Asparagine
- Aspartic acid
- Cysteine
- Glutamine acid
- Glutamine
- Glycine
- Praline
- Serine
- Tyrosine

## Functions of Proteins

The possible combination of protein structures is endless. Most health professionals agree that Americans eat more protein than what is recommended on a daily basis. Protein has many important functions such as:

- Hormones
- Enzymes
- Fluid balance
- Antibodies
- Acid-base balance
- Tissue growth and maintenance

### Hormones

A hormone is made in one part of the body and used in another. **Hormones** are large proteins that are made in response to the body's needs. Hormones are carried in the bloodstream to their target tissue. A good example of a hormone that is made in one part of the body and used in another is insulin. Remember that insulin is made in the pancreas. Insulin travels to the bloodstream in response to a rise in blood glucose.

### Enzymes

Enzymes are made of protein. **Enzymes** allow biochemical reactions to take place and are necessary for many body functions such as digestion, absorption, and metabolism. Enzymes also serve as **catalysts** which help to speed up reactions.

### Fluid Balance

A portion of the blood contains protein molecules. These proteins in the blood are too large to pass the cell membranes freely. Protein helps in fluid balance by attracting water molecules and pulling them across the cell membrane. On the surface of the cells there are sodium-potassium pumps that are also made out of proteins. When protein intake is inadequate, this can alter the fluid balance and cause a condition called edema. **Edema** is the movement of water from the inside of the cell to the outside of the cell and into the interstitial spaces between the cells.

## Antibodies

As you sit here and read this nutrition book your immune system is on alert. **Antibodies** are large proteins that are produced by the white blood cells. The antibodies can bind to a foreign agent and remove it from the body before it can cause harm. Each time the same foreign agent is introduced into the body again, the antibodies recognize it and can act even faster. Low protein status in the body can greatly affect the immune system.

## Acid-Base Balance

Normal body processes produce acids and bases within the body fluids daily. Acids and bases are carried to the lungs and kidneys for excretion. Alterations in this delicate balance between acids and bases can cause major health problems and possibly even death in some patients. A neutral pH in the body is about 7. Hydrogen ions are higher when the blood becomes more acidic and the pH falls below 7. Proteins can attract hydrogen ions to help raise the acidity and bring the blood back to a more neutral 7.

## Tissue Growth and Maintenance

The body is always in a state of **anabolism** and **catabolism**. Anabolism refers to the making of new material and structures in the body. Catabolism is the process of breaking down these structures which will eventually be excreted or reused in the body. Anabolism and catabolism occur simultaneously in the body. Nitrogen is excreted as a waste product of protein metabolism.

Nitrogen balance can be measured in the body. **Positive nitrogen balance** occurs when someone consumes more nitrogen than they excrete. Positive nitrogen balance primarily occurs during periods of growth in children and also in pregnant women. **Negative nitrogen balance** usually occurs in a patient who is not consuming enough protein; therefore less nitrogen is excreted. Negative nitrogen balance usually

EVERY DAY
## SUPERFOODS

Quality is just as important as quantity of protein. Complete proteins containing all essential amino acids mostly include animal products (egg whites being the best source). The plant kingdom also has complete protein super stars: quinoa, soybeans, and beet root!

occurs in burn patients or patients who are injured or experiencing infection or trauma. This negative nitrogen balance indicates that the patient may be experiencing lean body mass wasting which can greatly impact their ability to heal.

## Proteins in Food

Foods that contain protein can come from animal as well as plant sources. Animal sources of protein include beef, chicken, poultry, pork, and fish. We also get animal proteins from eggs, milk, and cheese. Plant sources of protein include beans and nuts. Almost all foods contain protein but in varying amounts. Animal sources of protein generally provide the highest amount of protein per serving when compared to plant protein. Animal sources of protein are more easily absorbed by the body and are considered to be high quality sources of protein.

© 2012, Shutterstock, Inc.

## NUTRITION NERD ALERT

For many years, the USDA meat inspection stamp was a dye extracted from blackberries.

## Protein Quality

The quality of a protein is determined by the number of essential amino acids a food contains. A high-quality or complete protein contains all nine essential amino acids. High-quality proteins are easily digested and absorbed by the body and generally come mostly from animal sources. The Protein Digestibility Corrected Amino Acid Score (PDCAAS) is a scoring system for protein containing foods. This scoring system evaluates different types of protein containing foods and assesses the quality of the protein and the body's ability to absorb the amino acids. According to this scoring system, eggs receive the highest score which makes it a high-quality protein.

Low-quality proteins do not contain all of the essential amino acids. These are also referred to as incomplete proteins. The human body does not digest these incomplete proteins as well as the complete proteins. Most plant proteins are considered low-quality proteins. The exception to this is soy protein; these are complete proteins but because they are plant based are still not absorbed as well as animal proteins.

## Digestion and Absorption of Protein

### Denaturation

The process of protein digestion begins when the bolus of food leaves the mouth, enters the esophagus, and proceeds to the stomach. The stomach acids (HCl) alter the protein structure via a process called **denaturation**. Denaturation of a protein occurs when a protein structure is exposed to an acid, heat, or alcohol. The process of denaturation can best be explained by using the following example. Take an egg and break it open in a pan on the stove. If there is no heat under the pan, the egg will not change its appearance. When heat is applied to the pan, the egg will begin to cook. The protein becomes denatured as a result and the protein structure becomes unraveled. Once the egg is cooked and the heat is turned off, does the egg go back to its original form and become uncooked again? Of course not, this is because denaturation is a one-way process. Once the protein has become unraveled, the polypeptides are exposed, which allows the digestive enzymes to break the peptide bonds for absorption.

### Digestion

Protein digestion requires the enzymes **pepsin** and **trypsin**. Pepsin works on the protein structure following the denaturation process by the stomach acids. Pepsin helps to break down the polypeptide chains into shorter chains. Once the proteins reach the small intestine, trypsin is released from the pancreas which further breaks down the chains of amino acids into smaller dipeptides and finally into single units of amino acids to prepare them for absorption.

### Absorption

Single amino acid units travel from the small intestine to the liver via the portal vein. These fresh nutrients enter the vascular system to be utilized by the body. Some of these amino acid units are converted into structures or used as energy, depending on the body's needs. Excess protein that is consumed in the diet and not utilized by the body will be converted into fat.

**Vegetarianism**

It has long been known that vegetarian diets can be healthy. The following are some reasons why people choose to adopt a vegetarian diet:

- Ethics

- Religion

- Economics

- Health

Adopting a vegetarian diet can be healthy but also needs to be well planned. Planning will ensure that the vegetarian diet provides plenty of nutrients and calories. There are different types of vegetarian diets, which include:

- Vegan-vegetarian

- Lacto-vegetarian

- Ovo-vegetarian

- Lacto-ovo-vegetarian

The **vegan-vegetarian** is the strictest of the vegetarian diets. Vegans eat only plant based foods and do not use animal products of any kind. Vegans may also exclude the use of clothing or shoes and other goods made from leather or other animal parts. The **lacto-vegetarian** diet includes milk and dairy products. The **ovo-vegetarian** diet includes eggs, and finally the **lacto-ovo-vegetarian** diet, which has the most variety of the vegetarian diets, includes plant based foods, eggs, milk, and dairy products.

**NUTRITION NERD ALERT**

Not all food programs are perfect. While trying to accommodate vegetarians, the National School Lunch Program requires 4 tablespoons of peanut butter to qualify for a reimbursable meal if used as a meat alternative in grades 4–12! That's a lot of peanut butter.

## Planning a Healthy Vegetarian Diet

Planning a healthy vegetarian diet can provide the right balance of carbohydrates, proteins, and fats. Of all the vegetarian diets discussed above, the vegan diet requires the most planning. Previously in this chapter, we discussed complementing plant proteins to ensure that a plant based diet includes all of the essential amino acids. All vegetarian diets benefit from adequate protein intake, and complementing proteins ensures that enough protein is consumed. In a vegan diet, some vitamins and minerals that may be lacking are:

- Vitamin D

- Vitamin B12

- Iron

- Zinc

- Calcium

Supplementing these vitamins may be necessary for some vegan-vegetarians. We will be discussing these vitamins in more detail in later chapters.

© 2012, Shutterstock, Inc.

## Recommended Protein Intakes

Protein intakes vary from person to person. In the United States protein intakes usually exceed the amount of 5.5 oz recommended by the Food Guide Pyramid. Most people think that an increase in protein intake can help them to build more muscle but, as previously mentioned, muscle builds muscle. Resistance training challenges the muscle to increase in size. Protein will help to repair the small tears that are made in the muscle fibers during resistance training.

## How Much Protein Do We Need?

Protein is important for growth and development and for maintaining overall health. The current RDA for protein is .8 g/kg of body weight. There are times when more protein would be beneficial. When the body is trying to heal itself from a major injury such as a third-degree burn, protein will aid in the healing process and tissue repair. Periods of growth and development like childhood and pregnancy may warrant additional protein. Endurance athletes and vegetarians may also benefit from some additional protein in the diet.

**EVERY DAY**
**SUPERFOODS**

Protein is found in every natural, whole food except butter and oils. Even vegetarians can easily get enough from these secret protein powerhouses: chickpeas/garbanzo beans, avocados, peanut butter, brown rice, and coconut milk!

**The following calculation can help you to determine your own protein needs:**

1. Take your weight in pounds and divide by 2.2 to get your weight in kilograms.

2. Take your weight in kilograms and multiply by .8 (RDA).

3. This is the amount of protein you need on a daily basis.

Example:

- A person's weight is 150 pounds
- Divided by 2.2 = 68 kg
- 68 kg X .8 (RDA) = 54.5 g of protein needed for an entire day.

You can add up the number of protein grams you consume on a daily basis by using the food labels. For measuring meat, poultry, or fish, an average 3 oz portion is approximately 21 grams of protein. If you are curious about how many grams of protein are in a variety of foods, visit the USDA website at www.nal.usda.gov/fnic/foodcomp/search/.

## Protein Energy Malnutrition

**Protein energy malnutrition (PEM)** is a condition that results from a chronic lack of food, especially protein containing foods. PEM is prevalent in underdeveloped countries such as Africa, parts of Central and South America, the Middle East, and Southeast Asia. PEM can also exist here in the United States.

PEM can occur for a number of reasons such as:

- Homelessness

- Inadequate access to protein containing foods due to financial hardships

- Hospitalized patients

- Eating disorders

The homeless population and those living in substandard conditions may be at risk for PEM as well as children and the elderly. Economic hardships may impact the access to nutritious foods; the reliance on lower protein foods that are less expensive may also be a contributing factor. Hospitalized patients may suffer from PEM associated with the progression of various diseases such as cancer and AIDS, both of which can result in wasting syndrome. **Wasting syndrome** is usually diagnosed when the patient has lost at least 10% of their body weight within a short period of time (1–2 months). A person with an eating disorder, especially anorexia, can suffer from PEM due to the severe restriction of food intake.

## FOOD IN FOCUS The Great Egg Debate

How many eggs should we eat per week? Aren't eggs high in cholesterol? What about increased risk of heart disease? All of these questions come up when it comes to discussing eggs and how to include them in a healthy diet. There is often some confusion as to what foods contain cholesterol. Consider these three foods: almonds, avocado, and turkey. Which one has cholesterol? Some people will choose the avocado or in some cases will choose all three foods. Only the turkey has cholesterol because it comes from an animal. "Cholesterol comes from anything that has parents." Egg lovers will be happy to know that recently eggs have been found to have less cholesterol than previously thought.

| Nutrition Facts | | |
|---|---|---|
| Serving Size 1 egg (50g) | | |
| Serving per Container 12 | | |
| **Amount Per Serving** | | |
| **Calories** 70 | Calories from Fat 45 | |
| | | % Daily Value* |
| **Total Fat** 5g | | **8%** |
| Saturated Fat 1.5g | | **8%** |
| Polyunsaturated Fat 1g | | |
| Monounsaturated Fat 2g | | |
| Trans Fat 0g | | |
| **Cholesterol** 185mg | | **60%** |
| **Sodium** 70mg | | **3%** |
| **Potassium** 70mg | | **2%** |
| **Total Carbohydrate** 0g | | **0%** |
| **Protein** 6g | | **13%** |
| Vitamin A 6% • Vitamin C 0% | | |
| Vitamin D 10% • Calcium 2% | | |
| Iron 4% • Thiamin 0% | | |
| Riboflavin 10% • Vitamin B-6 4% | | |
| Folate 6% • Vitamin B-12 8% | | |
| Phosphorus 10% • Zinc 4% | | |

Not a significant source of Dietary fiber or Sugars
* Percent Daily Values are based on a 2000 Calorie diet. Your daily volumes may be higher or lower depending on your calorie needs.

| | | Calories | 2,000 | 2,500 |
|---|---|---|---|---|
| Total Fat | Less than | | 65g | 80g |
| Sat fat | Less than | | 20g | 25g |
| Cholesterol | Less than | | 300mg | 300mg |
| Sodium | Less than | | 2,400mg | 2,400mg |
| Potassium | | | 3,500mg | 3,500mg |
| Total Carbohydrate | | | 300g | 375g |
| Dietary Fiber | | | 25g | 30g |
| Protein | | | 50g | 65g |

Calories per gram
Fat 9 - Carbohydrate 4 - Protein 4

In ancient times, man depended on eggs to provide a source of protein. Some evidence suggests that native fowl may have existed in America prior to the arrival of Columbus. On his second trip to America, Columbus' ships transported chickens similar to those that produce eggs today. Most people of the world eat eggs that come from chickens but there are other options. It is estimated that there are more than 200 breeds of chickens.

It is important to consume cholesterol in moderation. Current recommendations for cholesterol are 300mg per day or less. Recent studies have shown that eating cholesterol does not impact total cholesterol in the body as much as previously thought. It is suggested that eating an egg a day will not likely raise total cholesterol in the body if lower cholesterol or cholesterol free foods are consumed throughout the day. A recent sampling of eggs to analyze the nutrient content of eggs was completed by the United State Department of Agriculture (USDA) in 2010. The last sampling was done in 2002. Current sampling of large shell eggs showed that cholesterol content had slightly decreased from 215mg to 185mg per egg (note that the cholesterol is in the yolk).[1]

---

[1] http://www.incredibleedibleegg.org/healthandnutriton

# Acute and Chronic Forms of Protein Energy Malnutrition

## Kwashiorkor

There are both acute and chronic forms of PEM. The acute form of PEM is referred to as **kwashiorkor**. Kwashiorkor is a Ghanaian word that is interpreted as "the evil spirit that inflicts the first child when the second child is born." Kwashiorkor is commonly seen to reflect a sudden onset of deprivation of food. This sudden onset may be due to the birth of another child further straining the available food sources. Other reasons for the acute onset include illnesses such as measles or other infections (usually gastrointestinal infections). **Dysentery** is a common infection of the digestive tract that results from drinking unclean water. Dysentery can cause severe diarrhea with the additional loss of nutrients. Remember that antibodies are made up of protein and function to protect the immune system from various illnesses and infections. With PEM, this protection is compromised which can further weaken the immune system. Kwashiorkor typically inflicts children between the ages of 18 months to 2 years old.

© Stephen Morrison/epa/Corbis.

Symptoms of kwashiorkor include some weight loss and loss of body fat stores. Protein in the body is necessary to maintain fluid balance. With the sudden onset of deprivation of protein, fluid is shifted into the interstitial spaces. Children with kwashiorkor often present with edema and an enlarged liver. The abdomen will appear swollen as a result of a sudden lack of protein intake.

## Marasmus

Marasmus is the chronic onset of PEM. The word marasmus comes from the Greek word that is interpreted as "dying away." Marasmus is a more serious form of PEM which results from a long-term deprivation of food. Children who are inflicted with marasmus are usually between the ages of 6 and 18 months old. Marasmus usually exists in the overpopulated areas of the world where there are substandard living conditions.

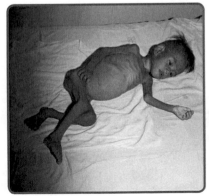

© Paul Almasy/CORBIS.

People often live in make-shift tents among refuse and waste products. There is limited availability of clean water and food. This grim picture of the living conditions is further blemished by the appearance of the children who suffer from marasmus. They are often very short in stature from stunted growth and development and have protruding ribs and "matchstick" arms. They are no bigger at four years of age than they were at two if they survive that long. The severe lack of protein containing foods damages the heart muscle and compromises the development of the brain.

## Summary

Protein plays numerous important roles in our bodies. Protein structures are made up of various amino acid structures. There are 20 different amino acids that we deal with in nutrition. These amino acids are divided up into two categories, essential and nonessential. The essential amino acids are those that we must obtain from the diet and there are nine of them. The nonessential amino acids are those we make in the body and there are 11 of them. There is also an amino acid that can be considered "conditionally essential" and that is phenylalanine which is the featured Highlight of this chapter.

Proteins function as hormones which are made in one part of the body and used in another. A classic example of this action is insulin which is made in the pancreas and then sent to the bloodstream to target the sugar molecules. Enzymes are protein structures that help to speed up chemical reactions that are necessary for a number of biochemical reactions. Protein assists in fluid balance by attracting water molecules and pulling them across the cell membrane. The sodium-potassium pumps are made out of protein and will malfunction when protein intake is inadequate. Antibodies are large proteins that aid in the protection of the immune system. Low protein status can cause a decline in the ability of the immune system to function at an optimum level. Acid-base balance is achieved by giving up or the taking of hydrogen ions across the cell membrane when there are changes in the acidity or alkalinity of the body. The body is in a constant state of anabolism and catabolism and protein must be readily available. Nitrogen is excreted as a waste product of protein metabolism. Negative and positive nitrogen balance is an indication of protein status in the body. When someone is in negative nitrogen balance it is assumed that inadequate protein is being consumed; therefore less nitrogen is excreted. Positive nitrogen balance is usually achieved during periods of growth and development of children and during pregnancy.

Protein in foods can come from animal as well as plant sources. The protein quality is determined by applying the protein digestibility corrected amino acid score

(PDCAAS) which determines how much of the protein is absorbed by the body. High-quality proteins, or complete proteins, consist of all of the nine essential amino acids. Most animal meats are high quality with the exception of tofu. Tofu is a complete protein, but its absorbability in the body is not as high as an animal protein.

Digestion of protein begins when the bolus of food arrives in the stomach. HCl alters the protein structure via denaturation. Denaturation of the protein structure can occur by heat, acid, or alcohol. In the stomach, HCl exposes the amino acid structure to the acid in preparation for absorption. Absorption of protein requires the enzymatic action of pepsin and trypsin to reduce the polypeptides down into dipeptides and finally into single units of amino acids which will then pass the cell membrane and travel to the liver via the portal vein. Excess protein consumed in the diet that is not used by the body is converted into fat and stored in the adipose tissue.

Vegetarian diets can be healthy but require some knowledge and preparation. The vegan-vegetarian is the strictest of the vegetarian diets. This option does not include any animal products of any kind, which may also exclude items made out of leather or other animal products. Several nutrients of concern that may be lacking in the vegan diet include vitamin D, vitamin B12, iron, zinc, and calcium. The lacto-ovo-vegetarian diet includes a variety of foods which includes eggs and milk products. Planning a healthy vegetarian diet should provide the right balance of carbohydrates, proteins, and fats. All vegetarian diets benefit from adequate protein intake. Complementing proteins ensures that all of the essential amino acids are included in the diet on a daily basis.

Recommended protein intakes vary from person to person. In the United States, protein intakes usually exceed current recommendations. Calculating an individual's protein needs can be achieved by using the RDA for protein which is .8 g/kg of body weight. This number is the amount of protein that is needed on a daily basis. Some health conditions and special situations require additional protein. Protein is necessary during times of growth and development and repair.

Protein energy malnutrition (PEM) is a condition that results from a lack of protein in the diet. PEM can occur for a variety of reasons such as homelessness, inadequate access to protein containing foods due to financial hardship, hospitalization, and eating disorders. PEM can be further divided into two categories. Kwashiorkor and marasmus are two forms of PEM, the former is acute and the latter is chronic.

# HOW MUCH PROTEIN DO YOU REALLY NEED?

Many people tend to think that protein is the most important nutrient when compared to carbohydrates and fats. A common misconception is that protein can build muscle. Drinking protein shakes and eating protein rich foods will not build muscle; muscle builds muscle. Protein can repair the muscle fibers after you work out, which will help the muscle to increase in size.

**Protein is found in the following foods:**

- Meats, poultry, beans, and fish
- Eggs
- Tofu
- Nuts and seeds
- Milk and milk products
- Small amounts in fruits and vegetables

© 2012, Shutterstock, Inc.

The chart below is based on the Recommended Dietary Allowance for protein, which is 0.8 grams per kilogram of body weight. To figure out your own protein needs, take your weight in pounds and divide by 2.2, this will give you your weight in kilograms. Multiply your weight in kilograms by 0.8.

- Children ages 1–3          13 grams/day
- Children ages 4–8          19 grams/day
- Children ages 9–13        34 grams/day
- Girls ages 14–18           46 grams/day
- Boys ages 14–18           52 grams/day
- Women ages 19–70        46 grams/day
- Men ages 19–70             56 grams/day[*]

Remember these recommendations are for those people who are in good health. There are some people who will need more or less protein under special circumstances. To better understand how to apply these recommendations to actual foods, consider the examples below:

- 1 cup of milk = 8 grams of protein
- 3 oz of meat = 21 grams of protein
- 3 oz of tofu = 8 grams of protein

[*] http://www.cdc.gov/nutrition/everyone/basics/protein.html

# CHAPTER 7

# The Water Soluble Vitamins: Building Blocks for Energy Metabolism

© 2012, Shutterstock, Inc.

## Learning Objectives

- List the water soluble vitamins
- Outline the different toxicities and deficiencies associated with water soluble vitamins
- List three food sources for each water soluble vitamin
- Explain how an antioxidant functions
- Understand how vitamin C functions as an antioxidant

### Functional Food Fact   Cranberry

Cranberry juice has long been known to play a role in the treatment of urinary tract infections. Studies have shown that cranberry juice can inhibit the adherence of E coli to the cells of the urinary tract. One cup of cranberry juice also provides about 100 mg of vitamin C.

## Introduction to Vitamins

It is estimated that 40% of the U.S. adult population takes a vitamin or mineral supplement. Some people believe that taking a vitamin or mineral supplement will provide them with extra protection from a disease or illness. People also believe that supplements would not be as widely available as they are if they were deemed to be harmful. The truth is that vitamin and mineral supplements are not regulated by the Food and Drug Administration. Taking in excessive amounts of a vitamin can be harmful and all consumers should be aware of potential interactions with other supplements and/ or medications.

## Basics about Vitamins

A vitamin is an organic (carbon containing) compound that assists in metabolic processes to produce energy. A vitamin can further be defined as:

- A compound that the body cannot make or make enough of to sustain health

- Naturally occurs in foods

- Could cause serious health problems (a deficiency) if not consumed in adequate amounts

- Could alleviate a deficiency if added back to the diet

The structure of the vitamin is organic in nature but much more complex in relation to our macronutrients such as carbohydrates, proteins, and fats. These macronutrients are needed in larger amounts in the body. Vitamins are considered to be micronutrients because they are required in smaller amounts in the body. Dietary reference intakes (DRI) for these vitamins are often measured in milligrams (mg) or micrograms (mcg or μ).

## Classes of Vitamins

### Water and Fat Soluble Vitamins

Vitamins are divided into two groups, water soluble and fat soluble. The water soluble vitamins will dissolve easily in what are considered to be the watery compartments of the body as well as food. We do not store the water soluble vitamins for long periods of time; therefore it is recommended that we intake these vitamins more often and perhaps even daily. Under most circumstances, the water soluble vitamins will not be toxic to the body when taken in large amounts, although it is not recommended that anyone intake excessive amounts of these vitamins above and beyond the recommended amounts as suggested by the RDA's. We will discuss potential toxicity problems when the vitamins are taken in excess of the UL.

Some vitamins have more than one form, each of which may perform different functions in the body. Some vitamins act as coenzymes which assist in chemical reactions or help chemical reactions to occur. Vitamins may exist in an inactive form in a food item and then become active when utilized by the body.

The water soluble vitamins include:

- Vitamin C

- Thiamin

- Niacin

- Vitamin B6

- Pantothenic acid

- Biotin

- Folate

- Vitamin B12

We will further investigate the importance of these B vitamins and the role that they play in energy metabolism. Any disturbances in the balance of these vitamins in the body can cause a deficiency that can be harmful to our health.

**NUTRITION NERD ALERT**

College students may not be getting even one serving of fruits and vegetables per day. Why is this important? This is where we find many micro- and macronutrients, as well as water soluble vitamins!

## Functions of Vitamins

Vitamins play many roles and perform many functions in the body. As previously mentioned, some of these vitamins contribute to energy metabolism, act similar to hormones and enzymes, as well as help with chemical reactions by donating or accepting electrons which occur during normal metabolism. Vitamins are important for growth and development at any stage in life and our needs change throughout our lifespan. It is important to understand that even though vitamins are organic, they do not provide calories or energy directly. When you consume a healthy diet, you can get adequate amounts of most vitamins and minerals from your foods. Most health professionals agree that is acceptable to take a multivitamin and mineral supplement on a daily basis but caution should be used when including other herbal supplements and various botanicals. The intake of multiple vitamins, minerals, or supplements should be discussed with your physician to avoid interactions with food or medications.

According to the National Institutes of Health from the Office of Dietary Supplements, Americans spend about 25 billion dollars per year on more than 50,000 different products that contain vitamins, minerals, herbs, and botanicals. The marketing

of vitamins to consumers may offer promises of optimal health and well being and sometimes even possible cures for certain health conditions or diseases. It is important to understand that vitamin supplements and other supplements are not regulated by the Food and Drug Administration.

## How Antioxidants Function

An antioxidant is defined as a substance that inhibits oxidation or reactions promoted by oxygen, peroxides, or free radicals. Figure 7.1 shows the action of the antioxidant donating its electron in an attempt to stabilize the free radical. If the free radical is not stabilized, damage to surrounding tissues can occur. The process of digestion and absorption of our foods causes the formation of free radicals. During metabolism, there are numerous oxidation and reduction reactions that occur where the cells exchange electrons. In order for the cell to remain stable, the electrons must exist in even numbers when surrounding the nucleus. When a cell loses an electron and becomes unstable it will immediately try to steal electrons from a nearby cell to stabilize itself. The formation of the free radicals can cause damage to the other cells.

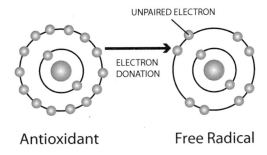

**Figure 7.1** How antioxidants stabilize free radicals

Diseases that are related to free radical production include:

- Diabetes
- Heart disease
- Alzheimer's
- Macular degeneration

The marketing of vitamins and minerals can also play up the antioxidant qualities of a supplement. It is not just foods that contain antioxidants. Many products today such as skincare, hair care, and various other beauty items contain antioxidants to offer the consumer younger, healthier skin. Most of these products are marketed strongly toward women in an attempt to promise youth and vitality.

## The Antioxidant Vitamins

The antioxidant vitamins that will be explored in this chapter are:

- Vitamin C
- Vitamin E
- Vitamin A
- Beta-carotene

**NUTRITION NERD ALERT**

Epigallocatechin gallate (EGCG), the powerful antioxidant found in green tea, may be up to 25 times more powerful than Vitamin E and 100 times more powerful than Vitamin C. Try cold brewing to keep cool in the summer.

### Vitamin C

The first antioxidant vitamin we will discuss is vitamin C. Vitamin C, as you recall, is a water soluble vitamin. The deficiency associated with vitamin C is called **scurvy**. Scurvy plagued sailors on long ocean voyages and many died as a result.

Symptoms of scurvy include:

- Pinpoint hemorrhages under the skin
- Poor wound healing
- Bleeding gums and loose teeth

These symptoms could start to develop in a relatively short amount of time. In as little as 20–30 days, symptoms could occur. Scurvy was not understood until the 1750s when a British physician by the name of James Lind described an experiment that he performed on a group of sailors that were suffering from the same symptoms. Some of the sailors were given cider, vinegar, sea water, nutmeg, and oranges and lemons. The only sailors who fully recovered from their symptoms were the sailors who were given the oranges and lemons. It was then discovered that citrus fruits were rich in vitamin C and scurvy was curable. British sailors acquired the name "limeys" because of this discovery when Dr. Lind found that a small amount of lime juice was all the sailors needed on a daily basis to protect against symptoms of scurvy.

### Functions of Vitamin C

Most animals can make their own vitamin C and therefore do not rely on outside sources of vitamin C coming from the diet. One animal that is an exception is the guinea pig. If you keep a guinea pig as a pet, you must provide a source of vitamin C to prevent a deficiency. Humans cannot make their own vitamin C either and therefore rely on rich sources from the diet.

Vitamin C has many important functions that contribute to maintaining our health and well being. These functions include:

- Antioxidant
- Collagen synthesis
- Immune function
- Iron absorption

### Antioxidant

Remember that an antioxidant's role is to prevent or stop the oxidative process. Vitamin C is one of our most impressive vitamins that can help to reduce the action of a free radical and prevent further cellular damage. The action of vitamin C is it has the ability to donate an electron to the free radical in order to stabilize the molecule and stop the cellular damage. Vitamin C may also help to reduce cancer causing agents that are consumed in the diet in the form of carcinogens. An example of this is nitrosamines that come from foods that are smoked or pickled. Vitamin C may help to reduce the action of these nitrosamines.

### Collagen Synthesis

Vitamin C plays a role in the synthesis of collagen. **Collagen** is an abundant protein in the body and is part of connective tissue, bone, teeth, tendons, and blood vessels. This makes vitamin C especially important for wound healing.

### Immune Function

The immune function also relies on the proper functioning of vitamin C. There is promising research that vitamin C could reduce the number of colds that people get. There are numerous products on the market that claim that vitamin C can help with the common cold. Although not proven, it may be beneficial to increase intake of vitamin C during a cold but the amount taken in should not exceed the upper limit (UL) amounts. High intakes of vitamin C (above 2000 mg) could cause nose bleeds and nausea.

### Iron Absorption

When foods rich in vitamin C are consumed in combination with foods that contain iron, iron absorption is enhanced. This can be important for those who consume few or no animal sources of iron such as vegetarians. Iron will be explored further in the next chapter when we discuss minerals that are important for blood health.

### Vitamin C Requirements and Food Sources

The RDA for vitamin C is 75 mg per day for women and 90 mg per day for men. Smokers may benefit from an additional amount of vitamin C (about 135 mg/day) due to their exposure to the toxins in the cigarette smoke.[1]

Fruits that are the highest sources of vitamin C include:

- Cantaloupe
- Citrus fruits and juices, such as orange and grapefruit
- Kiwi fruit
- Mango
- Papaya
- Pineapple
- Strawberries, raspberries, blueberries, cranberries
- Watermelon

© 2012, Shutterstock, Inc.

[1] http://www.nlm.nih.gov/medlineplus/ency/article/002404.htm

Vegetables that are the highest sources of vitamin C include:

- Broccoli, Brussels sprouts, cauliflower
- Green and red peppers
- Spinach, cabbage, turnip greens, and other leafy greens
- Sweet and white potatoes
- Tomatoes and tomato juice
- Winter squash

**NUTRITION NERD ALERT**

Red bell peppers have almost 3 times your daily vitamin C recommendations in 1 cup (raw). That is more than an entire orange!

Some cereals and other foods and beverages are fortified with vitamin C. **Fortified** means a vitamin or mineral has been added to the food.

Cooking vitamin C-rich foods or storing them for a long period of time can reduce the vitamin C content. Microwaving and steaming vitamin C-rich foods may reduce cooking losses. The best food sources of vitamin C are raw fruits and vegetables.[2]

## B Vitamins: Involved in Energy Metabolism

The B vitamins function in the body as coenzymes. Coenzymes are cofactors that aid in a chemical reaction. It is like fitting the pieces of a puzzle together. If the pieces do not fit properly, then the chemical reaction will not take place; when all the pieces fit, then the chemical reaction will take place. The B vitamins act as coenzymes in numerous chemical reactions that mostly have to do with energy metabolism.

The B vitamins help us to get energy from our foods. The metabolism of carbohydrates, fats, and proteins depends on the coenzymes that come from the B vitamins.

### The Enrichment Process: B Vitamins in Our Foods

Milling of wheat for flour compromises the B vitamins that are present in the grain. During the milling process, these B vitamins are removed and do not become part of

---

[2] http://www.nlm.nih.gov/medlineplus/ency/article/002404.htm

the flour. In the late 1930s and early 1940s many diseases related to vitamin B deficiencies were being recognized as serious health conditions. It became evident that something needed to be done to address these concerns. Enrichment of grains began in 1941. Key B vitamins such as riboflavin, niacin, and thiamin were the first ones to be added back to the refined grains. This eradicated several diseases associated with these vitamin B deficiencies to be discussed below.

The following list is the B vitamins we will discuss in this chapter:

- Thiamin

- Riboflavin

- Niacin

- Pantothenic acid

- Biotin

- Vitamin B6

- Folate

- Vitamin B12

## Thiamin

### Thiamin Recommendations and Food Sources

Thiamin is also known as B1 because it was the first of the B vitamins to be identified. Thiamin functions in the metabolism of carbohydrates and proteins. Thiamin is important for proper heart, muscle, and nervous system functioning. The RDA for adults is 1.2 mg/day for males and 1.1 mg/day for females.

Food sources of thiamin include:

- Eggs

- Enriched breads and grains

- Lean meats

- Legumes

- Nuts and seeds

- Organ meats

- Peas

© 2012, Shutterstock, Inc.

### Deficiencies and Toxicities of Thiamin

**Thiamin Deficiency**

A diet that is deficient in thiamin is most often seen in people who suffer from alcoholism. Alcohol intake interferes with the absorption of thiamin in the body. A deficiency of thiamin is called beriberi. A severe deficiency of thiamin is called Wernicke-Korsakoff syndrome, which can result in brain damage.[3]

**Thiamin Toxicity**

There are no known toxicities of thiamin.

## Niacin

### Niacin Recommendations and Food Sources

In the body niacin is converted into niacinamide when intake exceeds the amount needed in the body. Niacin and niacinamide are important for the metabolism of carbohydrates and fats in the body. The RDA is 16 mg/day for men and 14 mg/day for women.[4] In the past, high doses of niacin were sometimes prescribed by a doctor to treat high cholesterol, but is not a common practice today. Niacin food sources include:

- Meat
- Fish
- Milk
- Eggs
- Green vegetables
- Enriched grains and cereals
- Beans

### Toxicities and Deficiencies of Niacin

**Niacin Deficiency**

A niacin deficiency can cause a condition called pellagra. In the early twentieth century Dr. Joseph Goldberger was called upon to investigate a disease that was ravaging the American South. Thousands of people were suffering from what was later described as the four D's, dermatitis, diarrhea, dementia, and death. In this part of the South, people were poor and the diet consisted of mostly grain and corn. Meat was not commonly consumed in the diet of those who were poor, so protein intake was very low. Dr. Goldberger observed many people with these symptoms and he suspected that this disease was not contagious.

---

[3] www.nlm.nih.gov/medlineplus/ency/article/002401.htm
[4] www.nlm.nih.gov/medlineplus/ency/article/002409.htm

## FOOD IN FOCUS The History of Vitamin C

Throughout history there are many stories of nutrient deficiencies that plagued populations. As with many discoveries about nutrition and nutrient deficiencies, many people had to die until a solution was found. A deficiency of vitamin C called scurvy potentially killed some two million sailors somewhere between the years 1500 to 1700.

**The symptoms of scurvy include:**

- Poor wound healing
- Bleeding gums, tooth loss
- Extreme fatigue and nausea

By the seventeenth century, a discovery was made that small doses of lemon or lime juice solved the problem. Although this solution seemed to work, research was still ongoing to really figure out if this was caused by a deficiency of a nutrient or caused by something else.

Differences of opinions by different researchers attempted to prove that scurvy was in fact caused by a deficiency of a food source, and the other opinion was that scurvy was caused by "moist salty air."

Scurvy still existed and was reported in the late Victorian period. It was not until the early 1930s, experiments on guinea-pigs showed that vitamin C was in fact a deficiency disease. Other than humans, guinea-pigs cannot recycle their own vitamin C stores and therefore must be consumed in the diet. All other animals seem to be able to do this. It is thought that vitamin C deficiency symptoms can occur in a little as 30 days. Today, research on vitamin C includes using this antioxidant vitamin to possibly cure the common cold and to research its role in the treatment or prevention of cancer.

The next time you enjoy a glass of orange juice, think about all the benefits you get from including vitamin C rich foods in your diet on a daily basis.

**Here are some other food sources of vitamin C to enjoy:**

- Red and green hot chili peppers
- Guavas
- Bell peppers
- Dark leafy greens
- Oranges and strawberries

*all food sources above provide 2-3 times the RDA for vitamin C

http://www.ncbi.nlm.nih.gov/pmc/articles/PMC1139720/

## The Story of Dr. Goldberger and the Discovery of Niacin

The story of Dr. Goldberger was shared in Chapter 1. This story plays an important role in the discovery of how nutrition plays a role in our health and well being. Dr. Goldberger hypothesized that this disease was in fact dietary related and not contagious. Joseph Goldberger's theory on pellagra was not shared by other medical professionals. The work of Italian investigators as well as Goldberger's own observations in various settings convinced him that germs did not cause the disease. In such institutions as jail, inmates contracted the disease, but staff never did. Goldberger knew from his years of experience working on infectious diseases that germs did not distinguish between inmates and employees.

© Bettman/CORBIS.

Goldberger found no evidence for that hypothesis, but diet certainly seemed the crucial factor. Shipments of food which Goldberger had requested from Washington were provided to children in two Mississippi orphanages and to inmates at the Georgia State Asylum. Results were dramatic; those fed a diet of fresh meat, milk, and vegetables instead of a corn-based diet recovered from pellagra. Those without the disease who ate the new diet did not contract pellagra.

## Goldberger's Filth Parties

Angry and frustrated, Goldberger would not give up trying to persuade his critics that pellagra was a dietary disorder, not an infectious disease. He hoped that one final dramatic experiment would convince his critics. He and his colleagues swabbed out the secretions of the nose and throat of a person who had pellagra and rubbed them into their own noses and throats. They swallowed capsules containing scabs from the patients who had dermatitis. Others joined what Goldberger called his "filth parties," including his wife Mary Goldberger. None of the volunteers got pellagra. Despite Goldberger's heroic efforts, a few physicians maintained opposition to the dietary theory of pellagra.[5]

---

[5] http://history.nih.gov/exhibits/goldberger/docs/pellegra_5.htm

### Niacin Toxicity

As previously mentioned, niacin is a water soluble vitamin that is usually harmless in large amounts and is sometimes prescribed by doctors in high doses to treat high cholesterol. However, niacin toxicity can occur from consuming niacin supplements. The side effects of the niacin toxicity may result in a "flushing" of the hands and face characterized by a burning, tingling feeling with some redness on the face and chest.[6]

## Vitamin B12

Vitamin B12 is a water soluble vitamin that is present in some food sources and is also fortified in our foods. Natural sources of vitamin B12 are bound to protein in our foods. Vitamin B12 is mostly found in foods of animal origin. The absorption of vitamin B12 from our food sources requires hydrochloric acid in the stomach. In fortified foods and dietary supplements, vitamin B12 is in a "free form" and does not require this extra step for absorption.

### Vitamin B12 Recommendations and Food Sources

Vitamin B12 is important for the development of the red blood cells, neurological function, and the making of DNA. Vitamin B12 acts as a coenzyme for many reactions that involve amino acids. In the stomach, B12 is absorbed with the assistance of a substance produced in the stomach called intrinsic factor. As we age, hydrochloric acid production and intrinsic factor are decreased in the stomach which may increase our need for vitamin B12 later in life. The RDA for vitamin B12 is 2.4 mcg/day for adults.

The following foods are rich sources of vitamin B12:

| Food | mcg/serving | %DV |
|---|---|---|
| ▪ Beef liver (cooked) 1 slice | 48 | 800 |
| ▪ Clams (cooked) | 34.2 | 570 |
| ▪ 100% fortified cereals | 6 | 100 |
| ▪ Trout (cooked) 3 oz | 5.4 | 90 |
| ▪ Salmon (cooked) 3 oz | 4.9 | 80 |

---

[6] www.nlm.nih.gov/medlineplus/druginfo/natural/924.html

## Deficiencies and Toxicities of Vitamin B12

### Vitamin B12 Deficiency

Most deficiencies of vitamin B12 are the result of a decreased ability to absorb the vitamin and are not usually related to a decrease in the intake of the vitamin. As we get older, a condition called atrophic gastritis means that we produce less acid in the stomach. We need this acidic environment to help with the absorption of B12.

Vitamin B12 status can be measured in the blood. A deficiency of vitamin B12 can cause megaloblastic anemia. Megaloblastic anemia is characterized by large red blood cells that have a decreased ability to carry adequate amounts of oxygen around the body. This type of anemia presents with symptoms that include, fatigue, weakness, loss of appetite, and weight loss. Neurological damage can also occur. Various types of anemia will be discussed further in a later chapter.

### Vitamin B12 and Folic Acid

Folic acid can mask the deficiency of vitamin B12. If too much folate is taken in (usually in the form of supplements) B12 deficiencies are more difficult to detect.

### Groups at Risk of Vitamin B12 Deficiency

- Older adults

- Individuals with pernicious anemia

- Vegetarians (especially vegans)

- Pregnant and lactating women who follow vegan diets

### Vitamin B12 and Cardiovascular Disease

Cardiovascular disease is the number one killer of Americans. Homocysteine, which is an amino acid in the body, has been linked to an increased risk for cardiovascular disease. Elevated homocysteine levels in the blood have been shown to increase the likelihood of a heart attack or stroke. Vitamin B12 along with vitamin B6 and folate have been shown to be beneficial in lowering homocysteine levels in the blood.

### Vitamin B12 Toxicities

There are no known risks for toxicities to vitamin B12. Vitamin B12 is often promoted as an energy booster. Intramuscular injections of B12 are sometime given to patients as part

**EVERY DAY SUPERFOODS**

The water soluble B vitamins are found in many plant foods, but pork is a unique B vitamin super store. It contains at least 25% of the daily recommended intake of vitamins B1, B2, B3, B6, and B12. Be careful when cooking—water-soluble vitamins are easily lost if cooked too long or at too high of a temperature.

of a weight loss program. Remember that vitamin B12 is water soluble. The excess amount taken in the injections is excreted from the body. Vitamin B12 does not provide direct energy in the form of calories.

## Folate

Folate is a water soluble vitamin. Folate was found to be a key vitamin in the prevention of "pregnancy anemia" nearly 70 years ago. Folate is needed in the production of RNA and DNA which are building blocks for our cells. Folate is needed to produce red blood cells in the prevention of anemia. Folic acid is also important for the metabolism of homocysteine as previously mentioned.

### Folate Recommendations and Food Sources

Folic acid is the synthetic form of folate that is found in supplements and included in fortified foods. Unlike most vitamins that are better absorbed by the body when taken in by the diet, the synthetic form of folic acid is said to be better absorbed by the body. In the original enrichment of grains and cereals in the 1930s, folate was not one of the B vitamins that were added. It was not until 1996 that the Food and Drug Administration published regulations requiring the addition of folic acid to all grain products.

Folate can be found in the following foods.

| Food | mcg | %DV |
|---|---|---|
| ▪ Fortified cereals ¾ cup | 400 | 100 |
| ▪ Beef liver (cooked) 3 oz | 185 | 45 |
| ▪ Black-eyed peas ½ cup | 105 | 25 |
| ▪ Spinach (cooked) ½ cup | 100 | 25 |
| ▪ Great northern beans ½ cup | 90 | 20 |

### Folate and Pregnancy

Folate plays an important role in pregnancy and helps with the prevention of neural tube defects. Studies have shown that folic acid intake is critical for women who may become pregnant. Adequate folic acid before the women gets pregnant is important in the prevention of neural tube defects. When a woman gets pregnant, the critical period of development in the first trimester is when the neural tube defect can occur. In the first 17–30 days of gestation, the neural tube defect can form. There are two types of neural tube defects called spinabifida and anencephaly. Both of these neural tube defects will be discussed in further detail in a later chapter. The RDA for folate is 400 mcg for both men and women. It is recommended that women who are planning to get pregnant or may become pregnant receive 600 mcg of folic acid per day. The best benefits that folate can provide is before she gets pregnant and during pregnancy, especially during the first trimester.[7]

### Folate and Blood Health

Folate plays a role in blood health. Folate helps to make red blood cells. Normally, immature red blood cells divide to make additional red blood cells. Without adequate amounts of folate, the immature cells will not divide and the cells will remain large—referred to as megaloblasts—eventually leading to megaloblastic anemia. Megaloblastic anemia results in large immature red blood cells that cannot carry a sufficient amount of oxygen around the body.

## Riboflavin

Riboflavin, also known as B2, is important for blood cell production and aids in carbohydrate metabolism.

### Food Sources and Recommended Intakes for Riboflavin

The food sources that provide adequate amounts of riboflavin include:

- Dairy
- Eggs
- Green leafy vegetables
- Lean meats
- Legumes
- Fortified breads, grains, and cereals

© 2012, Shutterstock, Inc.

The recommended intake of riboflavin for adult males is 1.3 mg/day and 1.0 mg/day for women.[8]

### Deficiencies and Toxicities of Riboflavin

Before the grain enrichment process began back in the 1930s, riboflavin deficiency was more common. The symptoms of a riboflavin deficiency include a sore mouth and a swollen mucus membrane around the mouth, this condition was known as **ariboflavinosis**. Milk is a great source of riboflavin. During the days when milk was delivered to the door steps of many homes, milk was often left outside if no one was

---

[7] http://ods.od.nih.gov/factsheets/folate/
[8] http://nlm.nih.gov/medlineplus/ency/article/002411.htm

home to receive the delivery. It was later discovered that riboflavin in the milk was easily destroyed by the sunlight because the milk bottles were made out of clear glass. Because of this discovery, they began to use brown glass milk bottles which could protect the riboflavin from being destroyed by the sun. Toxicities of riboflavin are rare.

## Vitamin B6 (Pyridoxine)

Pyridoxine is also known as vitamin B6. Vitamin B6 is necessary for more than 100 enzymes that are involved in protein metabolism. Vitamin B6 is also important for red blood cell metabolism. The nervous system and the immune system also rely on vitamin B6 for optimal function.

### Vitamin B6 Food Sources and Recommendations

The following foods are good sources of vitamin B6:

- Fortified ready to eat cereals
- Baked potatoes
- Bananas
- Garbanzo beans
- Chicken breast

### Recommendations for Vitamin B6

For adult men and women between the age of 19 and 50 the RDA is 1.3 mg/day. For those who are 51 and older the RDA is 1.7 mg/day for men and 1.5 mg/day for women. For pregnancy and lactation the recommendations are slightly higher, 1.9 mg-2.0 mg/day.[9]

### Deficiencies and Toxicities of Vitamin B6

Although rarely seen in the United States, deficiencies of vitamin B6 can occur in individuals who have poor quality diets. Vitamin B6 deficiency can also result in anemia. Symptoms of vitamin B6 include glossitis (sore tongue), dermatitis (skin inflammation), depression, confusion, and possibly convulsions.

Vitamin B6 is a water soluble vitamin; toxicity of a water soluble vitamin is rare but can still occur. In studies where individuals took supplements in excess of the UL, which is 100 mg/day, documented cases have shown that the individuals suffered nerve damage.

---

[9] www.nlm.nih.gov/medlinepuls/ency/article/002411.htm

### Other Uses for Vitamin B6

Although not yet proven, the use of vitamin B6 is being researched for use in the following areas:

- Carpal tunnel syndrome
- Premenstrual syndrome
- The nervous system

## Pantothenic Acid and Biotin

Pantothenic acid plays a role in the production of hormones and cholesterol. Biotin is necessary for growth.

### Food Sources for Pantothenic Acid and Biotin and Recommended Intakes

### Pantothenic Acid

- Avocado
- Cruciferous vegetables such as cabbage
- Eggs
- Legumes
- Mushrooms

Recommended AI for pantothenic acid is 5 mg/day for both men and women.

© 2012, Shutterstock, Inc.

### Biotin

- Fortified cereals and grains
- Chocolate
- Egg yolk
- Legumes
- Milk

Recommended AI for biotin is 30 mcg/day for both men and women.

### Toxicities and Deficiencies of Pantothenic Acid and Biotin

There are no known toxicities or deficiencies associated with these two vitamins. A discovery of biotin deficiency was found in body-builders who consumed raw egg whites as a source of protein in their diets. Research found that raw egg whites contain a protein called avidin. Avidin in the raw egg whites binds with biotin and causes excess excretion of the vitamin. Symptoms of a biotin deficiency include redness or discoloration on the face and hair thinning or pigment lost from the hair causing the hair to turn white. The study was later duplicated in animal studies.

**NUTRITION NERD ALERT**

Caffeic acid, a water-soluble phytochemical found in skin of pears (and many other fruits and vegetables) is an antioxidant, anti-inflammatory agent, and anticarcinogenic. The skins of fruits and vegetables often have bonus nutrients that cannot be found in the inner flesh.

## Summary

There are two classes of vitamins, the water soluble vitamins and the fat soluble vitamins. The water soluble vitamins are stored in the watery compartments of the body. We do not store water soluble vitamins for very long; therefore our need for these vitamins is higher. Fat soluble vitamins are stored in the adipose tissue as well as the liver. Fat soluble vitamins are stored longer in the body; therefore we do not require them on a daily basis.

Vitamins can function as coenzymes, hormones, and antioxidants. Vitamins are important for growth and development at all stages of our lifespan. Vitamins are organic but they do not provide energy in the form of calories. Consuming a healthy diet that includes a variety of foods is a great way to get an adequate amount of vitamins. Most health professionals agree that it is acceptable to take a multivitamin with minerals. Toxicities and deficiencies can occur with many of these vitamins. Toxicities are more commonly related to the intake of supplements above the recommended amounts. It is often agreed that toxicity of water soluble vitamins is uncommon but can still occur.

An antioxidant is defined as a substance that inhibits oxidation. Oxidation occurs during various biochemical reactions when molecules gain and lose electrons. Atoms gain and lose electrons all the time in the body. This process is referred to as oxidation-reduction reactions. When an atom loses an electron and becomes unstable it is referred to as a free radical. A free radical will try to steal electrons from nearby molecules and cause damage as a result.

## Vitamin C

Vitamin C is an antioxidant that aids in the destruction of free radicals. A vitamin C deficiency is called scurvy. Most animals can make their own vitamin C and therefore do not rely on food sources. Humans are one of the few exceptions (as well as guinea pigs) who require a steady supply of vitamin C coming from the diet. Vitamin C functions as an antioxidant by donating an electron to stop the free radical from harming other nearby molecules. Vitamin C is also important for collagen synthesis. Collagen is the most abundant protein in the body, and is important for bones, teeth, tendons, blood vessels, and wound healing. Vitamin C enhances absorption of iron. Vitamin C is reduced in foods that are cooked for long periods of time or at high temperatures.

## Vitamins Involved in Energy Metabolism

The B vitamins are involved in energy metabolism and act as coenzymes. All of the B vitamins are instrumental in the metabolism of carbohydrates, proteins, and fats. Milling of wheat compromises the amount of available B vitamins in products made with flour. Other food items have B vitamins but they are not always consumed on a daily basis. It was not until the late 1930s that B vitamins were enriched (put back) into grains, breads, and cereals.

### Thiamin

Thiamin is also known as B1. Thiamin functions in the metabolism of the nutrients, especially carbohydrates and proteins. A deficiency of thiamin causes a condition called beriberi. Alcoholics may also experience a thiamin deficiency which can lead to a condition called Wernicke-Korsakoff syndrome which can lead to serious brain damage. There are no known toxicities of thiamin.

### Niacin

Niacin is important for the metabolism of carbohydrates and fats in the body. A deficiency of niacin can lead to a disease called pellagra. Pellagra is characterized by the 4 D's, dermatitis, diarrhea, dementia, and death. Dr. Joseph Goldberger was the scientist who discovered the deficiency of niacin. Dr. Goldberger went to great lengths to prove that pellagra was not a contagious disease. Niacin remains bound in the body when protein intake is too low. A toxicity of niacin occurs when supplementation exceeds the UL. Niacin toxicity is characterized by symptoms that produce tingling in the hands and feet as well as redness on the face and chest.

## Vitamin B12

Vitamin B12 comes mostly from foods of animal origin. Vegetarians (especially vegans) may not get adequate amounts of vitamin B12 on a daily basis. Natural sources of B12 remain bound in the body. Adequate absorption of vitamin B12 is dependent upon the acids in our stomach. Vitamin B12 is important for the production of red blood cells. A deficiency of vitamin B12 can cause an anemia called megaloblastic anemia. Low B12 levels will cause symptoms that are consistent with anemia such as lethargy and difficulty concentrating. Vitamin B12 has also been used as an "energy booster" and is given as an injection, but remember that this vitamin is water soluble and excess is excreted from the body. Vitamin B12 is also important in the metabolism of the amino acid homocysteine which plays a protective role in cardiovascular disease. There are no known risks in taking high amounts of vitamin B12.

## Folate

Folate is necessary for the production of RNA and DNA which are building blocks for our cells. Folic acid is a synthetic form of folate and is fortified in our foods especially breads, grains, and cereals. Folic acid is said to be more absorbable by the body. Folic acid plays a significant role in the prevention of neural tube defects. Folate also plays a role in blood health. Toxicities of folic acid can mask a vitamin B12 deficiency. Deficiencies of folate could lead to megaloblastic anemia.

## Riboflavin

Riboflavin is important for blood cell production and assists with carbohydrate metabolism. Riboflavin is found naturally in milk and dairy sources. A deficiency of riboflavin could cause a condition referred to as ariboflavinosis. Before riboflavin was added to our foods, intakes of riboflavin were not sufficient if you did not consume milk or dairy products. Riboflavin is easily destroyed by sunlight. There are no known toxicities of riboflavin.

## Vitamin B6

Vitamin B6 is also known as pyridoxine. Vitamin B6 plays an important role as an enzyme in more than 100 different reactions. Vitamin B6 is also important for protein metabolism. Deficiencies of vitamin B6 are rarely seen in the United States. As in most cases, poor quality diets can be a risk factor for developing a deficiency. Unlike most B vitamins, where toxicity is not very likely because they are water soluble, toxicity can occur with high levels of vitamin B6. Several studies have found that vitamin B6 could be instrumental in the treatment of carpal tunnel syndrome and pre-menstrual syndrome. One study has shown that, when patients took in amounts in excess of the UL for a long period of time, toxicities can occur.

## Pantothenic Acid and Biotin

Pantothenic acid plays a role in the production of hormones and cholesterol. Biotin is needed for growth and development. There are no known common deficiencies or toxicities of pantothenic acid. A biotin deficiency can occur with the consumption of raw egg whites. There is a protein in the raw egg white called avidin. Avidin can bind with biotin and cause excess to be excreted from the body. This discovery was found in body-builders who consumed large amounts of raw egg whites as a source of protein.

# ARE YOU SUPPLEMENT SAVVY?

Consumers spend billions of dollars on supplements every year. Supplements come in many forms such as pills, drinks, bars, and powders. Current regulations do not require manufacturers to prove their products are safe according to the Food and Drug Administration (FDA). The FDA does not get involved until after the product is released on the market.

© 2012, Shutterstock, Inc.

The FDA recommends that consumers take these steps to be safe with supplements:

- Let your doctor know which supplements you are taking to avoid possible drug/nutrient interactions

- Contact the manufacturer for additional information for the supplement if you are questioning the safety of the product

- Be aware that some supplement ingredients can be toxic and harmful when consumed in large amounts

- Consumers should avoid self-diagnosis and work with their healthcare professional

- Do not substitute supplements for medications prescribed by your doctor

- Do not assume the word "natural" means that the product is safe

- Be aware of any claims made by the manufacturer, check for research studies done on the product

- If it seems to good to be true, it probably is not true*

The FDA also recommends that consumers report problems to the FDA as soon as possible. Adverse reactions to products may be serious and require immediate medical care.

To protect your family and yourself, you can use the following websites as recommended by the FDA:

- Protect your Health at: www.webmd.com/fda

- Fortify your knowledge about Vitamins at: www.fda.gov/updates.vitamins111907.html

- Tips for Savvy Supplement User at: www.fda.gov/fdac/features/2002/202_supp.html

* http://www.fda.gov/ForConsumers/ConsumerUpdates/ucm050803.htm

# CHAPTER 8

# The Fat Soluble Vitamins: Building Blocks for Vision, Bone, and Blood Health

© 2012, Shutterstock, Inc.

## Learning Objectives

- Describe what a dietary supplement is
- List the fat soluble vitamins
- Explain the function of the fat soluble vitamins in the health of our eyes, bone, and blood
- List three food sources for each fat soluble vitamin
- Describe toxicity and deficiencies associated with each vitamin
- Understand how vitamins A and E function as antioxidants

## Functional Food Fact \ Pumpkins and Beta-Carotene

**Beta-carotene** is a water soluble provitamin. A **provitamin** is activated in the body when the food is eaten. Beta-carotene is known for its antioxidant properties. As you will learn in this chapter, beta-carotene is the plant form of vitamin A. Beta-carotene is also known for enhancing the immune system and assisting with the communication between cells in the body. Proper communication between cells could be a way to prevent cancer. Pumpkins are a great way to get a generous dose of beta-carotene. Although there is no RDA or AI for beta-carotene, 1 cup of pumpkin puree will provide over 5,000 micrograms of beta-carotene and when cooked it is even better for us. So have that slice of pumpkin pie! But just a slice!

## The Scoop on Dietary Supplements

What exactly is a dietary supplement? As defined by the Dietary Supplement Health and Education Act of 1994, a dietary supplement is a product (does not include tobacco) that:

- Is intended to supplement the diet

- Contains one or more dietary ingredients such as vitamins, minerals, or herbs

- Is intended to be taken by mouth, pill, capsule, tablet, or liquid

- Is labeled on the front panel of the product as being a dietary supplement

Dietary supplements may not make claims that will lead the consumer to believe that they will be diagnosed, treated, cured, or prevented from getting a disease or illness. The following claims may be used:

- Health claim—may include the claim that the supplement may reduce the risk of disease

- Nutrient content claim—describes the amount of the nutrient in the product

- Structure/function claim—a statement describing how the product is supposed to act on the body. Must be submitted to the FDA in writing within 30 days of putting the product on the market.

It is important to note that the FDA does not directly regulate or endorse the sale of supplements. Any new dietary products introduced to the market after 1994 must be reviewed by the FDA for safety before being sold. The manufacturer must provide sufficient evidence about the safety of the product for human use. In 2007, the FDA issued Good Manufacturing Practices (GMPs) which are a set of requirements and expectations by which the supplement company must abide to ensure a good quality product.[1]

Dietary supplements are not required to be standardized; therefore the product could be inconsistent in quality. The FDA also does not require dietary supplements to be tested for safety before they are marketed. This can result in the misuse of the supplement by consumers and therefore may be dangerous for some people.

## Fat Soluble Vitamins

The fat soluble vitamins include vitamin A, vitamin D, vitamin E, and vitamin K. The fat soluble vitamins are stored with the adipose tissue (fat) in the body. The fat soluble vitamins are also transported in the body via the lymphatic system along with fat as discussed in the chapter on lipids. Because we store these vitamins for a longer period of time, we are not required to consume them on a daily basis. In contrast to the water

---

[1] http://ods.od.nih.gov/factsheets/dietarysupplements

soluble vitamins, the fat soluble vitamins can be toxic if taken in large amounts (in the form of supplements).

## Vitamin E

### Recommendations and Food Sources

Vitamin E is a fat soluble vitamin that has eight different chemical forms. The form that we will discuss is alpha-tocopherol which is the form that is necessary to meet our biological requirements. Vitamin E functions primarily as an antioxidant, protecting polyunsaturated fatty acids from oxidation. Oxidative damage to polyunsaturated fatty acids can lead to atherosclerosis which can lead to heart attack or stroke. Vitamin E also functions to protect the immune system and metabolic processes. The RDA for vitamin E is 15 mg for both men and women.[2]

© 2012, Shutterstock, Inc.

The following food sources are rich in vitamin E:

| Food | mg per serving | %DV |
|---|---|---|
| Wheat germ oil | 20.3 | 100% |
| Sunflower seeds | 7.4 | 37% |
| Almonds (dry roasted) | 6.8 | 34% |
| Sunflower oil, 1 Tblsp | 5.6 | 28% |
| Hazelnuts (dry roasted) | 4.3 | 22% |

[2] http://ods.od.nih.gov/factsheets/vitaminE/

### The Antioxidant Function of Vitamin E

The alpha-tocopherol form of vitamin E is said to protect the outer layer of the cell membranes from oxidation. This is especially important for oxidative damage that is seen in the arteries and can further promote plaque formation. Damaged phospholipids can lead to further damage to the arteries in the development of atherosclerosis. If the membrane is damaged by oxidation, the membrane will lose its functionality.

© 2012, Shutterstock, Inc.

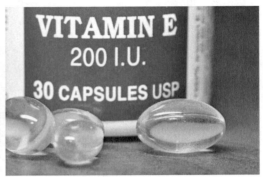
© 2012, Shutterstock, Inc.

**Figure 8.1** Almonds and hazel nuts are foods rich in vitamin E, but when diet does not provide enough vitamin E, supplements are available over the counter.

### Deficiencies and Toxicities of Vitamin E

**Vitamin E Deficiency**

Vitamin E deficiencies are rare and are not commonly found in healthy people. Most people obtain adequate amounts from the diet. Premature babies may be deficient and will most often require supplementation. People with malabsorption disorders caused by Crohn's disease and cystic fibrosis are also at risk for a deficiency of vitamin E due to decreased absorption of fat soluble vitamins especially in the small intestine. Deficiency symptoms include peripheral neuropathy (nerve damage to the hands and feet), retinopathy (eye damage), and impaired immunity.

**Vitamin E Toxicity**

As with most vitamins, toxicity is not related to food intake. Supplement use is the most common cause of vitamin E toxicity. The UL for vitamin E is 1000 mg/day. In some studies, increased intake of vitamin E was associated with an increased risk of hemorrhagic stroke and could decrease blood clotting time. Vitamin E may also interact with some blood thinning medications.

## Vitamin A

### Recommendations and Food Sources

© 2012, Shutterstock, Inc.

Vitamin A is a fat soluble vitamin and has some antioxidant properties. Vitamin A has two forms, the animal form and the plant form. Vitamin A is composed of a variety of compounds that includes retinol. Retinol is the most active form of vitamin A in the body. Retinol is the animal form of vitamin A. The plant form is made up of a variety of yellow-orange pigments called carotenoids. The primary function of vitamin A is the role that it plays in eye health. The RDA for vitamin A for adults is 900 mcg for men and 700 mcg for women.[3]

The following foods are plant (beta-carotene) sources of Vitamin A:

| Food | IU per serving | %DV |
|---|---|---|
| ▪ Carrot juice, ½ cup | 22,567 | 450 |
| ▪ Boiled carrots, ½ cup | 13,418 | 270 |
| ▪ Boiled frozen spinach, ½ cup | 11,458 | 230 |
| ▪ Kale boiled, ½ cup | 9,558 | 190 |
| ▪ Cantaloupe, 1 cup | 5,411 | 110 |

---

[3] http://ods.od.nih.gov/factsheets/vitamina/

The following foods are animal sources of Vitamin A:

| Food | IU per serving | %DV |
|---|---|---|
| ■ Beef liver, 3 oz | 27,185 | 545 |
| ■ Chicken liver, 3 oz | 12,325 | 245 |
| ■ Fortified milk, 1 cup | 500 | 10 |
| ■ Cheddar cheese, 1 oz | 284 | 6 |
| ■ Egg substitute, ¼ cup | 226 | 5 |

## Functions of Vitamin A

All cells require vitamin A to function in a variety of ways such as:

- Growth and development
- Health of mucous membranes
- Reproductive health
- Bone health
- Eye health

### Vitamin A and Eye Health

The health of our eyes depends on vitamin A. The name of the part of the eye called the *retina* bears a resemblance to *retinol,* which is a form of vitamin A that is essential for proper vision. Vision begins when light rays are reflected off an object and enter the eyes through the cornea, the transparent outer covering of the eye. The cornea bends or refracts the rays that pass through a round hole called the pupil. The iris, or colored portion of the eye that surrounds the pupil, opens and closes (making the pupil bigger or smaller) to regulate the amount of light passing through. The light rays then pass through the lens, which actually changes shape so it can further bend the rays and focus them on the retina at the back of the eye. The retina is a thin layer of tissue at the back of the eye that contains millions of tiny light-sensing nerve cells called rods and cones, which are named for their distinct shapes. Cones are concentrated in the center of the retina, in an area called the macula. In bright light conditions, cones provide clear, sharp central vision and detect colors and fine details. Rods are located outside the macula and extend all the way to the outer edge of the retina. They provide peripheral or side vision. Rods also allow the eyes to detect motion and help us see in dim light and at night. These cells in the retina convert the light into electrical impulses. The optic nerve sends these impulses to the brain where an image is produced. Vitamin A helps to keep the cornea, which is the lens on the front of the eye, clear and healthy.

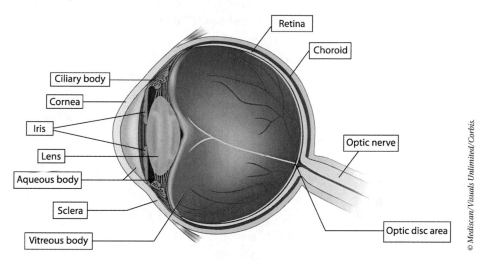

© Mediscan/Visuals Unlimited/Corbis.

**NUTRITION NERD ALERT**

There are fat-soluble nutrients, called carotenoids, that have many health benefits. Carrots are known for their eye health benefits (from beta-carotene, a precursor to Vitamin A). However, two other carotenoids—lutein and zeaxanthin—are also important for eye health. Beets are an excellent source of both.

## Deficiencies and Toxicities of Vitamin A

### Vitamin A Deficiency

You are in a theatre watching a movie and the lights are dim. After the movie is over, the lights in the theatre come on and it takes a few seconds for your eyes to adjust to the bright light. The retina is the area of the eye that is responsible for the sensitivity to light. With adequate vitamin A intake, the ability of the eye to adjust to the bright light is maintained. In some under-developed nations, deficiencies of vitamin A can occur. Foods that are rich in vitamin A and beta-carotene may not be available. A condition called night blindness is an inability to see in dim light due to a vitamin A deficiency. People who suffer from night blindness are at risk for total vision loss—referred to as xeropthalmia—which is a severe form of vitamin A deficiency.

### Vitamin A Toxicity

The UL for vitamin A is 3000 mcg/day for adults. Vitamin A supplementation is the likely source for vitamin A toxicity. Excessive supplementation with vitamin A can cause liver damage. The liver is the primary site for storing vitamin A. Birth defects can also result from excess vitamin A supplementation. Women who are pregnant or might become pregnant should not be taking more than what is recommended.

Too much beta-carotene can also be a form of toxicity. Remember that beta-carotene is the plant form of vitamin A. Although harmless, excessive amounts of beta-carotene will cause the skin to appear slightly yellow or orange. This condition can sometimes be seen in infants who are fed baby foods that contain carrots, yams, squash, and other bright yellow or orange colors. This condition is harmless and the skin color will return to normal after a few hours.[4]

### NUTRITION NERD ALERT

Think those yams are the same as sweet potatoes? Yams have only a small amount of beta-carotene (the precursor to vitamin A). One cup of sweet potatoes has over 300% of your daily value!!

## Vitamin D

### Vitamin D Recommendations and Food Sources

Vitamin D (calciferol) is a fat soluble vitamin. Vitamin D is also known as the sunshine vitamin. In the past, it was believed that most or all of the vitamin D we needed came from the sun. There are very few foods that contain vitamin D. In areas where there is not enough sunshine, vitamin D deficiencies can be a problem. In the United States, most milk and dairy products are sold with added vitamin D to prevent deficiencies. The individual dairies are responsible for adding a recommended amount of vitamin D.

---

[4] http://ods.od.nih.gov/factsheets/vitaminA/

Vitamin D could also be considered a hormone because we make it in one part of the body and utilize it in another. Vitamin D works with cholesterol in the body to convert vitamin D from the sun into the active form of vitamin D that is necessary for the body. In most circumstances, vitamin D can be obtained from the sun. UVB exposure will provide about 80–100% of the vitamin D that is needed; although this will depend on the color of your skin and the amount of time spent in the sun. It is suggested by some researchers that 5–30 minutes of sun exposure between 10am and 3pm at least twice a week without sunscreen is a sufficient amount of time to convert the active form of vitamin D in the body.[5]

## Vitamin D Food Sources

Vitamin D does not occur naturally in many food items. Fatty fish such as sardines and salmon are good sources but most of our vitamin D comes from the sun or fortified foods. Milk and dairy products are the most common foods to be fortified with vitamin D, along with some cereal and grain products.

## Vitamin D Recommendations

The RDA for vitamin D is 600 IU for both male and females. Because vitamin D is a fat soluble vitamin, deficiency of vitamin D was once thought to be rare in most cases as long as there was adequate sun exposure. Recent research has come out that more people are being tested and showing deficient serum levels of vitamin D. One theory is that we are using sunscreens to protect our skin and this may result in a decrease in vitamin D absorption.

## Vitamin D and Bone Health

Osteoporosis is a serious disease that results in low bone density. Low bone density can lead to numerous bone breaks and fractures. Women are 80% more likely to develop osteoporosis than men. Osteoporosis is often thought to result from an inadequate intake of calcium but vitamin D also plays an important role in bone health. Vitamin D helps to regulate bone metabolism and works closely with two hormones called **parathyroid hormone (PTH)** and **calcitonin**. We will discuss these two hormones in more detail in the minerals chapter. These two hormones work together to carefully balance the calcium levels in the blood along with vitamin D. Vitamin D helps to move calcium into the bones when an adequate dietary intake is maintained, or it can also help in taking away calcium from the bones when dietary intakes are not adequate.

---

[5] http://ods.od.nih.gov/factsheets/vitaminD/

## Toxicities and Deficiencies of Vitamin D

### Deficiencies of Vitamin D

Deficiencies of vitamin D occur most often in those populations in which adequate sunlight is not available or intake of vitamin D is too low. In children a vitamin D deficiency is called rickets. Rickets is characterized by a "bowing" of the legs due to the bones being too soft. Vitamin D is important for the mineralization of the bones which makes the bones stronger. Without adequate vitamin D, the bones cannot support the weight of a growing child.

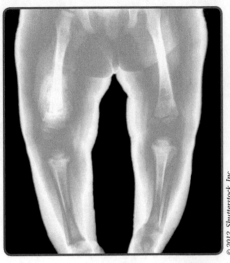

© 2012, Shutterstock, Inc.

Another vitamin D deficiency disease that can occur in adults is called **osteomalacia**. Osteomalacia means "soft bones" and is similar to what happens to the bones in rickets. Inefficient calcium absorption along with low vitamin D intake or sun exposure can lead to soft bones which can cause fractures in hips or other bones. Vitamin D deficiency is common in older adults especially those with limited sun exposure or those who are in long term care or convalescent hospitals. As we age, the amount of vitamin D we get from sun exposure is decreased. It is recommended that older people get sun exposure during the early morning hours or late afternoon, times of day when the risk of skin cancer is minimized. Vitamin D supplements should be used only when recommended by your physician.

### Toxicities of Vitamin D

Toxicity of vitamin D cannot occur from too much sun exposure. Toxicity of vitamin D occurs from over-supplementation. Vitamin D toxicity can cause non-specific weight loss, excessive urination, and possible heart problems. Serious symptoms of toxicity can lead to higher levels of calcium in the blood which can cause calcification and damage to the heart and other vital organs.[6] Higher doses of vitamin D supplements are currently being studied in the prevention of breast and possibly other cancers. High doses in excess of 10,000–40,000 IU/day can cause some of the symptoms outlined above. High doses of vitamin D supplementation should be only be prescribed by and monitored by your physician.

---

[6] http://ods.od.nih.gov/factsheets/vitaminD-HealthProfessional/

Mushrooms are in season all year long. Mushrooms have selenium (a type of antioxidant), potassium, folic acid, and are one of the few food sources that is a non-animal source of vitamin D.

## FOOD IN FOCUS  Could Milk and Dairy Be Bad For Us?

Some websites are making claims that dairy products may be bad for our bones. As we have learned, vitamin D and calcium are needed in the body to build strong bones. A claim that milk may actually deplete calcium in the bones does not make much sense. The weak argument behind this claim is that the consumption of dietary protein, especially from milk and animal sources may increase urinary calcium excretion. This is true but the calcium that is being excreted from the body is coming from the foods and not from the bones, experts say.

There are also discussions about the benefits of milk and the possible prevention of colon cancer. The Harvard School of Public Health looked at studies where people consumed at least one cup of milk per day were less likely to develop colorectal cancer than compared to those that consumed less than two cups per week. It is not quite clear yet whether it is the calcium or something else in the milk. Another study showed that patients who have had precancerous lesions removed from their colons had a lower risk for a recurrence of the lesions when they took 1200 mg of a calcium supplement. It may also be that vitamin D plays an important role in lowering the risk of a recurrence.

Dairy also provides potassium which has been shown to be a great way to lower blood pressure. Some ethnicities are at a higher risk for developing hypertension than compared to others. The DASH diet has shown the best evidence in using high potassium, low sodium foods to lower blood pressure. Adding milk and dairy to this diet can add even greater benefits.

Can milk and dairy help with weight loss? Claims about the consumption of milk and dairy leading to weight loss were popular in 2007. The government pulled the ad campaign claiming that there was not enough evidence to prove this claim. Milk and dairy contain protein which can provide some satiation and make you feel full, which may help to curb the appetite.[*]

The benefits outweigh the risk when it comes to consuming adequate amounts of milk and dairy in the diet. Milk and dairy provide the main source of vitamin D that we need on a daily basis. Low vitamin D intake may also be associated with an increase risk for developing certain types of cancer such as breast cancer.

[*] Nutrition Action Healthletter, July/August 2011

## Vitamin K

### Vitamin K Recommendations and Sources

Vitamin K is the last fat soluble vitamin that plays a role in blood health. Vitamin K is necessary for blood clotting. We produce our own vitamin K in the large intestine. There are two forms of vitamin K, the plant form and the animal form. The plant form of vitamin K is called phylloquinone. The animal form comes from meat and fish oils and is called menaquinone; this is also the form that is produced in the large intestine. There is an established AI for vitamin K. For men the recommendation is 120 mcg/day, and for women the recommendation is 90 mcg/day.[7]

Good food sources of vitamin K:

- Green leafy vegetables such as spinach, kale, Swiss chard, and mustard greens

- Brussels sprouts, broccoli, and cauliflower

- Fish, liver, meat, and eggs contain smaller amounts

**EVERY DAY**
**SUPERFOODS**

K is for kale! Vitamin K that is. With over 600% of your daily needs, kale is the best choice for getting your daily dose of Vitamin K. Who needs supplements?!

### Vitamin K Deficiency

Deficiencies of vitamin K are rare. As previously mentioned, we produce vitamin K in the large intestine. Without adequate vitamin K, the ability to clot our blood would be difficult. In newborns, vitamin K is not yet present in the large intestine; they have what is referred to as a "sterile gut." Most newborns born in the United States are given a dose of vitamin K at birth as a preventive measure.

### Vitamin K Toxicity

Vitamin K toxicity is not common. High intake of vitamin K rich foods will not cause toxicity. A UL has not been established for vitamin K. High doses of vitamin K may interfere with anticoagulant medications that are prescribed to patients. Anticoagulant medications are used to prevent blood clotting. A patient who is prescribed an anticoagulant medication will need to monitor their intake of vitamin K rich foods so as to not interfere with the action of the medication.

---

[7] http://www.nlm.nih.gov/medlineplus/ency/article/002407.htm

*Nutrition Intuition*

## Summary

The fat soluble vitamins are involved in numerous important functions that involve bone health, blood health, and healthy vision. The fat soluble vitamins are primarily stored in the liver and adipose tissue and are transported around the body through the lymphatic system. Concentrations of these fat soluble vitamins in the blood can be steadily maintained when the need arises. The vitamins can be retrieved from the liver or adipose tissue when necessary. The storage of the fat soluble vitamins in the liver and adipose tissue ensures that we have a steady supply and will not run out any time soon, so deficiencies of these vitamins are rare. It is also important to mention that because of the extended storage of these vitamins there is a greater risk of toxicity.

## Vitamin E

The main function of vitamin E is as an antioxidant. Vitamin E acts to stop free radicals by donating an electron to stabilize the molecule. Vitamin E is mostly found in oils and is added commercially to most oils to prevent oxidation and give the oil a longer shelf-life.

## Vitamin A

Vitamin A is a fat soluble vitamin that plays a role in vision, immune function, and cell differentiation and acts as an antioxidant. The precursor of vitamin A is beta-carotene and is also the plant form of vitamin A. Excess intake of vitamin A supplements can be toxic, especially in pregnant women. Vitamin A rich foods include liver, fish, and fish oils. Beta-carotene is found in fruits and vegetables that are rich red and orange colors as well as dark green leafy vegetables.

## Vitamin D

Vitamin D acts both as a vitamin and a hormone. Vitamin D is also referred to as the sunshine vitamin because we get it from the sun. Few foods contain vitamin D; therefore we rely on sun exposure to get adequate amounts. In cases where individuals do not get adequate sunlight a supplement may be necessary. In the United States, milk and dairy products are fortified with vitamin D. Vitamin D helps to regulate blood calcium levels and helps with the calcification of the bones. Vitamin D deficiencies may occur in both adults and children. In children who do not get adequate amounts of vitamin D, the deficiency is called rickets, which is characterized by a softening of the bones. In adults a vitamin D deficiency is called osteomalacia.

## Vitamin K

Vitamin K is made in the large intestine. Vitamin K plays a major role in the blood clotting process. In newborns, a shot of vitamin K is often administered because the infant does not have the proper bacteria established in the large intestine. Vitamin K also plays a small role in bone health. Vitamin K rich foods such as dark green leafy vegetables may interfere with blood thinning medications such as coumadin or warfarin.

# DRUG/NUTRIENT INTERACTIONS

Medications or drugs are prescribed to treat various diseases and illnesses. Absorption of medications by the body often takes a similar pathway in the body as many of our nutrients. Sometimes drugs and nutrients can interact with each other and possibly cause adverse reactions or decrease the effectiveness of the drug. A food may speed up or slow down the action of a drug. If you or your family members are taking any of the medications listed below, the doctor or pharmacist should explain possible interactions.

© 2012, Shutterstock, Inc.

Below are some common drug/nutrient interactions to be aware of:

| Drug Name | Use | Interaction |
|---|---|---|
| Coumadin | blood thinner | vitamin K containing foods such as dark, green leafy vegetables are natural foods that help to clot blood and interfere with coumadin |
| Aspirin | anti-inflammatory | can cause loss of vitamin C |
| Birth Control Pills | oral contraceptive | lowers levels of folic acid, Vitamin B6 |
| Tetracycline | antibiotic | calcium may interact with the antibiotic and should be taken 2-3 hours before and after the medicine |
| Lipitor | cholesterol lowering | may interact with vitamins A, C, E, B, and folic acid |
| Prednisone | corticosteroid | may increase appetite and cause weight gain |
| Lasix | diuretic | may decrease appetite |

http://www.faqs.org/nutrition/Met-Obe/Nutrient-Drug-Interactions.html

# CHAPTER 9

# Water: Essential to Life
# Electrolytes: Fluid Balance

© 2012, Shutterstock, Inc.

## Learning Objectives

- Discuss the roles of sodium and potassium and their influence on blood pressure
- Describe the importance of calcium in the prevention of osteoporosis
- List and explain the functions of water
- Discuss healthy amounts of water intake and output to maintain proper balance
- Outline the different sources of water, caffeine, and alcohol in the diet

## Functional Food Fact  Tea

Tea is second to water as the most widely consumed beverage worldwide. Healing properties of drinking tea have long been recognized in ancient literature. Today's health benefits of tea have mostly focused on green teas, but all tea contains polyphenols which are shown to have antioxidant properties. Studies on tea consumption and a reduced risk of cancer development are being done today. Animal studies have shown the best evidence of tea and cancer prevention but studies on humans are still in the works.

© 2012, Shutterstock, Inc.

# Introduction to Water and Electrolytes

Water is essential to life. You can survive about 20–30 days without food but only a few days without water. Water provides an environment in which our cells can perform their duties and keep us functioning optimally. It may seem trivial to spend an entire chapter on water, but you will find that water has numerous important functions. The electrolytes that we will discuss in this chapter are also important. Sodium, potassium, phosphorus, and chloride all assist in maintaining fluid balance in the body and work very closely with water.

## Water: Basic Components

### Water Balance in the Body

The human body is made up of approximately 50–70% water. The amount of water in the body depends on several different factors such as:

- Age

- Gender

- Muscle mass

Infants require more water because their body fat percentage is higher. Older adults also require more water because as we age we lose lean body mass that is replaced with fat. Men have more lean body mass than compared to women; therefore men have more water in their bodies. Women tend to have higher body fat percentages compared to men so women have less water in their bodies.

### Functions of Water

Water has various functions. Water is a major solvent which means that many substances can be easily dissolved in water and this allows many chemical reactions to occur.

Other functions of water include:

- Body temperature regulation

- Help removing waste products

© 2012, Shutterstock, Inc.

- Amniotic fluid

- Cushion between the joints (synovial fluid)

## Fluid Needs

Fluid needs vary depending on the person, the climate, physical activity level, health status, and the environment. Hotter or more humid climates require that a person drink more water. Illnesses that cause excessive vomiting or diarrhea will cause a person to become dehydrated faster and thus the fluids lost through vomiting or diarrhea need to be replaced quickly. The consensus on how much water someone should drink is difficult to define because of the numerous variations in our needs for water. A general recommendation is eight 8-oz glasses of water per day. This could be too much for one person or too little for someone else. Thirst and total fluid intake will determine the hydration status of a person.

## NUTRITION NERD ALERT

Feeling fatigued? Make sure you are properly hydrated! The kidneys release fatigue-causing toxins (e.g., mercury from fish and dioxins absorbed from pollution) through urine but need lots of water to do this efficiently! Sweating can also help release toxins (among the benefits of exercising daily)—but keep in mind that less that 1% of toxins are lost due to sweat.

## Thirst Mechanism

The thirst mechanism is regulated by the hypothalamus. Just as with hunger, the hypothalamus sends signals regarding the hydration status in the body. If you do not drink enough fluid, the body will eventually signal thirst. There are minimum amounts of waste products that are to be excreted from the body to maintain good health. The minimum amount of waste that should be excreted is about 500 ml or 2 cups. Ignoring the thirst mechanism can cause a build-up of a waste product called urea. Urea is a by-product of protein metabolism. Urine that is very concentrated will appear darker in color. The heavy concentration of the urine could be a cause of kidney stones in some people.

## Water Is Water?

When you are thirsty, does it matter what kind of fluids you drink? Water should be the fluid of choice when you are thirsty or dehydrated. Another way that we can get water is from our fruits and vegetables. Be wary of beverages that contain caffeine;

caffeine is known to act as a diuretic in the body, a diuretic draws water out of the cells. Alcohol is also known to be a diuretic and can cause loss of water from the body.

**NUTRITION NERD ALERT**

It may be cold outside during the winter months, but do not forget to hydrate! Winter fruits and veggies high in water content include: grapefruit, broccoli, winter greens, and tomatoes.

### Dehydrated vs. Over Hydrated

Did you know that you could become dehydrated from drinking too much water? Remember that the electrolytes play an important role in balancing water inside and outside of the cells. Drinking too much water can cause those electrolytes to become diluted which can be dangerous. That is why you see sports beverages that contain a mixture of sodium and potassium and other minerals, especially at sporting events or marathons where the athletes need more fluids. When a person has excessive sweating, vomiting, or diarrhea, the use of sports drinks can be beneficial. Many children and teens believe that they need sports drinks to remain hydrated during recess or playing in sporting events. Commercials about sports drinks usually have athletes and celebrities that encourage consumption of these beverages. We try to educate children and teens that unless they are competing at the same level as the professionals, water will do just fine. The sports drinks often have as much sugar in them as a can of soda.

Dehydration is possible when the thirst response has been ignored, with excessive vomiting or diarrhea due to an illness, or it can occur with excessive sweating. Normally, most of our water lost is through urination. Water is also lost from the body via exhalation, and small amounts in the bowel movements.

Some symptoms of dehydration include:

- Headache
- Dizziness
- Nausea
- Mental confusion

It is estimated that we can live only about three days without water; replacing fluids when we are dehydrated is vital. Those who are at the highest risk for dehydration are infants and the elderly because of the higher percent of fat in their bodies.

## Fluid and Electrolyte Balance

Water is essential to life. There are two major fluid compartments within the body which are referred to as intracellular water and extracellular water. Intracellular water is found inside of the cells. Extracellular water is found outside of the cell, which also includes plasma (the fluid component of blood). The balance of water inside and outside of the cell is maintained by the electrolytes sodium, potassium, chloride, and phosphorus. These electrolytes all work closely together. These minerals carry positive and negative charges and are collectively referred to as **ions**. We have positively charged ions and we have negatively charged ions. The positive and negative charges are what help the water to move in and out of the cell to maintain balance. These positive and negative charges also serve a purpose in helping to assist with nerve transmission and muscle contraction.

Even now as you hold your pencil or pen, type on your computer, or read this text, your electrolytes are assisting in the transmission of messages to nerves and sending electrical currents to where they are needed. Electrolytes exist both inside and outside of the cell membrane. The electrical charges must be even on both sides of the cell membrane to function adequately, meaning that there is always one negative and one positively charged ion inside the cell and one negative and one positively charged ion outside the cell.

Sodium and potassium are the two positively charged ions or cations. Phosphorus and chloride are the two negatively charged ions or anions. Sodium and potassium have a unique relationship because they have the ability to switch places across the cell membrane temporarily during nerve transmission of messages and muscle contraction. Remember that the balance of the charges needs to remain the same on both sides of the cell membrane. The imbalance of these charges can be dangerous. For example, potassium is responsible for controlling the heartbeat; an imbalance of potassium in the body could cause a heart attack.

Phosphorus and chloride do not switch places. Calcium, which is a trace mineral, has somewhat of an electrolyte function and plays a small but important role in muscle contraction and relaxation of the muscle. When the muscle contracts, calcium is pumped into the cell and during relaxation calcium is pumped back out of the cell. We will discuss calcium later in this chapter.

The overall health and well being of the cell depends on the balance of the water inside and out. Too much water inside the cell can cause the cell to burst, and too little water inside the cell can cause the cell to die. It is ironic to think that if you were shipwrecked and floating around the ocean in a lifeboat, you could die of dehydration surrounded by all that water. Why? Because the ocean water contains too much salt and would cause more dehydration when consumed. When water balance is off, the body tries to compensate and make adjustments. Dehydration can be caused by a number of conditions such as:

- Excessive vomiting

- Diarrhea

- Heat stroke

- High fever

- Infections

Whenever there are significant losses of water from the body, the cells become dehydrated and the concentration of the electrolytes becomes higher outside of the cells causing the electrical charges to malfunction, which may lead to death.

## Sodium

### How Much do we Need?

Sodium is a positively charged ion and the major extracellular electrolyte. Our main source of sodium comes from the diet. Table salt, which is sodium chloride (NaCl), is made up of 60% sodium and 40% chloride. It is estimated that the average American consumes over 3000 mg of sodium per day, which exceeds the current recommendation of 2400 mg. The consumption of too much sodium is contraindicated for people with hypertension (high blood pressure). Current recommendations suggest that for optimal heart health we should consume only about 1500 mg of sodium per day.

© 2012, Shutterstock, Inc.

## Sources of Sodium

We get sodium from a variety of foods. Sodium is used in processed foods, canned goods, and frozen foods, just to name a few. Sodium is a good preservative and adds flavor to foods. Do you know someone who salts their food at the table before they even taste it? Have you ever had the low sodium version of a food you typically consume? The taste is often bland at first, but with gradual decreases in sodium intake, your taste buds will begin to adjust. Listed below are some typical foods and their sodium amounts.

### High Sodium Foods

| Food | Serving | mg of Sodium |
| --- | --- | --- |
| ▪ Potato salad | 1 cup | 1323 |
| ▪ Cheeseburger | 1 each | 1314 |
| ▪ Canned tomato sauce | 1 cup | 1284 |
| ▪ Tuna sandwich | 6 inch | 1293 |
| ▪ Egg and sausage biscuit | 1 each | 1210 |

### Low Sodium Foods

| Food | Serving | mg of Sodium |
| --- | --- | --- |
| ▪ Garden salad | 1 tbsp of dressing | 142 |
| ▪ Cheese pizza | 1 slice | 282 |
| ▪ Fresh tomato | 1 medium | 6 |
| ▪ Low sodium soup | 1 cup | 60 |
| ▪ Frosted Flakes cereal | ¾ cup | 143 |

*source: www.ars.usda.gov/SP2UserFiles/Place/12354500/Data/SR22/nutrlist/

## Toxicities and Deficiencies of Sodium

As discussed earlier, sodium is important for fluid balance, nerve transmission, and muscle contraction. Can you eat too many potato chips and cause a toxicity of sodium? The answer is no. Sodium toxicities and deficiencies usually occur when there is an imbalance of sodium in the body. Toxicities and deficiencies are rarely caused by eating too much or not eating enough of sodium.

A toxicity of sodium is called **hypernatremia**. Hypernatremia is a condition characterized by high sodium levels in the blood. Common causes are:

- Kidney dysfunction

- Drinking large amounts of salt water

The kidneys filter sodium along with other nutrients and waste. When the kidneys are not functioning properly sodium can be retained in the body and can raise the levels in the blood. As previously mentioned, if someone were floating around in the middle of the ocean surrounded by water he or she could not drink the salt water. High intake of salt water in a short amount of time could lead to hypernatremia.

A deficiency of sodium is called **hyponatremia**. Hyponatremia is a condition characterized by low sodium levels in the blood. Common causes are:

- Drinking too much water (over hydration)

- Excessive sweating or vomiting

Symptoms of hyponatremia include muscle cramps, nausea, vomiting, dizziness, and the possibility of coma or death. Losses of sodium from the body can quickly lower blood sodium levels. This may occur in marathon runners who drink too much water and lose too much sodium from excessive sweating. Maybe you have heard stories of people drinking large amounts of water in a short amount of time to win contest or prizes and then end up going into a coma and possibly dying as a result of hyponatremia. Hyponatremia can be very serious and must be treated immediately.

**Hypertension and Sodium**

**Hypertension** is a condition characterized by an increased pressure exerted on the arterial walls. It is estimated that 1 in 5 adults has hypertension. Hypertension is often referred to as "the silent killer" because it is asymptomatic. A blood pressure reading is expressed as systolic over diastolic. Systolic is the top number and measures the heart's force of contraction. The diastolic reading measures the heart at rest. A recommended adult blood pressure reading is 120/80. Stage 1 hypertension is diagnosed when the blood pressure exceeds 140/90. Stage 2 hypertension is diagnosed when the blood pressure exceeds 160/100. When a patient is diagnosed with hypertension, the doctor often prescribes antihypertensive medications. It is estimated that 95% of diagnosed cases of hypertension are from an unknown etiology. This means that we do not quite understand why people get hypertension. Only 5% of diagnosed cases of hypertension are from other conditions such as kidney failure.

Lowering sodium in the diet is an effective way to treat high blood pressure. The exact mechanism of how lowering sodium in the diet lowers blood pressure is not very well understood. Often patients with hypertension are prescribed a special diet called the DASH diet. DASH stands for Dietary Approaches to Stop Hypertension. The DASH diet is a heart healthy eating plan that strives to limit total fat, saturated fat, and cholesterol in the diet. The DASH diet also focuses on including foods that are rich in potassium, magnesium, calcium, and magnesium. The DASH diet is our Food in Focus topic for this chapter.

## Potassium

### How Much do we Need?

Potassium has many of the same functions that sodium has. Potassium is a positively charged ion and is the major intracellular electrolyte. Potassium also helps with fluid balance, nerve transmission, and muscle contraction. Although potassium has similar functions to sodium, potassium helps to lower blood pressure rather than increase it. The recommended daily intake for potassium is 4700 mg per day for adult men and women.

© 2012, Shutterstock, Inc.

### Sources of Potassium

| Food | mg |
| --- | --- |
| ▪ Tomato paste, canned 1 cup | 2657 |
| ▪ Beans, white 1 cup | 1309 |
| ▪ Milk, condensed, sweetened 1 cup | 1135 |
| ▪ Raisins, seedless 1 cup | 1086 |
| ▪ Potato, baked with skin 1 medium | 1081 |

Foods that are high in potassium are mostly unprocessed foods. Many fruits and vegetables are good sources of potassium such as bananas, tomatoes, potatoes, milk, and milk products. As mentioned earlier higher potassium intake is usually associated with lower blood pressure.

### Toxicities and Deficiencies of Potassium

### Toxicities of Potassium

Toxicities of potassium do not come from eating too many fruits and vegetables. The toxicity of potassium is called **hyperkalemia** which means high blood potassium. Potassium is processed through the kidneys. Reduced renal function or abnormal functioning of the kidneys can cause a build-up of potassium in the blood. In such a case, a doctor might prescribe a medication to decrease potassium levels in the blood.

### Deficiencies of Potassium

Potassium deficiency may occur if someone is taking a diuretic medication. Diuretics are also called water pills and are used in the treatment of high blood pressure and congestive heart failure. Other types of medications can also cause excessive potassium to be lost from the body. Low blood potassium is called **hypokalemia**. Hypokalemia can also be caused from excessive vomiting or diarrhea.

**NUTRITION NERD ALERT**

Hydration is important year round. In the summer, fresh fruits and vegetables high in water help keep you hydrated *and cool* (watermelon, cantaloupe, grapefruit, strawberries, lettuce, spinach, and zucchini all top 90% water). Add hot peppers to your favorite dish or salad (capsaicin helps you sweat—cooling you down) and eat a handful of frozen grapes as dessert or a snack.

## Phosphorus

### Phosphorus Recommendations and Food Sources

The recommended RDA of phosphorus for adult males and females is 700 mg per day.[1] Phosphorus is the negatively charged electrolyte that exists inside the cell along with potassium. Phosphorus functions as an electrolyte to help maintain fluid balance, contraction and relaxation of the muscles, as well as nerve transmission. Although this is an important function for phosphorus, this is not its the main function. The main function for phosphorus is the role that it plays in bone health, which will be discussed in the next chapter. Foods high in protein such as meat and dairy are high in phosphorus.

---

[1] http://www.nlm.nih.gov/medlineplus/ency/article/002424.htm

## FOOD IN FOCUS  The DASH Diet

By Victoria Buxton-Pacheco

The DASH eating plan focuses on heart healthy guidelines that will help to reduce blood pressure. The DASH Diet guidelines are presented below and are based on a 2100 calorie diet.

### Daily Nutrient Goals—2100 Calorie Eating Plan

| | | | |
|---|---|---|---|
| **Total Fat** | 27% of calories | **Sodium** | 2300 mg |
| **Saturated Fat** | 6% of calories | **Potassium** | 4700 mg |
| **Protein** | 18% of calories | **Calcium** | 1250 mg |
| **Carbohydrates** | 55% of calories | **Magnesium** | 500 mg |
| **Cholesterol** | 150 mg | **Fiber** | 30 g[*] |

Researchers conducted studies on the effectiveness of following the guidelines listed above. Their findings showed that blood pressure was lowered from choosing a diet rich in fruits and vegetables, whole grain, low fat dairy, and lean meats. Red meat, added sugars, and sugar-containing beverages were kept to a minimum. Overall the diet is a healthy approach to including plenty of fruits and vegetables. High potassium-containing foods have been shown to aid in the lowering of blood pressure.

Rich potassium containing foods include:

- Bananas
- Tomatoes
- Potatoes
- Dark green leafy vegetables
- Milk and dairy products

The diet is largely plant based with little animal meat. Choosing more non-animal sources of protein such as tofu and beans will help to lower the cholesterol intake. Fiber is also important to add in the diet.

Good sources of fiber include:

- Whole wheat grains and pastas
- Fruits and vegetables

[*] http://www.nhlbi.nih.gov/health/public/heart/hbp/dash/new_dash.pdf

## Chloride

### Chloride Recommendations and Food Sources

The AI recommendations for chloride are 2.3 g per day for males and females age 14–50 years old. For males and females aged 51–70, the AI recommendation is 2.0 g per day and for males and females ages 71 and over, the AI recommendation is 1.8 g per day. Chloride is the negatively charged ion that exists outside of the cell along with sodium. Chloride's main function is as an electrolyte which helps to maintain fluid balance. Chloride is mainly found in table salt or sea salt as sodium chloride. Chloride can also be found in some vegetables such as seaweed, tomatoes, lettuces, celery, and olives.[3]

## Summary

Water is essential to life. Without water you can survive for only a few days. Water provides an optimal environment for our cells to function properly. The human body is made up mostly of water. Water comprises 50–70% of our bodies. Several factors play a role in how much water we have in the body, such as our age, gender, and how much muscle mass we have. Women have less water in their bodies compared to men because men have more muscle. Infants and the elderly also have less water in their bodies and therefore have an increased need for water.

Water is a solvent; many substances can be easily dissolved in water which allows chemical reactions to take place. Water functions to aid in body temperature regulation and waste product removal; it also functions as amniotic fluid and provides cushion between the joints. Fluid needs vary from person to person depending on several factors such as age, gender, environment, and different types of activities.

Proper hydration is essential for good health. Thirst is regulated by the hypothalamus. Drinking plenty of fluids will help to ensure that waste products are excreted from the body. The minimum amount of waste that should be excreted is about 500 ml per day. What you drink is almost as important as how much you drink. Drinks that contain caffeine and alcohol are known to act as a diuretic. Sources of fluid can come from foods as well as beverages. Fruits and vegetables can provide some fluids to the body but in smaller amounts.

---

[3] http://www.nlm.nih.gov/medlineplus/ency/article/002417.htm

It is important that hydration is balanced in the body. Dehydration as well as over hydration can cause an imbalance of the electrolytes in the body. Dehydration can occur when the thirst response has been ignored, through excessive sweating and during excessive vomiting and diarrhea. Dehydration needs to be treated right away and can be life-threatening. Over hydration can also be life-threatening and can occur from drinking too much water, this can cause an imbalance in the electrolytes.

Fluid balance in the body is achieved with the help of the electrolytes, sodium, potassium, phosphorus, and chloride. Although fluid balance is important, this is not the only function of the electrolytes. Contraction and relaxation of the muscles and messages sent along the nerve cells are also important functions. Calcium also plays a small role as an electrolyte. During a muscle contraction, calcium is pumped into the cell, and during relaxation of the muscle, calcium is pumped back out of the cell. The electrical charges inside and outside of the cells also have to be in balance for optimal function.

Sodium is a positively charged ion. Sodium is the main extracellular ion. Sources of sodium primarily come from our foods. Processed, canned, and frozen foods are among the highest food sources in our diet. A toxicity of sodium is called hypernatremia and is rare. A toxicity of sodium is a condition characterized by high blood sodium levels usually caused by kidney dysfunction or drinking large amounts of water that contains sodium. A deficiency of sodium is called hyponatremia, is more common, and is caused by excessive sweating, vomiting, or diarrhea. The loss of excess sodium via sweating will cause the blood sodium levels to decrease. In such extreme cases, drinking water alone will not be adequate in replacing the sodium needed by the body. Sports drinks that contain various electrolytes will help to regain the sodium balance in the body.

Hypertension is a condition in which the blood pressure is elevated above normal levels. It is estimated that 95% of diagnosed cases of hypertension are from an unknown etiology. A healthy blood pressure reading is 120/80. Hypertension is often referred to as the "silent killer" because it often presents without symptoms. Lowering sodium in the diet along with antihypertensive medications are effective treatments for hypertension. Weight loss can also be effective in lowering the blood pressure.

Potassium is the major positive ion in the intracellular fluid. Potassium plays a role in fluid balance, muscle contraction and relaxation, and nerve transmission. Potassium is found in a variety of fruits and vegetables. A toxicity of potassium is referred to as hyperkalemia and characterized by a high blood potassium level. Hyperkalemia can occur as a result of kidney dysfunction. Potassium is filtered through the kidneys.

When the kidneys are not functioning properly, potassium will remain in the body. A deficiency of potassium is referred to as hypokalemia and is characterized by low blood potassium levels commonly caused from excessive vomiting or diarrhea. Hypokalemia can also be caused by a patient taking a diuretic. Potassium in the diet can help to lower blood pressure. The DASH diet is often used to help patients lower their blood pressure.

Phosphorus and chloride are the negatively charged electrolytes. Chloride is located outside of the cell along with sodium. Phosphorus is located inside of the cell along with potassium. Both phosphorus and chloride have similar functions to sodium and potassium. Phosphorus plays a bigger role in bone health and will be discussed in more detail in a later chapter.

# WAYS TO LOWER YOUR SODIUM INTAKE

Lowering the sodium in your diet can be beneficial and is a step in the right direction to better your heart health. Current recommendations suggest that we consume about 1500–2400 mg of sodium per day. For optimal heart health and if you have high blood pressure, 1500 mg is recommended. Sodium is found in many processed, frozen, and canned foods. Lowering the sodium in your diet does not mean that you have to sacrifice taste.

© 2012, Shutterstock, Inc.

**The following is a list of alternatives for salt that can add great flavor to your foods:**

- Garlic powder and onion powder
- Herbs such as basil, thyme, bay leaves, and oregano
- Curry powder, cumin, turmeric
- Celery seeds - crush for a "salty flavor"
- Mrs. Dash® or other no-salt alternatives
- Bragg® liquid aminos - great alternative for soy sauce
- Bragg® nutritional yeast seasoning

**What to look for on food labels:**

- Remember to look at the serving size first, then determine how much sodium is in each serving
- Low sodium foods contain less than 140 mg of sodium per serving
- Try to choose frozen foods with less than 300–400 mg per serving
- If you must buy canned vegetables, choose the low sodium varieties

# CHAPTER 10

# Minerals: Small Amounts, Big Impact

## Learning Objectives

- Outline the major and trace minerals, and define their functions
- Understand conditions that may influence the absorption of minerals
- List food sources for minerals and identify possible toxicities and deficiencies
- Describe the minerals important for blood and bone health
- Learn the importance of adequate calcium intake for the prevention of osteoporosis

© 2012, Shutterstock, Inc.

## Functional Food Fact  Milk

Could milk be bad for your bones? Calcium is a key mineral in bone health. The claim that one company makes is that calcium coming from animal products may actually cause more calcium excretion from your bones so they recommend calcium rich fruits and vegetables. Actually the scientific evidence shows that this is not the case. Calcium consumed from animal sources, such as milk, does not increase urinary calcium excretion as the company claims. Cannot drink milk? Try soy milk, rice milk, or almond milk; just make sure that the product is fortified with calcium.

© 2012, Shutterstock, Inc.

# Introduction to Minerals: Major and Trace Minerals

Minerals are inorganic elements, meaning they do not contain carbon. Minerals can carry electrical charges and can gain and lose electrons. Minerals do not break down during metabolism and can be combined with other elements in the body. Even in small amounts, minerals play very important roles in the body. A good example of this is the mineral iron. Iron is known as a trace mineral, meaning we only need a small amount. Improper intakes of iron can lead to iron deficiency anemia. This deficiency not only impacts us here in the United States but also is a common deficiency that impacts many on a global basis.

## Major vs. Trace Minerals

**Major minerals** are those that we need to consume at least 100 mg of per day. The major minerals that we will discuss in this chapter include:

- Sodium
- Potassium
- Phosphorus
- Magnesium
- Sulfur
- Chloride
- Calcium

**Trace minerals** are those that we need to consume less than 100 mg of per day. The trace minerals are not less important, even though they are needed in smaller amounts. The trace minerals to be discussed in this chapter include:

- Iron
- Zinc
- Copper
- Selenium
- Fluoride
- Iodide
- Chromium
- Manganese

## Minerals Involved in Blood Health

### Iron

Iron is a trace mineral that has long been recognized for its importance in blood health. Iron deficiency anemia is a deficiency that is shared worldwide. Iron is a component of hemoglobin and myoglobin. **Hemoglobin** is the iron-containing protein in the red blood cells. **Myoglobin** is the iron-containing protein that is found in the muscle. Strength is often associated with iron. Images of the beloved Popeye cartoon charac-

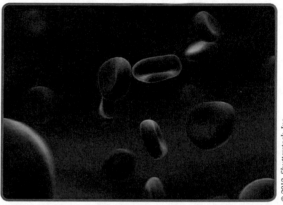

ter gobbling up his can of spinach to gain his strength to battle the enemy comes to mind. Inadequate intake of iron is often associated with feelings of tiredness.

### Iron Recommendations and Food Sources

Food sources of iron can come from animal and plant sources. Heme sources of iron come from animals and nonheme sources of iron come from plants. Heme sources of iron are more readily absorbed by the body. Meat is the main source of heme iron in the typical American diet. Fortified foods are also a good source of iron.

The current recommendations for iron are 8 mg/per day for men and 18 mg/day for women of childbearing age. After the age of 50, the recommendation for women drops to 8 mg/day, the same as for men. Pregnant women will need almost triple the amount of iron (about 27 mg/day) than men. Iron needs for pregnant women will be discussed in a later chapter.

### Food Sources of Iron: Heme and Nonheme Iron

The following food sources of iron are from *heme* sources:

| Food | mg/serving | %DV |
|---|---|---|
| ▪ Chicken liver, cooked (3.5 oz) | 12.8 mg | 70% |
| ▪ Oysters, breaded and fried (6 pc) | 4.5 mg | 25% |
| ▪ Beef, roasted (3 oz) | 3.0 mg | 15% |
| ▪ Clams, breaded and fried (3/4 cup) | 3.0 mg | 15% |
| ▪ Turkey, dark meat cooked (3 oz) | 2.3 mg | 10% |

The following food sources of iron are from *nonheme* sources:

| Food | mg/serving | %DV |
|---|---|---|
| ▪ Fortified cereal (3/4 cup) | 18.0 mg | 100% |
| ▪ Oatmeal, instant fortified (1 cup) | 10.0 mg | 60% |
| ▪ Soybeans, boiled (1 cup) | 8.8 mg | 50% |
| ▪ Lentils, boiled (1 cup) | 6.6 mg | 35% |
| ▪ Kidney beans, boiled (1 cup) | 5.2 mg | 25% |

## Functions of Iron

Iron is a very abundant metal found here on earth. Iron needs for the human body are essential to normal growth and development. Iron helps to carry oxygen throughout the body. About 75% of iron is found in the **hemoglobin** which is also known as red blood cells. A smaller amount of iron is found in the muscle tissue and is referred to as **myoglobin**. Iron is also found in other protein molecules that serve to store iron for future use in the body. When iron stores are depleted the symptoms are consistent with how someone would feel due to a lack of oxygen such as fatigue, a decrease in the immune system, and overall poor work performance.

## Absorption of Iron

There are several factors that can increase and decrease iron absorption. Competing factors may decrease iron absorption. As previously mentioned, calcium will compete with iron for absorption because both minerals require an acidic environment. The body can regulate iron absorption by increasing or decreasing absorption in the intestinal tract depending on its needs.

Heme sources of iron are better absorbed by the body than nonheme sources. Non-heme sources of iron are better absorbed when eaten with heme sources of iron as well as vitamin C. There are also dietary factors that decrease iron absorption, such as tannins found in tea and polyphenols and phytates which are found in beans and whole grains. Iron absorption may also be limited with high fiber diets. Iron absorption and adequacy in the diet is also a concern in the various vegetarian diets that were mentioned in our previous chapter on protein.

The liver can store iron and can recycle iron. The stored form of iron is called **ferritin**. Iron is lost from the body during the menstruation cycle in women; trace amounts are lost in the urine and even the skin. Replenishing iron that is lost from the body is important in trying to prevent a deficiency.

Iron needs are significantly higher in certain populations such as children, women of childbearing age, and pregnant women. For women of childbearing age, the main reason for increased needs is the menstrual cycle. For children, iron needs are important for growth and development. In children the lack of iron in the body is usually due to inadequate dietary intake of iron rich foods. In pregnant women the iron needs are increased due to the increase in blood volume associated with the pregnancy. Iron needs for pregnant women will be discussed in more detail in a future chapter that addresses pregnancy and nutrition.

### Toxicities and Deficiencies of Iron

### Iron Deficiency Anemia

According to the World Health Organization (WHO), iron deficiency anemia is the one nutritional disorder that we share on a worldwide basis. WHO further states that as much as 80% of the world's population may be deficient in iron with about one-third of those having iron deficiency anemia.

**Iron deficiency anemia** can occur due to several factors such as a lack of dietary intake, low absorption of iron, loss of iron via the blood, or a combination of all of these factors. A deficiency of iron can be detected by the measurement of lab values. Lab values that are helpful in assessing iron status include hemoglobin and hematocrit. There are other lab values to assess iron status but these are the most common ways to diagnose a deficiency.

The following list is signs of iron deficiency anemia:

- Feeling tired and weak
- Decreased work and school performance
- Slow cognitive and social development in children

- Difficulty maintaining body temperature
- Decreased immune function
- Glossitis (inflamed tongue) [1]

**Iron Toxicity**

Iron toxicity is not very common in the United States. Iron toxicity has been known to be a cause of death in children who have mistaken iron supplements for candy and ingested too many. As with all medications, supplements and vitamins should also be kept out of reach of children.

A rare genetic condition called **hemachromatosis** is another way that iron toxicity can occur. In this case iron that is consumed in the diet is highly absorbable by the body which can eventually lead to damage to many of the major organs.

## Minerals Involved in Immune Health

### Selenium

Selenium is a trace mineral that is required is small amounts which are important for antioxidant enzymes. Selenoproteins are made by combining selenium and protein and are found to play an antioxidant role in the prevention of cellular damage from free radicals. Selenium also plays a role in thyroid function.

### Selenium Recommendations and Food Sources

The RDA for selenium is 55 µg/day for both men and women. Most Americans get adequate amounts of selenium in the diet on a daily basis. Food sources of selenium are found are follows:

| Food | µg/day | %DV |
|---|---|---|
| Brazil nuts (1 oz) | 544 | 780 |
| Tuna, light canned in oil (3 oz) | 63 | 95 |
| Beef, cooked (3 ½ oz) | 35 | 50 |
| Spaghetti with meat sauce | 34 | 50 |
| Cod, cooked (3 oz) | 32 | 452 |

---

[1] http://ods.od.nih.gov/factsheets/Iron-HealthProfessional

## Selenium Deficiencies and Toxicities

### Selenium Deficiency

Selenium deficiencies are uncommon in the United States, but there were a few cases found in China. The soil concentration of selenium was found to be low due to a depletion of nutrients over time when rice is planted and harvested over and over again. The depletion of selenium caused the development of a certain type of heart disease that caused an enlarged heart muscle which then resulted in heart dysfunction. Keshan disease is the name of the heart disease found in selenium deficient persons. Kashin-Beck disease results in a severe deforming type of arthritis that causes a deformity of the hands.

### Selenium Toxicity

Selenium toxicity is rare in the United States.

## Zinc

Zinc is a trace mineral that is necessary for a healthy immune system. Studies have shown that zinc can also help in wound healing. Zinc can help to fight off invading bacteria and viruses. Up to 200 enzymes rely on zinc as a cofactor for proper functioning. Zinc is also involved in DNA, cell growth, and cell differentiation, and the senses of taste and smell.

### Zinc Recommendations and Food Sources

Zinc recommendations are 11 mg/day for adult men and 8 mg/day for adult women. The following foods are good sources of zinc.

- Oysters
- Red meat, poultry, seafood such as crab and lobsters
- Fortified cereals
- Beans, nuts, whole grains, and dairy products

### Zinc Deficiencies and Toxicities

### Deficiencies of Zinc

Deficiencies of zinc were recognized in the early 1960s in Egypt and Iran. Zinc deficiencies caused growth retardation and poor sexual development in certain groups

**EVERY DAY SUPERFOODS**

One Brazil nut can have between 90 and 170% of your daily selenium needs. Pair them with broccoli or other cruciferous vegetables (that contain sulforaphane) to have an even greater anti-carcinogenic effect than either selenium—or sulforaphane—containing foods alone!

of people. The cause of the deficiency appeared to be due to a lack of bioavailability of the mineral in the diet. Zinc was being consumed in the diet but it was not being utilized correctly in the body. Zinc deficiencies can occur in those who consume a diet that is high in phytic acids. Phytic acids are found in unleavened breads (a traditional food consumed in the Middle East) which can decrease the amount of zinc that is available in the body. Zinc absorption depends on how much zinc the body needs. Zinc is better absorbed in the presence of protein. Zinc also competes with iron and copper for absorption, which may cause a decrease in absorption.

**Toxicities of Zinc**

Toxicities of zinc are usually taken in the form of supplements. Toxicity symptoms include nausea, vomiting, loss of appetite, cramping, diarrhea, and headaches. The UL limit for zinc is 40 mg/day. Zinc supplements can also interfere with certain medications such as:

- Certain antibiotics (reduce zinc absorption)

- Penicillamine (a drug that treats rheumatoid arthritis)

- Some diuretics (increase zinc excretion)[3]

## Minerals Involved in Bone Health

### Calcium

#### Calcium Recommendations and Food Sources

Calcium is the most abundant mineral in the body, and 99% of the calcium that is in the body is in the bones and teeth. The other 1% is in the blood. Calcium has a similar function to electrolytes because it aids in muscle contraction and relaxation, blood clot formation, nerve cell transmission, and cellular metabolism. Calcium may

also play a role in keeping your blood pressure and your weight within a healthy range. Calcium recommendations vary slightly across the lifespan. For adults ages 19–50, the AI recommendation is 1000 mg/day. For adults ages 51–70, the AI recommendation is 1000 mg for men and is increased to 1200 mg for women. Women over the age of 50 require

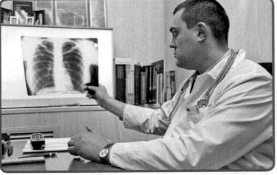

© 2012, Shutterstock, Inc.

---

[3] http://ods.od.nih.gov/factsheets/Zinc-QuickFacts/

additional calcium due to decreased absorption rates, especially in post-menopausal women.

## Food Sources of Calcium

### Dairy Sources

| Food | Serving size | mg of calcium |
|------|--------------|---------------|
| Cheese, ricotta (part skim) | 1 cup | 669 mg |
| Yogurt, plain (non fat) | 1 cup | 452 mg |
| Milk, 1% fat | 1 cup | 290 mg |
| Swiss cheese | 1 oz | 229 mg |
| Vanilla pudding | 4 oz | 99 mg |

© 2012, Shutterstock, Inc.

### Non-Dairy Sources

| Food | Serving size | mg of calcium |
|------|--------------|---------------|
| Sardines (canned in oil) | 3 oz | 325 mg |
| Tofu, firm (with calcium) | ¼ block | 163 mg |
| Molasses (blackstrap) | 1 Tblsp | 172 mg |
| Almonds | 1 oz (24 nuts) | 70 mg |
| Tahini | 1 Tblsp | 64 mg |

© 2012, Shutterstock, Inc.

### Fruit and Vegetable Sources

| Food | Serving size | mg of calcium |
|------|--------------|---------------|
| Rhubarb (cooked) | 1 cup | 348 mg |
| Kale (cooked) | 1 cup | 179 mg |
| Mustard greens (cooked) | 1 cup | 104 mg |
| Okra (cooked) | 1 cup | 123 mg |
| Figs (dried) | 2 each | 62 mg |

© 2012, Shutterstock, Inc.

## Calcium Regulation in the Body

The major role of calcium is in the formation and maintenance of bone health. Think of your calcium intake as a bank. When you go to the bank to withdraw money, your bank account gets smaller. If you do not deposit any money in the bank, eventually you will go broke. The same thing happens with our bones. If you do not deposit enough in your "calcium bank," eventually your bones can "go broke."

When calcium intake is low, adequate absorption of calcium depends on several factors. The acidity of the stomach and dietary intake of calcium both play a role in how much calcium is absorbed in the body. Calcium may also compete for absorption in the stomach with other minerals (such as iron). During different stages in our life cycle, the amount of calcium that we are able to absorb in the body varies. When we are infants and children, our absorption rates are much higher due to bone growth and development. During pregnancy, women can absorb higher amounts of calcium to support fetal growth and development. As we age, our ability to absorb calcium decreases.

**EVERY DAY
SUPERFOODS**

Milk is recommended for its 300 mg of calcium per cup (8 ounces). Other superstars include seaweed (400 mg per ¼ cup), sardines (with bones; 325 mg per 1/3 cup), and tofu (255 mg per ½ cup).

Factors that increase calcium absorption include:

- Increased blood levels in the body
- More calcium consumed in the diet
- Functioning digestion and absorption of calcium
- Pregnancy, infancy, and childhood

Factors that decrease calcium absorption include:

- High intakes of phytic acids (from grain products)
- Excess intake of phosphorus (in the form of supplements)
- High intakes of tannins (found in tea)
- Vitamin D deficiency
- Aging

As previously mentioned, 99% of calcium in the body is found in our bones and teeth. The other 1% is found in the blood and is carefully regulated by two hormones called

## FOOD IN FOCUS  Calcium Bioavailability

By Jennifer Jackson

Calcium bioavailability determines how much calcium we can absorb at one time. For women especially, adequate calcium intake is very important to bone health. Most sources of calcium come in the form of dairy. Due to a large percentage of people that are lactose intolerant, getting enough calcium can be challenging for some. Other foods do contain calcium but in much smaller amounts.

- Bioavailability is the difference between what you consume and what is actually available to your body. There are many things that can affect this quality of nutrients in foods.

- In addition to bioavailability, the content of nutrients in foods determines how much of them can be absorbed. If there is only a small amount, only a small amount can be absorbed.

- If a person is deficient in the vitamin, mineral, or other nutrient – they will also absorb more naturally.

- The environment within the body also affects absorption of nutrients, including pH and the presence of antagonists to absorption.

Soy milk has gained popularity in recent years. When fortified with calcium, soy milk can be a good source of calcium. Common calcium fortifiers include tricalcium phosphate (TCP) and calcium carbonate (CC). Other sources of milk that also contain calcium are almond milk and rice milk. Just make sure to read the label. Some companies that produce these products do not always add calcium.

Studies have shown that the TCP and CC that are added to these products have a similar bioavailability to the calcium that is found in cow's milk. The body's ability to absorb the calcium from the cow's milk and from the fortified soy milk was equivalent in a study done on young women by researchers at Purdue University.[1] Getting adequate calcium in the diet can prevent bone health problems in the future.

[1] Zhao, Yongdong; Martin, Berdine R.; Weaver, Connie M. Calcium Bioavailability of Calcium Carbonate Fortified Soy Milk is Equivalent to Cow's Milk in Young Women. *Amer. Society for Nutrition 2005*:2379-2382.

---

**calcitonin** and the **parathyroid hormone (PTH)**. Just as the hormones insulin and glucagon carefully regulate the blood glucose levels in the body, calcitonin and PTH regulate blood calcium levels. Calcitonin is the hormone that is activated when blood calcium levels are high which will signal **osteoblasts** to remove excess calcium from the blood and helps to promote the building of bone tissue. PTH is the hormone that is signaled when blood calcium levels fall below optimal ranges. PTH signals **osteoclasts** to break down bone tissue.

## Supplements and Bioavailability

The dietary calcium recommendations mentioned above may not always be met on a daily basis. A person who is lactose intolerant may not consume an adequate amount of calcium on a daily basis and therefore might rely on supplements. Calcium supplements can be found in a variety of forms. Most multivitamin and mineral supplements do contain calcium but in varying amounts. Calcium supplements may be combined with vitamin D and other minerals to help with absorption. There are two main types of calcium supplements. Calcium carbonate is recommended to take with food. The other is calcium citrate, which has been found to be more absorbable and is better taken on an empty stomach. Another form of a calcium supplement is found in antacids such as Tums, which are used to treat heartburn.

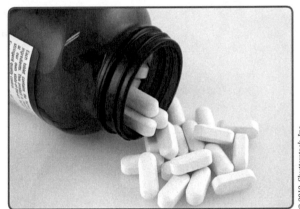

© 2012, Shutterstock, Inc.

**Bioavailability** of a vitamin means that we can absorb only a certain amount of a vitamin or mineral at one time. With calcium, it is estimated that we can absorb only about 500 mg at a time. If someone is taking a 1000 mg supplement, only about half of that will be absorbed.

## Calcium and Bone Health

Our bones are composed of two different structures. The first structure is the outer dense bone structure called **cortical bone**. The second structure is the **trabecular bone**. Trabecular bone acts to provide strength and support to the cortical bone. Our bones are constantly going through stages of modeling and re-modeling. Bone modeling begins in the womb and continues throughout adulthood. Bone re-modeling occurs from early childhood.

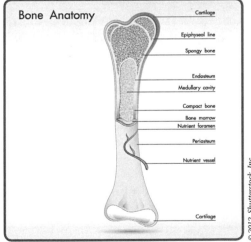

Bone Anatomy

Cartilage
Epiphyseal line
Spongy bone
Endosteum
Medullary cavity
Compact bone
Bone marrow
Nutrient foramen
Periosteum
Nutrient vessel
Cartilage

© 2012, Shutterstock, Inc.

### Calcium Deficiencies and Toxicities

A toxicity of calcium is called **hypercalcemia** which means high blood calcium levels. Hypercalcemia is usually caused by taking too many calcium-containing supplements such as antacids or regular calcium supplements. Too much calcium could cause constipation and make it more difficult for your body to absorb iron and zinc. Too much calcium can also increase the chance of getting kidney stones in those who are at risk.[4] Remember, as with most toxicity, supplements are usually the cause, not the food source.

A common calcium deficiency disease is called osteoporosis and will be discussed in more detail later in this chapter. Calcium deficiencies have also been linked to:

- High blood pressure

- Cancer

- Kidney stones

- Weight loss

The conditions above are currently being studied for their effect on our health. For more information visit the Office of Dietary Supplements to track the progress of these and other studies related to calcium.

NUTRITION NERD ALERT

Did you know? Adequate calcium intake helps naturally block lead absorption! Rhubarb, tempeh (fermented tofu), and turnip greens are good plant sources of calcium. Collard greens are especially low in mineral-blocking phytates, which make them an even better plant source of calcium.

## Osteoporosis

### What Is Osteoporosis?

**Osteoporosis** is a chronic condition and is characterized by low bone density. Osteoporosis causes weak bones and increases the chances of bone fractures or breaks. It is estimated that 1.5 million Americans experience bone fractures related to osteoporosis every year. Bone density is dependent on several factors. Women are 80% more likely to get osteoporosis than men. There are several reasons why women are at more risk than men. An increase in our life expectancy and a growing aging population

---

[4] Calcium Quickfacts Sheet

has a large impact on the number of people (especially women) who will experience bone breaks or fractures during their lifespan. It is estimated that 90% of our total bone mineral content (BMC) is generated before the age of 17 years old, and female adolescence is the time when the accumulation of bone density is at its best. Some health professionals believe that prevention of osteoporosis should be focused on at an earlier age.[5] The strength of the bones is related to a person's bone mass and bone density. Peak bone density is reached at an early age. It is estimated that we reach peak bone density in our late twenties and early thirties. After that, we must work to maintain our bone density.

## What Causes Osteoporosis?

Several factors can contribute to bone loss. Some factors are modifiable, meaning we can do something to change the outcome, but other factors are non-modifiable. The following factors (both modifiable and non-modifiable) are thought to contribute to bone loss:

- Excessive alcohol intake

- High protein intake

- Cigarette smoking

- Family history of osteoporosis

- Gender

- Frame size

- Absence of menstruation

Bone loss can also occur due to vitamin D deficiencies as discussed in a previous chapter. To determine a person's risk for osteoporosis, bone density can be measured. The optimal way to measure bone density involves a dual energy X-ray absorptiometry (DEXA) machine. A DEXA machine is able to scan the whole body using small doses of X-ray radiation. The procedure is a non-invasive procedure. Bone density scores are determined by comparing your bone density with that of a healthy thirty-year-old. Scores are given in and interpreted as a T score as indicated below:

- 0 to –1 is considered normal

- –1 to –2.5 is considered low bone mineral density (osteopenia)

- –2.5 or lower is considered to be osteoporosis[6]

---

[5] *Am J Clin Nutr* 2008; 88:1670-7.

[6] www.nlm.nih.gov/medlineplus/ency/article/007197.htm

## How Can I Prevent or Reduce My Risk for Osteoporosis?

Being proactive at a young age can help to decrease your risk of getting osteoporosis. The challenge is that, with most young people, education about osteoporosis is usually not a priority. Knowing your family history is also important when it comes to assessing your risk for osteoporosis. There are several great websites that are designed to help you assess your risk for osteoporosis. One of the tools that can be accessed online is called FRAX®. The FRAX® tool was developed by the World Health Organization (WHO). This online assessment tool can help to determine your risk associated with fractures using clinical risk factors as well as bone mineral density (BMD) measurements at the neck of the femur. Understanding your need for calcium and how to get adequate amounts of calcium in the diet is important. Understanding the various food sources available is also important.

One of the best ways to prevent osteoporosis is by exercising regularly. Regular exercises, especially weight bearing exercises, are a great way to build and maintain bone density. Weight bearing exercises such as walking, running, jogging, dancing, and strength training exercises are great ways to increase tension on the muscles, which in turn can help to strengthen bones.

## Other Minerals Important to Bone Health

### Magnesium

Magnesium is the fourth most abundant mineral in the body. More than half of the magnesium in the body is found in our bones. Magnesium is needed for various biochemical reactions. Magnesium supports normal muscle and nerve functions, especially the steady rhythm of the heartbeat. Other functions of magnesium include the regulation of blood sugar levels, blood pressure regulation, energy metabolism and protein synthesis, and heart health.[7]

### Magnesium Recommendations and Food Sources

The DRI for magnesium for adult males aged 19–30 is 400 mg/day. For females aged 19–30 the DRI is 310 mg/day. For males over the age of 30 the DRI is 420 mg/day and for females over the age of 30 the DRI is 320 mg/day.

---

[7] http://ods.od.nih.gov/factsheets/Magnesium

Good sources of magnesium include the following foods:

| Food | mg/serving | %DV |
|---|---|---|
| ▪ Halibut (3 oz) | 90 mg | 20% |
| ▪ Almonds, dry roasted  (1 oz) | 80 mg | 20% |
| ▪ Cashews, dry roasted (1 oz) | 75 mg | 20% |
| ▪ Soybeans, cooked (1/2 cup) | 75 mg | 20% |
| ▪ Spinach, frozen, cooked (1/2 cup) | 75 mg | 20%[8] |

### Magnesium Deficiencies and Toxicities

### Deficiencies

Deficiencies of magnesium are rarely seen in the United States. The health status of the digestive system and the kidneys can greatly influence the amount of magnesium in the body. Gastrointestinal disorders can be a cause of a magnesium deficiency. Excessive sweating or vomiting can cause rapid losses of magnesium from the body. Deficiency symptoms include loss of appetite, nausea, vomiting, excessive tiredness, and weakness. Severe cases of magnesium deficiency can also lead to numbness and tingling and possible alterations in brain activity which could also alter the heart's rhythm.

### Toxicities

As with most cases of toxicity, the risk does not come from dietary sources of magnesium. The over-consumption of magnesium supplements can cause symptoms such as diarrhea and abdominal cramping. Because magnesium is excreted via the kidneys, kidney failure could also result in a toxicity of magnesium because excess is not being excreted.

## Phosphorus

Phosphorus is a mineral that plays a role in bone health. About 85% of phosphorus in the body is in the bones and plays a role as a structural element. The body absorbs phosphorus from a wide variety of food sources. Just like calcium, vitamin D also helps with phosphorus absorption. Phosphorus also functions as a component of enzymes and DNA.

---

[8] http://ods.od.nih.gov/factsheets/Magnesium

### Phosphorus Recommendations and Food Sources

The recommendation for phosphorus is 700 mg per day for adult men and women. The main food sources for phosphorus include foods high in protein such as meat and dairy. Whole grain breads and cereals can also provide more phosphorus than breads and cereals made from refined or enriched flours. There is a storage form of phosphorus called phytin which is not absorbed by humans.[9] Fruits and vegetables are low in phosphorus and are therefore not considered good sources.

### Deficiencies and Toxicities of Phosphorus

Deficiencies of phosphorus are rare since we absorb phosphorus adequately in the body. Phosphorus is eliminated by the kidneys. A toxicity of phosphorus can occur if someone has kidney disease, which would cause a buildup of this mineral. Excessive phosphorus levels in the blood could cause calcium deposits in the soft tissues in the body.[10]

## Fluoride

### Fluoride Recommendations and the History of Fluoridation

Small amounts of fluoride occur in the body and are found in the bones and teeth in the form of calcium fluoride. The most common way that we get fluoride is through our water. The fluoridation of water came about in the 1940s. To this day, fluoridation of water is still a controversial topic because fluoride can be toxic in large doses. The history behind fluoridation goes back to research that was done on fluoride and the prevention of dental caries. Before the fluoridation of water, people would lose their teeth before the age of 40 years old.[11] Nutritional implications became a concern because if people did not have teeth, proper nutrition would be challenging for many. Possible nutrient deficiencies that could occur with decreased intake of food, include protein containing foods such as meat that is difficult to chew without teeth.

Recommendations for fluoride are 4.0 mg per day for males and 3.0 mg per day for females.[12]

---

[9] http://www.nlm.nih.gov/medline/ency/article/002424.htm
[10] http://www.nlm.nih.gov/medline/ency/article/002424.htm
[11] http://history.nih.gov/museum/education_fluoride.html
[12] www.nlm.nih.gov/medlineplus/ency/article/002420.htm

### Toxicities and Deficiencies of Fluoride

### Deficiencies of Fluoride

A deficiency of fluoride may lead to increased cavities and weak bones and teeth. Fluoride can contribute to bone strength and development. Deficiencies of fluoride are rare in the United States.

### Toxicities of Fluoride

Just as a deficiency of fluoride can affect the teeth, a toxicity of fluoride can also impact the teeth. Too much exposure to fluoride, which may occur due to over fluoridation of the water, can cause staining and pitting on the enamel of the teeth referred to as mottling. Mottling of the teeth will cause the teeth to appear brown, pitted, and stained.

## Minerals Involved in Thyroid Health

## Iodine and Iodide

### Iodine Recommendations and Food Sources

Iodine is an important nutrient at all stages of the life cycle. Iodine rarely occurs as the element, which is a gas in nature. It more commonly appears as a salt, and is therefore referred to as iodide.[13] Iodized salt is the most common supplemented form of iodide and has been added to table salt since the early 1920s. Some foods do naturally contain some iodine. Iodide plays an important role in the function of the thyroid hormones. Proper thyroid function also plays a role in the regulation of our metabolic rate. The recommendation for iodine is 150 mcg per day for both men and women over the age of 19. The recommendation is slightly higher for pregnancy and lactation at 220 mcg per day and 290 mcg per day respectively.

© 2012, Shutterstock, Inc.

---

[13] http://ods.od.nih.gov/factsheets/Iodine-QuickFacts

### Food Sources of Iodine*

| Food | mcg/serving | %DV |
|---|---|---|
| ■ Cod, baked 3 oz | 99 | 66% |
| ■ Yogurt, plain low fat, 1 cup | 75 | 50% |
| ■ Iodized salt, ¼ teaspoon | 71 | 47% |
| ■ Milk, reduced fat, 1 cup | 56 | 37% |
| ■ Fish sticks, 3oz | 54 | 36% |

*The best source of iodine is seaweed. The iodine content of seaweed can vary from 16 mcg to 2,984 mcg which provides 11% to 1,989% of the daily value.

## Toxicities and Deficiencies of Iodine

### Iodine Toxicities

The UL for iodide is 1.1 mg per day. Consumption of high amounts of iodide can cause a thyroid gland enlargement called a goiter. A goiter can develop from both a toxicity and a deficiency of iodide—which is discussed further below.

### Iodine Deficiencies

Iodine deficiencies remain a public health concern today. Approximately 38% of the world's population lives in areas where iodine deficiencies are common.[14] An iodine deficiency can cause a goiter. A goiter is an enlargement of the thyroid gland located near the neck area. Goiters often occur in areas where iodine is deficient in the soil; these areas are also further inland. Living closer to the ocean provides better sources of iodine. An iodide deficiency during pregnancy can cause a condition in the baby called **cretinism**. Cretinism is characterized by brain damage, reduced intellectual capabilities, and reduced growth and development. This condition is permanent once the child has been born. Because of the large number of people who still suffer from iodide deficiencies, worldwide efforts are being made to promote the use of iodized salt and iodide fortified foods.

© Alison Wright/Corbis

---

[14] http://www.nlm.nih.gov/medlineplus/ency/article/002421.htm

## Other Minerals

### Chromium

Chromium is a trace mineral. The functions of or needs for chromium are not clearly understood at this time. There are two forms of chromium, one that is biologically active and found in foods, and the other that is toxic and is found as part of industrial pollution. Studies on chromium include the effects chromium has on insulin. Studies have shown that chromium may play an important role that helps to enhance the action of insulin uptake into the cells. The studies found this to be valid in animal studies; human studies are still inconclusive about the benefits of chromium and insulin.

The AI for chromium is 35 mcg/day for adult males ages 19–50 and 25 mcg/day for females ages 19–50. In people over the age of 50, 30 mcg/day is recommended for men and 20 mcg is recommended for women.[15]

Food Sources for chromium

| Food | mcg (micrograms) |
| --- | --- |
| ▪ Broccoli, ½ cup | 11 |
| ▪ Grape juice, 1 cup | 8 |
| ▪ English muffin, whole wheat (1) | 4 |
| ▪ Potatoes, mashed 1 cup | 3 |
| ▪ Garlic, dried 1 tsp | 3 |

---

[15] http://ods.od.nih.gov/factsheets/Chromium-HealthProfessional

## Summary

Minerals are inorganic elements. Minerals carry electrical charges and can gain and lose electrons. There are two classes of minerals, major and trace minerals. The role of minerals in the diet is to combine with other elements to perform many important functions in the body. Major minerals include sodium, potassium, phosphorus, magnesium, sulfur, chloride, and calcium. Trace minerals include iron, zinc, copper, selenium, fluoride, iodide, chromium, and manganese.

Iron is a trace mineral that has long been recognized for the role it plays in blood health. Iron deficiency is a common nutrient deficiency that affects many people worldwide. Iron is a component of myoglobin and hemoglobin, which are both iron-containing proteins. Food sources of iron include heme and nonheme sources. Iron deficiency is more common in women of childbearing age and in children. Several factors can increase or decrease iron absorption. Toxicities of iron or iron overdose are the most common cause of poisoning deaths in children under the age of four. Iron toxicity can also be seen in a rare genetic condition called hemachromatosis.

Selenium is a trace mineral that plays a role as antioxidant, which makes it important to our immune system. Selenium may help to protect our cells from oxidative damage and also plays a role in our thyroid function. Food sources of selenium are varied; most people in the United States get adequate amounts of selenium on a daily basis. Toxicities and deficiencies of selenium are rare in the United States.

Zinc is also an important trace mineral to our immune system. Zinc has been shown to help fight off bacteria and viruses. Zinc is also involved in the proper functioning of our taste and smell. Zinc deficiencies were studied in Middle Eastern countries and they found that mothers who were zinc deficient during pregnancy gave birth to children who had delayed sexual development and growth retardation. Toxicities of zinc are usually taken in the form of supplements. Some factors can also decrease the absorption of zinc.

Calcium is the most abundant mineral in the body. Calcium is important for our bone health. Calcium also plays a small role as an electrolyte for muscle contraction and relaxation. Calcium is regulated in the body by two hormones. The parathyroid hormone (or PTH) and calcitonin help to balance calcium levels in the blood. There are many factors that can increase and decrease calcium absorption. Osteoporosis is the deficiency associated with a calcium deficiency. Osteoporosis affects women more than men and is characterized by the weakening of the bones which can cause fractures or breaks. Calcium toxicities are not common but can occur when excess calcium supplements are taken on a regular basis.

There are several websites that you can access to assess your risk for osteoporosis. You can decrease your risk of osteoporosis by exercising regularly, especially including weight bearing exercises. Being proactive about your calcium intake is important. Young women should be taught the importance of calcium in the diet in an effort to prevent osteoporosis.

Magnesium is the fourth most abundant mineral in the body. More than half of our body's magnesium is in our bones. Magnesium plays a role in bone health as well as assisting with the steady rhythm of the heartbeat.

Phosphorus is another mineral important for bone health; 85% of phosphorus is in the bones and plays a role in the bone structure. Phosphorus is available in a wide variety of foods, especially protein containing foods. Excess phosphorus in the diet may not be good for our bones and may cause more calcium excretion from the bones. See Food in Focus earlier in this chapter for more details.

Fluoride is a trace mineral that is found in the bones and teeth. Fluoride helps to give bones their hardness, especially the enamel on the teeth. Fluoride is commonly found in our tap water. Fluoridation of water began in the 1940s. The role that fluoride plays in the prevention of dental caries came about because many people ere losing their teeth. Loss of teeth can have an impact on nutrition and health because the inability to chew foods properly can lead to malnutrition.

Iodine is important at all stages of the lifecycle. Iodine is important for proper functioning of the thyroid gland. Too much or too little iodine in the diet can cause a goiter which is characterized by the gland enlargement on the side of the neck. Goiters are rare in the United States due to our use of iodized salt.

Chromium is a trace mineral that assists the hormone insulin to move glucose into the cells. Research on chromium and insulin is currently being done to find out if this mechanism can benefit people with diabetes, but currently there is no conclusive evidence.

# EATING GREEN

Eating green is more than eating green vegetables. Fruits and vegetables of course are rich in vitamins and minerals but knowing where our food comes from is important when eating green. Here are some tips for eating green:

- Shop Locally- buying locally grown produce will help to support local farmers and reduce emissions from long-distance shipping

- Eat Less Meat- opt for eating a vegetarian based meal at least once or twice per week. It takes more energy, water and other resources to produce a pound of meat than compared to a pound of grain

- Look for the 9- Check fruits and veggies that display the number 9. These fruits and vegetables are grown organically

- Not everything has to be Organic- check out the website www.ewg.org. The Environmental Working Group lists

© 2012, Shutterstock, Inc.

the "clean fifteen" and the "dirty dozen" so you can be informed on which fruits and vegetables you might want to buy organic

- Recycle- sort your recyclables and reduce waste in the land fills

- Grow a Small Garden- small gardens that provide fresh fruits, vegetables, and herbs can be grown in small areas. Most can be grown in containers that save space

- Compost- take your kitchen scraps and lawn clippings to make a nutrient-rich compost pile that you can use to increase the nutrients in your soil

- Cook Outdoors- grilling outdoors can save energy and is a healthy way of cooking

- Clean Green- using cleaning products that are typically found in your pantry is a great way to reduce chemicals that go down the drain.

Green eating is an easy way to be friendlier to the environment. Taking small steps to change the way we buy our food can help to preserve precious resources. Read the labels and understand where your food comes from can help you to make better decisions about your health and well being.

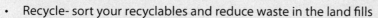

# CHAPTER 11

# Energy Balance and Weight Control: Healthy Body, Healthy Mind

© 2012, Shutterstock, Inc.

## Learning Objectives

- Describe the obesity epidemic
- Learn how to calculate and assess body mass index (BMI)
- Understand different methods used to assess body composition
- Understand the different components of energy expenditure
- Evaluate different theories of obesity
- Explain the health risks of being underweight and overweight
- Discuss the characteristics of a reliable weight-loss program
- Evaluate popular weight loss diets and discuss possible health risks associated with frequent dieting
- Discuss the importance of behavior modification for successful weight loss
- Distinguish between the different surgical treatments for obesity
- Learn the difference between eating disorders and disordered eating behaviors
- Understand the difference between movement and exercise
- List the benefits of exercise

## Functional Food Fact | Foods to Enhance Weight Loss

It is no secret that to maintain body weight requires a balance between energy intake and energy expenditure. For weight loss, energy expenditure needs to exceed energy intake. Some foods such as tea, milk, and nuts may be beneficial functional foods to help with weight loss, especially for appetite control. Green tea contains antioxidants and some varieties contain caffeine that can help to sustain a workout. Calcium in milk may play a role in fat metabolism at a cellular level. Nuts contain good fats which can help you feel full longer. As with any functional foods and weight loss, exercise and healthy eating are the keys to successful weight loss.

© 2012, Shutterstock, Inc.

# Introduction to Energy Balance and Weight Control

## The Obesity Epidemic

The epidemic of obesity is often a hot topic of discussion in the news. The percentage of people who are overweight or obese continues to climb. Children who are overweight or obese are also gaining attention on a national level. Michelle Obama has taken steps to institute a campaign called "Let's Move" in an effort to fight childhood obesity. With the rise in obesity rates comes an increase in the onset of chronic diseases such as diabetes, cancer, and heart disease to name just a few. Some research suggests that obesity in America is possibly more of an economic issue. Are the food manufacturers responsible for providing low cost healthier foods for low-income consumers? Is it more expensive to eat healthier? These are just some of the questions that arise when faced with the problems of obesity and how to solve them.

According to the Centers for Disease Control and Prevention (CDC) 72 million adults in the United States are obese. The medical costs for those who are obese will be about $1,500 more per year than someone who is not obese. Currently there are nine states that have obesity rates that exceed 30% of the population. There are no states that have obesity rates less than 15%. The total estimated cost associated with the growing epidemic of obesity is estimated at $147 billion.[1] The incidence of obesity is particularly high among some racial and ethnic minority populations.

## What Is a Healthy Weight?

Traditionally height and weight tables were used to assess body weight. Many health professionals today agree that the use of these tables is outdated. Today many health professionals use body mass index (BMI) to assess body weight and the risk for developing chronic diseases. **BMI** is a measurement expressed as a height to weight ratio. This ratio is expressed as a number 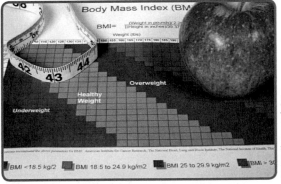 that is used to define weight as healthy or un-healthy and the consequences of being overweight or underweight. A BMI of 18.5–24.9 is considered healthy, a BMI of 25.0–29.9 is considered overweight, and a BMI of 30.0–39.9 is considered obese, which is associated with a greater risk for the development of chronic diseases. A BMI under

---

[1] http://www.cdc.gov/vitalsigns/pdf/2010-08-vitalsigns.pdf

*Nutrition Intuition*

18.5 can be considered underweight and a BMI over 40 is considered to be extremely obese. Both of these BMI's are also associated with health risks. There are cases in which BMI would not be accurate in assessing the risk for the development of chronic diseases. Individuals who have more muscle than fat in their bodies are an example. Muscle is denser than fat, and thus the BMI would be higher and the person would appear overweight or obese. The adult BMI tables do not apply to children, some elderly that appear to have healthy BMI's may be frail, and pregnant and lactating women need to be measured on a different BMI scale.

The calculation for BMI is shown below.

### Formula

$$\frac{\text{Weight in (lbs)}}{[\text{Height (in) squared}] \times 703}$$

### Example

A person who weighs 155 lbs and is 5'4" (64 inches) would have a BMI of

$$[155 \text{ divided by } (64) \text{ squared}] \times 703$$

$$(155 \text{ divided by } 4096) \times 703$$

$$0.03784 \times 703 = 26.6 \text{ BMI}$$

This person would be categorized as being slightly overweight.

## Waist Circumference

Research has also shown that waist circumference is an important measurement in assessing the risk for chronic diseases. Where the excess weight is on the body is important too. Weight that is centered on or around the waist is related to a higher risk for heart disease. **Waist circumference** is measured by placing a measuring tape around your bare abdomen just above your hip bone. The measuring tape should be snug against your skin but not pressed too far into your skin. Relax your muscles and exhale. Women with a waist circumference of more than 35 inches and men with a waist circumference of more than 40 inches are likely to develop obesity-related health problems. This measurement can be useful when determining successful weight loss.[2]

© 2012, Shutterstock, Inc.

---

[2] http://win.niddk.nih.gov/publications/tools.htm#circumf

## Positive Body Image

A healthy weight can also be defined as a weight with which you feel comfortable. Being comfortable and confident with your weight improves your self-esteem. Being overweight or obese is often associated with negative feelings about oneself. There are many prejudices that overweight or obese people face. Studies find that overweight or obese people are sometimes underpaid in the workplace and may get passed up for promotions. Negative stereotypes associated with obesity include lack of self-discipline, laziness, and overeating.

## Overnutrition vs. Undernutrition

**Overnutrition** is simply defined as excessive intake of foods that are unhealthy or provide little nutrients. Many foods eaten today are more calorie dense than they are nutrient dense. **Undernutrition** is defined as having inadequate food intake. It is said that today our children are "overfed and undernourished." We live in a "toxic food environment" where food is available every day, 24 hours a day. The availability of cheap, calorie dense foods is partially to blame for our obesity problems.

We have progressed from undernutrition to overnutrition in less than a generation. Obesity is not only affecting the United States, but has increased globally and many countries are seeing the consequences on mortality and morbidity rates. The cost of obesity is staggering and is increasing at rates which nations are no longer able to afford. In the United States, increasing healthcare costs related to obesity are putting a strain on insurance companies that are passing the costs down to employers who then pass on the costs to the employees. Obesity is related to so many other chronic diseases. Strong evidence about obesity and cancer risk suggests that being overweight can increase your risk for getting cancer. Common cancers such as colon, postmenopausal breast cancer, uterine, esophageal, and renal cell cancers may be related to being overweight and/or lack of physical activity.[3]

> **EVERY DAY**
> **SUPERFOODS**
> Pinot noir has the highest level of resveratrol, a polyphenol antioxidant, within wines. Grape juice has double the resveratrol content when compared to fermented grape juice (aka wine) without any of the harmful side products produced during fermentation.

---

[3] http://progressreport.cancer.gov/doc

## Energy In vs. Energy Out

What is the secret to weight loss? Is it about calories in versus calories out? The truth is, if you eat less and exercise more you will lose weight. The opposite is true too; if you eat more and exercise less you will gain weight. Of course this concept sounds very simplistic and there are many other factors to take into consideration when it comes to obesity. The truth is that an energy deficit will lead to weight loss just as an energy excess will lead to weight gain. A diet that consists of junk food is not going to be healthy, but when this same diet is con-

© 2012, Shutterstock, Inc.

sumed and there is an energy deficit, weight loss can occur. Energy balance is a comparison of your calories consumed (energy in) to the amount of physical activity that you do to burn off those calories (energy out). Table 11.1 below shows us how many calories you might need based on your activity level and age.

**Table 11.1** Estimated Calorie Requirements (in kilocalories) for Each Gender and Age Group at Three Levels of Physical Activity[4]

| Gender | Age (years) | Activity Level | | |
| --- | --- | --- | --- | --- |
| | | Sedentary | Moderately Active | Active |
| Child | 2-3 | 1,000 | 1,000-1,400 | 1,000-1,400 |
| Female | 4-8 | 1,200 | 1,400-1,600 | 1,400-1,800 |
| Female | 9-13 | 1,600 | 1,600-2,000 | 1,800-2,000 |
| Female | 14-18 | 1,800 | 2,000 | 2,400 |
| Female | 19-30 | 2,000 | 2,000-2,200 | 2,400 |
| Female | 31-50 | 1,800 | 2,000 | 2,400 |
| Female | 51+ | 1,600 | 1,800 | 2,000-2,200 |
| Male | 4-8 | 1,400 | 1,400-1,600 | 1,600-2,000 |
| Male | 9-13 | 1,800 | 1,800-2,200 | 2,000-2,600 |
| Male | 14-18 | 2,200 | 2,400-2,800 | 2,800-3,200 |
| Male | 19-30 | 2,400 | 2,600-2,800 | 3,000 |
| Male | 31-50 | 2,200 | 2,400-2,600 | 2,800-3,000 |
| Male | 50+ | 2,000 | 2,200-2,400 | 2,400-2,800 |

[4] http://www.nhlbi.nih.gov/health/public/heart/obesity/wecan/healthy-weight-basics/balance.htm

# Measuring Body Composition

Every cell in the body contains some fat. The main storage facility for our fat is the adipose or "fat cell." The fat cell is the specialized area in which we store extra fat. When fat is plentiful in the diet, the adipose tissue signals the fat cells to take up excess fat from the bloodstream. The fat cells can increase in size and also divide. As the cells increase in size, weight gain will soon follow.

Fat patterns vary in the body. There is **subcutaneous fat** which is closer to the surface of the skin and there is **visceral fat** which is closer to the organs. The distribution of fat in the body also varies. The distribution of the body fat is often described by referring to people as apple shaped or pear shaped. **Apple shaped** refers to body fat that has accumulated around the abdomen and is closer to the heart. The **pear shaped** fat pattern is where the fat is located more on the hips. Men tend to be apple shaped and women tend to be more commonly pear shaped. The apple shape is said to be more associated with an increase in heart disease because the fat is accumulated around the heart.

## Dual Energy X-Ray Absorptiometry (DEXA)

DEXA is a non-invasive means of measuring body fat which uses a low-energy X-ray technology. The subject lays down on a flat surface and the DEXA machine scans the patient from top to bottom and provides a detailed picture of where the body fat is distributed in the body. DEXA is the "gold standard" for measuring body fat, but it is not widely available. A gold standard usually means that this method has been researched and agreed upon as being an accurate and acceptable measure. DEXA is also used for measuring bone density.

## Under Water Weighing

This method requires a specialized tank of water in which the subject is submerged under water. This technique of estimating total body fat is done by weighing the subject on a standard scale first and then weighing the subject when submerged under water. The difference between the two weights is determined and used to estimate the total body volume. This number results in an estimation of body fat percentage. This method is very accurate but not easily accessible.

## Bioelectrical Impedance

Bioelectrical impedance is an instrument that is used to estimate body fat using a low-energy electrical current. The subject has electrodes placed on the skin, the electrical current (which is painless) travels through the electrodes and converts information about the subject's body fat. The principle of bioelectrical impedance is based on the fact that water and electrolytes conduct electricity and body fat resists electricity.

## Skinfold Thickness

Skinfold thickness measurements are more commonly used in gym settings because they are quick and easy. A caliper is a tool that is used to measure the thickness of the skin at different sites on the body. A person who has been properly trained will pinch the skin of the subject and gently pull it away from the muscle tissue. After the measurements are recorded, the values are calculated and can provide a fairly accurate body fat percentage. The accuracy of this method is dependent upon the person using the calipers and how accurately the mathematical equation is applied.

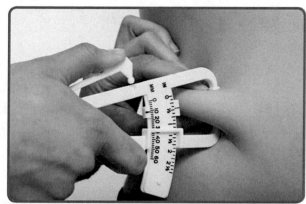

© 2012, Shutterstock, Inc.

### NUTRITION NERD ALERT

A 2011 study found that the benefits of whole food on overall health outweigh supplements. In fact, the use of supplements in older adults was shown to increase the risk of certain diseases in some study participants. There is such a thing as too much of a good thing.

## Components of Energy Expenditure

## Basal Metabolic Rate and Resting Metabolic Rate

Basal metabolism represents the minimal amount of calories that are expended in a fasting state (fasting means that you have not eaten for at least 12 hours). Basal metabolism is expressed as **basal metabolic rate (BMR)**. BMR is responsible for basic but important body functions such as the heartbeat, breathing in and out, as well as keeping other organs functioning such as the brain, liver, and kidneys. For someone who is sedentary, BMR accounts for about 60–75% of the total energy used by the body.

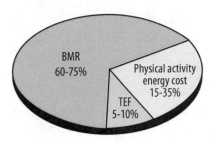

**Figure 11.1** Components of energy expenditure

**Resting metabolic rate (RMR)** is measured when the person is at rest. This measurement is not done during fasting and is about 6% higher than the BMR. There are several factors that can increase and decrease our metabolic rate. Some factors are listed below, in Table 11.2.

**Table 11.2** Factors That Influence Basal Metabolic Rate (BMR)

| Factors That Increase BMR | Factors That Decrease BMR |
| --- | --- |
| More lean body mass | Starvation |
| Male | Age (getting older) |
| Fever | Frequent dieting |
| Pregnancy | |
| Caffeine | |

## Physical Activity

Physical activity accounts for about 15–35% of energy expenditure. This component varies the most among individuals. Some people do more physical activity than others. Physical activity adds many benefits to our health. We will discuss more details about physical activity later in the chapter.

## Thermic Effect of Food

The **thermic effect of food (TEF)** is the amount of calories that are expended during digestion and absorption of nutrients. It is estimated that TEF accounts for about 5–10% of our total daily expenditure. If a person eats 2000 calories, it can be estimated that 200 calories were burned during this process.

# What Are Causes of Obesity?

## Theories of Obesity

It is said that obesity is a multifactorial disease. Obesity cannot be blamed on one particular reason. There are several theories that attempt to scientifically explain causes of obesity. Environmental influences of obesity are often blamed for the epidemic that we face today. Most health professionals agree that we live in a "toxic food environment." The availability of cheap, calorie dense foods is largely to blame. It is proposed that obesity problems arise from larger portion sizes and dramatic decreases in physical activity. Advertising of foods reaches audiences of all ages. The marketing of high sugar foods is especially of concern when the intended audience is children. Children are very susceptible to marketing and begin making their own food choices at a very young age. As previously mentioned, is obesity an economic issue? Do people with more money eat healthier than people who make less money?

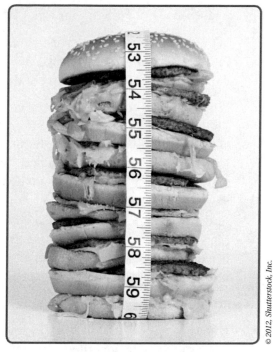

© 2012, Shutterstock, Inc.

## Hyperplastic and Hypertrophic Obesity

We are born with millions of fat cells in the body. Fat cells can increase both in size and number. **Hyperplastic obesity** is the increase in the number of fat cells in the body. **Hypertrophic obesity** is the increase in the size of the fat cells. The number of fat cells increases rapidly during childhood and then slows down in early puberty. When energy in exceeds energy out, the fat cells get larger, which then stimulates the cells to divide. The division of the cells increases the overall number of fat cells in the body and obesity occurs. When a person tries to lose weight, the fat cells can shrink but the number of cells remains constant.

Is there a way to decrease the number of fat cells in the body? Some people try **liposuction** which is a surgical procedure that removes fat cells from the subcutaneous layer of fat closest to the skin. Small tubes are inserted into various areas in the body where fat has accumulated. This procedure can be risky and can cause infections and damage to the skin. People who have liposuction think that they are removing fat from the body but the truth is that with millions of fat cells, the procedure only removes a very small percentage of fat from the body and is not a treatment for obesity.

## Set-Point Theory

What is a theory? A **theory** is a set of formulated ideas that are based on research or known facts to explain a probable cause. How is a theory proven? Further research can sometimes lead to proving or disproving a theory.

The **set-point theory** suggests that our body weight is genetically predetermined. The set point acts like a temperature gauge except it regulates our body weight. The set-point theory says that our body is satisfied with a particular weight. We may not agree with the weight that the body is comfortable with, so we attempt to lose or gain weight; but that is made difficult by the fact that our bodies will try to rebalance any weight loss or weight gain. The set-point theory proposes that when you lose weight and you go below the weight at which the body is satisfied, the body will adjust the basal metabolism rate and cause you to regain the weight that was lost. The opposite is true with the set-point theory as well. If a person is trying to gain weight, the body will speed up the metabolism in an attempt to lose the weight that was gained.

## Genetics

Genetic factors play a role in the development of obesity. Body shape, size, and metabolic rates can be inherited. If one parent is overweight or obese, the chance that their child is overweight is about 25%. If both parents are overweight or obese, the child has a 50–60% chance of being overweight.

Animal studies have revealed possible explanations about genetics and obesity but there is still much research to be done in this area. Genes that control hormones that influence growth and development are being studied as possible treatments for obesity. Some of these hormones and proteins act on the brain, specifically in the hypothalamus. One such protein is called ghrelin. **Ghrelin** is a large protein that acts as a hormone on the hypothalamus and sends messages to signal hunger. When you are hungry, blood levels of ghrelin are higher. When you are full, ghrelin levels fall in the blood. Some research suggests that increased ghrelin levels in the blood could develop when calories are consumed in excess of the body's needs, which could lead to further weight gain in an obese person. It is also suggested that ghrelin levels may increase in response to a diet that is low in calories.[5]

Leptin is another hormone that is being studied. **Leptin** is produced by the fat cells which receive signals from certain genes and act to decrease the appetite and

---

[5] http://www.ncbi.nih.gov/pmc/articles/PMC2967656/pdf/nihms231921.pdf

increase energy expenditure. The action of leptin is not completely understood, but the research has shown that overweight or obese people have less leptin in the blood. Those people who are normal weight tend to have higher leptin levels in the blood.

## FOOD IN FOCUS  Healthy Dining Out

Eating outside of the home gives us the chance to eat our favorite foods and offers us many opportunities to try new foods. Eating out at restaurants or fast food places does not have to be un-healthy if you use these suggestions when ordering.

- Practice portion control. Take half of your meal home or share a meal.
- Double the veggies on your plate.
- Look for appetizers and side salads.
- Get salad dressing on the side so you have control of how much you use.
- If you are going to have a steak, try sirloin steaks or filet mignon which is very lean red meat.
- Try thin crust pizza with roasted vegetables.
- Ask for items without cheese.
- Baked potatoes with sour cream, no butter can save you hundreds of calories.
- At Chinese restaurants, go with stir-fry vegetables and leave the fried noodles.
- Try brown rice instead of white rice.
- Have broth based soups instead of cream soups.
- Try the "kids" size at fast food restaurants.
- Try your coffee drinks "light" or "skinny" which uses non-fat milk and sugar-free syrups.
- Share a dessert.
- Pass on the chips and bread that come before your meal.

If you are not sure how something is cooked, kindly ask the server how certain foods are prepared. Beware of foods with heavy sauces or gravies that can be calorie busters. Go for dishes that are grilled or steamed and avoid dishes that are fried.

Remember that eating out should be a fun experience, enjoy your food. If you are watching your calories and you are going out to dinner in the evening, have a healthy breakfast and a light lunch and try to get some exercise so you can enjoy your dinner without guilt. Remember it is all about moderation.

## Consequences of Obesity

### Health Risks of Obesity

Too much fat in the body can be just as risky to our health as having too little fat in the body. Having some body fat is important for your health. The distribution of the body fat and where it resides in the body is also important, as previously mentioned. There are two different types of fat in the body, visceral fat and subcutaneous fat. **Visceral fat** is the fat that is closest to the organs. A higher amount of visceral fat in the body is related to an increased risk for developing insulin resistance and cardiovascular disease. Visceral fat is more difficult to lose. People who are sedentary tend to have higher amounts of visceral fat compared to active people. **Subcutaneous fat** is the fat that is located closer to the surface of the skin. Subcutaneous fat functions as a cushion and contains blood vessels that supply oxygen to our tissues. Subcutaneous fat is more visible and sometimes causes a dimpling effect on the surface of the skin which is also known as cellulite.

Health risks of obesity include:

- Increased risk for cancer
- Increased risk for heart disease
- Gallbladder disease and gallstones
- Fatty liver
- GERD
- Osteoarthritis
- Gout
- Breathing problems (including sleep apnea)
- Reproductive problems (especially in women)

### Health Risks of Underweight

Just as with being overweight, there are health risks with being underweight. Being underweight is far less common than being overweight. Some people tend to associate being underweight with being healthier. Societal pressures to be thin can contribute to this idea that being thin or underweight is more acceptable than being overweight. For people who have difficulty gaining weight, being underweight can be frustrating. Women who are underweight may not have regular menstrual cycles and may also have difficulty getting pregnant. Senior citizens who are underweight may have longer healing times and weaker immune systems. Recommendations for weight gain would include increasing calories from protein in the diet along with adequate amounts of carbohydrates and fat. However, weight gain is not beneficial if it simply adds excess fat, that is why increasing calories is combined with exercise—extra weight gain should be muscle weight.

NUTRITION NERD ALERT

Green and black tea have been shown to boost your immune system. L-theanine (also found in mushrooms) works with caffeine to improve mood too. But remember that the tannins in tea also decrease calcium absorption, so women especially should drink tea in moderation.

## Dieting Fads and Facts

### What Is a Fad Diet?

Fad diets and weight loss supplements are billion dollar industries. People are always looking for the latest and greatest ways to lose weight. If you closely examine the word diet, it is "die" with a "t" on the end. How do you feel when you go on a diet? Are you thinking about what foods you have to give up? Are you hungry all the time? Most diets fail in the first 24–48 hours. Feeling deprived and hungry is often associated with a higher rate of dieting failure. Statistics tell us that 95% of people who go on a diet end up gaining back their weight and sometimes more. Fad diets focus on gadgets and gimmicks to help sell the product. Often the purchase of a weight loss program requires special foods, drinks, shakes, or supplements that need to be purchased separately. The cost of the products is often expensive and the products are not well researched in regards to effectiveness. Some fad diets can even be hazardous to your health. Supplements that are used to lose weight can cause headaches, nausea, vomiting, and sometimes even death.

### Calories In vs. Calories Out

New research has shown that the composition of the diet does not seem to play a big role in the success of a weight loss diet. Does this mean that you can eat a diet of cakes and cookies? As long as the calorie restriction is followed, then yes you could lose weight on a 1200 calorie diet of cakes and cookies. It is definitely not the healthiest way to lose weight but it would work. The real way to lose weight is to eat less and exercise more. Of course this concept sounds overly simplistic. Where are the gadgets, gimmicks, and celebrities for this diet?

When you are cooking your vegetables today, make sure that they stay crisp yet tender (as opposed to mushy) to retain nutrients and reduce your use of heating energy! These al dente veggies also retain more of their color for prettier plates.

## The Low-down on Low Carbohydrate Diets

Have you tried a low carbohydrate, high protein diet? Have you heard of the cookie diet? I am sure you can name at least five more. All fad diets tend to have one thing in common, they offer quick weight loss. Low or no carbohydrate diets were the big trend for a long time because they promised quick, fast weight loss. The science behind this popular diet is relatively simple. When fat is broken down in the metabolic pathways, fat requires carbohydrates in order to be broken down adequately. Without carbohydrates in the diet, your body is forced to burn fat and produce ketones as a by-product of incomplete fat metabolism. This sounds great in theory but the truth is that the formation of ketones in the body is not a normal function. Ketone formation may cause the blood to become more acidic and the excessive protein intake may be difficult for the kidneys. Kidney damage may occur in those people who are susceptible to renal insufficiency or have a family history of renal disease. It is also suggested that when the blood becomes more acidic due to ketones, excess calcium excretion could occur. This would not be beneficial, especially for women.

## How To Be Successful in Weight Loss

Research has shown that the best way to lose weight is to keep a food journal. Writing down what you eat and how much you eat can lead to successful weight loss. It is often difficult for people to keep track of their food intake and amounts. Researchers and professionals agree that people tend to under-report the amount of food that is eaten and over-report the amount of exercise they have done. A food journal can help you to identify problem areas in your eating patterns and can also be a rude awakening to the actual amounts of food you do eat. Keeping track of foods and amounts eaten has gotten easier to track. Writing down foods in a journal can get boring for some people. Thankfully there are online resources and phone apps for keeping track of your foods that can even include detailed reports of the breakdown of macro and micronutrients.

The following is a list of websites (just to name a few) and phone apps that provide calorie tracking and analysis:

- Lose it - iPhone app

- Weightwatchers.com

- Livestrong.com

- Sparkspeople.com

Successful weight loss also requires adequate exercise, healthy eating, and behavior modification. Changing our behavior is not an easy task. We are more comfortable with our bad habits and often have difficulty in adopting good ones. Here are some suggestions on how to take some simple steps to change behaviors for successful weight loss.

## Behavior Modification

### Change Is Difficult

Calorie control is an important factor in weight loss, but behavior modification is the key to lifelong success with weight loss. Changing behavior can be a difficult process. People are often uncomfortable with change. We prefer our bad habits more than we are willing adopt good ones.

Motivation to make a change in behavior is important in the behavior change process. The following guidelines are helpful suggestions in assisting with the challenges of making behavioral changes.

### Your Weight Is Important

Some people want to lose weight for health reasons such as high blood pressure, high cholesterol, and diabetes. Maybe your doctor has told you that you need to lose weight even if you think you do not and you might be offended or self-conscious about your weight. Other people want to lose weight for vanity purposes because they fall victim to societal pressures of being thin. Whatever the reasons are for losing weight, understand that successful weight loss and weight management is challenging. Weight can affect your self-esteem. Too much body weight is visible to other people and those who are overweight or obese are usually judged unfairly. Stereotypes about fat people usually include laziness, they eat too much and all the wrong foods, and they do not exercise. The good news is that research has shown that even small amounts of weight loss can have a big impact on your health. A weight loss of just 5–10% of your baseline weight has shown to significantly decrease the risk of many chronic diseases such as diabetes, cardiovascular disease, and hypertension, just to name a few.

## Setting Goals

Goals need to be specific, attainable, measurable, and forgiving. Most people trying to lose weight have just one goal, to "lose weight." This goal of "losing weight" does not tell us who, where, what, when, and why. You need more detail when making goals for yourself. Setting a goal of losing 5 pounds in one month by exercising 3 times per week for 45 minutes to lower your blood pressure is a more detailed and measurable goal. Goals also have to be forgiving. When you do not reach a goal, go back and look at your actions. Did you exercise as much as you planned? Did you keep track of your caloric intake? Not achieving your goals can be disappointing, but do not give up. Forgiving yourself and moving forward will help you to succeed. It is also important to set short-term and long-term goals for yourself. Short-term goals help you to achieve your overall long-term goals. Behavior changes take time and setting short-term goals helps you to stay on track during the process. Achieving smaller goals gives you the motivation to achieve your long-term goals.

## Reward Yourself

It is important to reward yourself along the way. Of course you would not use food as a reward system because that could cause set-backs in your efforts. Reward yourself with items such as CDs, treat yourself to a movie, or my favorite reward, shoes!! Whatever the reward you think of, make it special for you.

## Checks and Balances

Just like keeping your check book balanced, it is important to keep your food intake balanced. Self monitoring your food intake will allow you to make better decisions about your food choices. It is very important to keep track of your food intake on a daily basis. Research has shown that journaling your food intake is one of the best tools that can help with weight loss. Keep track of exercise too to keep yourself motivated.

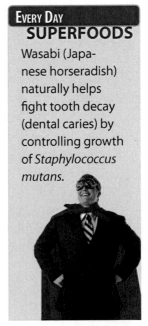

**EVERY DAY**
**SUPERFOODS**
Wasabi (Japanese horseradish) naturally helps fight tooth decay (dental caries) by controlling growth of *Staphylococcus mutans.*

## Triggers

**Triggers** are stimuli that may cause you to eat when you are not hungry. For example, stress can be a trigger that can lead to overeating for some people. Other triggers can be food related. Having too many sweets or junk food in the house can be a trigger that will lead to overeating. I have a saying that says "if you are tempted by it, don't buy it," meaning do not bring it in the house if you know that you are going to be tempted to eat it.

## Feeling Full

It takes 20 minutes to get a message to the brain that you are full. Have you ever timed yourself while you were eating? Did it take you longer than 20 minutes? Did it take less? Today we eat with so many distractions. We watch television, work on the computer, and talk on the phone. Distractions often lead to excessive intakes of food. Here is a challenge for you. Try setting a timer for 20 minutes, turn off the television and the computer, and do not answer phone calls. Focus on your meal, taste your food, put down your fork in between bites. Do you "feel full"? Did your brain get the message to "stop eating"? This is a great technique for someone who is trying to be more aware of what they are eating and how much they are eating.

## Medications

If weight loss is not achieved by making behavioral changes, some people turn to medications for help. Medications for weight loss are constantly being researched and developed by drug companies. Both over the counter and prescription medications for weight loss are used by millions of people every year, most of whom are women. Currently there are only a few widely used prescription medications available for weight loss. Below is a chart of current FDA approved weight loss medications along with common side effects.

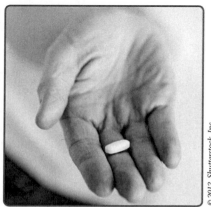

© 2012, Shutterstock, Inc.

**Table 11.3** FDA Approved Weight Loss Medications[6]

| Generic Name | Food and Drug Administration Approval for Weight Loss | Drug Type | Common Side Effects |
|---|---|---|---|
| Phentermine | Yes; short term (up to 12 weeks) for adults | Appetite Suppressant | Increased blood pressure and heart rate, sleeplessness, nervousness |
| Diethylpropion | Yes; short term (up to 12 weeks) for adults | Appetite Suppressant | Dizziness, headache, sleeplessness, nervousness |
| Phendimetrazine | Yes; short term (up to 12 weeks) for adults | Appetite Suppressant | Sleeplessness, nervousness |
| Orlistat | Yes; long term (up to 1 year) for adults and children age 12 and older | Lipase Inhibitor | Gastrointestinal issues (cramping, diarrhea, oily spotting), rare cases of severe liver injury reported |

[6] http://win.niddk.nih.gov/publications/prescription.htm

The weight loss success of any of these drugs requires a low calorie diet along with exercise. Once the medication is stopped, the weight is often re-gained if lifelong habits have not been changed. Most challenges with weight loss are the ability to change our behaviors.

## Weight Loss Surgery

When all other attempts at weight loss have been tried and failed, surgery may be the only other solution. Weight loss surgery is the most extreme approach to weight loss. Long term success and safety of weight loss surgeries depends primarily on the behavior changes and dietary compliance of the person who chooses this option. Weight loss surgery can be a life-saving operation for some who have tried and failed on many weight loss diets. Weight loss surgery should not be thought of as a permanent solution; it takes work and dedication to keep the weight off. Gastric bypass surgery and the lap band procedures are the two most popular weight loss surgeries.

**Gastric bypass surgery** is the more invasive procedure of the two surgeries to be discussed. The gastric bypass procedure reduces the size of the stomach from its normal 6 oz down to 1 oz. The surgeon then connects the jejunum to the new pouch and this causes the body to absorb fewer calories. This procedure is usually referred to as malabsorptive. This means that some nutrients will not be absorbed adequately by the body. A person who has had gastric bypass surgery will require vitamin and mineral supplementation for a lifetime. Gastric bypass surgery is not reversible. As with any surgery there are risks. Most people lose 10 to 20 pounds per month for the first year after surgery.[7]

The **lap band procedure** requires a restrictive banding that is placed around the top portion of the stomach to make the stomach smaller. The band contains an inflatable balloon. A port is accessible near the band and is located under the skin. This port can be used to loosen or tighten the band when necessary. This port can be filled

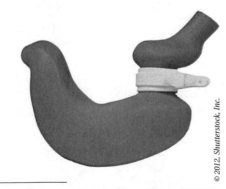

© 2012, Shutterstock, Inc.

© 2012, Shutterstock, Inc.

[7] www.nlm.nih.gov/medlineplus/ency/article/007199

with saline solution to restrict food going into the stomach until a desired amount of weight loss is achieved. The lap band procedure is reversible but usually at the expense of the patient. The weight loss that is achieved may not be as great compared to gastric bypass and the weight is also lost at a slower rate.[8]

As with any surgery there are risks involved. Weight loss surgery should not be taken lightly. Permanent behavior modification is the key to successful weight loss. Patients benefit and are more successful when they participate in support groups and follow up as directed by their doctor.

## Disordered Eating vs. Eating Disorders

It is estimated that 24 million Americans suffer from eating disorders. This statistic would include anorexia nervosa, bulimia, and binge eating. Eating disorders have the highest mortality rate of any mental illness.[9] The pressure to be thin in a society that is obsessed with dieting is a harsh reality. Media and magazines present unrealistic body images and most are led to believe that they too should look like a super-model. The truth is that the average American female is about 5'4" and weighs 165 pounds; the average American male is about 5'9" and weighs 195 pounds.[10] Here is another thought, the average size of a female movie star at the Golden Globes is probably about a size 2.

### Disordered Eating

Disordered eating is a combination of many behaviors that lead to unhealthy eating habits. Skipping meals, following fad diets, eating when stressed, and binge eating disorder are just a few unhealthy eating habits.

© 2012, Shutterstock, Inc.

© 2012, Shutterstock, Inc.

---

[9] http://www.anad.org/get-information/about-eating-disorders/eating-disorders-statistics/
[10] http://www.cdc.gov/nchs/fastats/bodymeas.htm

**Binge eating** is a disorder in which the person eats a large amount of food. Many people have eaten until they feel uncomfortable, but people with binge eating often feel out of control. The following is a list of other factors involved in binge eating behaviors.

- Eating very quickly during a binge episode

- Eating until they feel uncomfortable

- Eating when not hungry

- Eating alone because of embarrassment

- Feeling depressed, angry, or guilty from overeating[11]

Binge eating disorder affects about 3% of the population and is more common in adults aged 46–55. It is unclear what the exact cause of binge eating disorder is. Many health professionals agree that it may come from frequent dieting (i.e., "yo yo" dieting) and seen in those who turn to food for comfort during times when they are stressed, bored, or depressed.[12]

## Night Eating Syndrome

Night eating syndrome is characterized by the consumption of as much as 25% of total daily caloric intake taken in after dinner due to feelings of extreme hunger. Other characteristics of night eating syndrome include patients reporting that they wake up with food wrappers in their bed without any recollection of getting up during the night. Research in this area is just beginning to understand the mechanisms of this disorder. Some studies have found that people with night eating syndrome report higher amounts of stress and anxiety. Stress and anxiety can lower serotonin levels in the body and cause more cravings for food. Studies are showing that medications to treat stress and anxiety show improvements in patients suffering from this disorder.[13]

## Eating Disorders

Eating disorders are psychological based diseases that are diagnosed by a doctor. Eating disorders commonly occur in female adolescents, but recent research has shown a disturbing trend in the increase of adolescent males being diagnosed with eating disorders. Certain personality traits and behaviors seem to be a common thread in those who develop eating disorders. Some individuals are obsessed with cleanliness and order as well as perfectionism in many if not all areas of their lives. Other commonalities in those diagnosed with eating disorders include low self-esteem

---

[11] http://www.win.niddk.nih.gov/publications/binge.htm
[12] http://www.win.niddk.nih.gov/publications/binge.htm
[13] Issues for DSM-V: Night Eating Syndrome. *Am J Psychiatry* 165:4, April 2008.

and those who were victims of sexual abuse. There are two types of eating disorders, anorexia nervosa and bulimia.

### Anorexia Nervosa (AN)

Anorexia nervosa is an eating disorder characterized by self-imposed starvation. A person with anorexia nervosa will often deny or ignore the hunger signals in the body. Negative body image and societal pressures are common causes of anorexia nervosa. Distorted body image will often lead to body hate. Rigid expectations and perfectionist behaviors are often part of the disorder that lead to needing to feel in control of eating when other areas of their lives are out of control. The ability to control their food intake when other areas in their lives are out of their control can make them feel empowered and therefore further restrict food intake. The following is a list of adverse health consequences associated with anorexia:

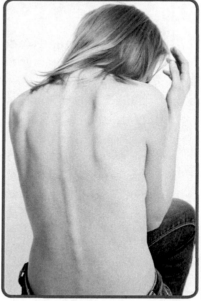
© 2012, Shutterstock, Inc.

- Rapid weight loss

- Fear of "fattening foods"

- Lower body temperature

- Lanugo - downy hairs on the body (body trying to warm itself)

- Decreased heart rate, low blood potassium levels (could lead to a heart attack)

- Iron deficiency anemia

- Rough, dry, and cold skin

- Decreased immune system

- Loss of hair

- Loss of menstruation cycle (body fat is too low, lower estrogen levels)

- Loss of bone density

- Feelings of bloating or fullness

- Constipation

- Depression

Effective treatments for patients with anorexia nervosa must include a team of qualified health professionals. Registered dietitians, registered nurses, psychologists, and physicians work together in treating the patient. Goals for treatment include a relatively slow and safe weight gain close to a healthy BMI range.

**Bulimia**

Bulimia is an eating disorder characterized by episodes of binge eating followed by the use of laxatives, diuretics, or self-induced vomiting. Genetic factors may also play a role in the development of bulimia. Low self-esteem and feelings of hopelessness are often centered on the illness. Certain lifestyle patterns may also predispose someone to the development of an eating disorder. Frequent dieting can lead to the development of both anorexia and bulimia.

© 2012, Shutterstock, Inc.

Someone with bulimia often thinks about food constantly and may be preoccupied with planning their meals, especially when a binge is being planned. A binge can last a few hours to an all day event. Large amounts of foods may be purchased and consumed with frequent bouts of vomiting in between. People with bulimia are often depressed and will turn to food when stressful events come up in their lives. Bulimics also tend to be impulsive. Suicide attempts and increased alcohol or drug use may also complicate the healing process.

Most commonly, high calorie, high carbohydrate foods are consumed during a binge. The common thought process behind the vomiting is that the calories will not be absorbed. However, since digestion begins in the mouth, it is estimated that one-third to two-thirds of the calories still may be absorbed. A binge is usually followed by strict dieting which then leads to hunger and the process begins all over again. The following is a list of adverse health consequences associated with bulimia:

- Erosion of tooth enamel (from vomiting)

- Low blood potassium (can cause a heart attack)

- Swelling of salivary glands

- Stomach ulcers, esophageal tears

- Constipation (from frequent laxative abuse)

- Calluses on the knuckles (from inducing vomiting)

Treatment of bulimia nervosa is consistent with the treatment that is required for anorexia nervosa. A qualified team of health professionals is important. Family involvement and support is also important. Teaching a person with bulimia about developing a healthier relationship with food can be challenging. Bulimics often adopt an all or nothing approach to eating. Therapy for the bulimic patient will include changes in beliefs and attitudes to try to decrease binging and purging episodes.

## NUTRITION NERD ALERT

A small handful of mixed, unsalted nuts in the afternoon is a healthy way to give you the energy you need to finish your day. It provides a healthy source of fat, protein, and micronutrients—such as phytochemical antioxidants—that help fight oxidative damage and keep your body healthy and in working order.

## Physical Activity

Despite the fact that exercise can reduce the risk of a number of chronic diseases, most adults in the United States do not exercise. Current statistics show that most adults do not get enough physical activity on a daily basis. It is estimated that only 31% of U.S. adults report engaging in physical activity on a regular basis (defined as 3–5 times per week). About 40% of adults report doing no leisure-time activity at all.[14]

© 2012, Shutterstock, Inc.

---

[14] http://win.niddk.nih.gov/publications/PDFs/stat904z.pdf

Physical activity is an important part of being healthy. Physical activity is not only recommended for losing weight, it is also recommended for maintaining overall good health and wellness. The amount of physical activity that is done on a daily basis varies greatly between individuals.

## What Is Exercise?

Is there a difference between exercise and movement? **Movement** would be considered a physical activity that you do because you have to get from one place to another. Movement of your body is required to do various activities such as getting dressed or other activities of daily living. **Exercises** are related to physical activities that are purposeful and planned. Planned physical activity would mean that you schedule these activities outside of your usual daily activities. Some people tend to think that walking from your car to class is exercise. Unless you are parking far away and planning a 10-minute walk to class, then it is not considered exercise, it would be movement, meaning you had to move to get there.

People tend to think that their jobs can count as exercise, for example, a waiter or waitress who has a very physical job. Some jobs require being more physical, but this is not considered exercise. The body makes adaptations according to the amount of physical activity someone does during work. The body can adapt to repetitive motions and the performance of usual routines at work. You need to be in good physical condition to do such a job but it is not counted as exercise. This type of physical activity would be considered occupational-related physical activity.

## Different Types of Exercise

Setting goals will help you to achieve the maximum benefits of exercise. Remember that goals need to be measurable and realistic. Think about what you want to achieve. Do you want to exercise for weight loss, overall health, or are you training for an athletic event? What your goals are will determine the type of exercises you will be doing. Different types of exercises can benefit different parts of the body. The following is a list of exercises and benefits:

- Cardiovascular—to help strengthen the heart

- Musculoskeletal—to help strengthen the muscles

- Stretching—for warm up and cool down

**EVERY DAY**
**SUPERFOODS**

Oatmeal is an exercise super food. It protects the heart through soluble fiber, provides carbohydrates to be used for energy, and has an added bonus of protein to help rebuild muscles after a good workout.

The intensity of the exercise is also important. Moderate physical activities include:

- Walking briskly
- Bicycling
- Gardening
- Dancing
- Golfing (carrying the clubs)
- Tennis (doubles)

Vigorous physical activities include[15]:

- Running or jogging
- Bicycling (more than 10 miles per hour)
- Heavy yard work (chopping wood)
- Swimming (freestyle laps)
- Aerobics
- Basketball
- Tennis (singles)

**Benefits of Exercise**

The benefits of exercise are obvious. Once an exercise routine is started, most people report feeling better and having more energy. The following list outlines the benefits of exercise:

- Reduces stress
- Promotes well being
- Reduces the risk of many types of cancer
- Reduces the risk of heart disease
- Reduces the risk of type 2 diabetes
- Improves immune function
- Strengthens the muscles and bones
- Aids in weight loss and weight maintenance

---

[15] www.choosemyplate.gov/foodgroups/physicalactivity.html

- Reduces blood pressure
- Decreases depression

Regular exercise may also slow the aging process and improve brain function. As previously mentioned, despite the clear benefits of exercise, people still do not do enough. I hope this list of benefits has inspired you to start a regular exercise program.

### Recommendations for Exercise

Adults 18 years and older need at least 30 minutes of physical activity most days of the week; children and teens need at least 60 minutes per day. For optimal health and weight loss benefits for adults, it is recommended that you exercise at least 45–60 minutes per day.[16]

The fact is that most people do not like to exercise. The most common excuses for not exercising include not having the time, not knowing which exercises to do, not a member of a gym, and many more. Can you think of excuses that you use when you do not want to exercise? The funny thing is that we find time to watch our favorite television programs, we drive to our favorite restaurants, and we always have time for checking our Facebook page.

The total number of minutes that we exercise per day is important, but not all exercise has to be done at once. Most health professionals agree that breaking up exercise into smaller increments throughout the day is also beneficial. For example if 30 minutes per day is your goal you can take a brisk walk for 15 minutes in the morning and 15 minutes in the evening.

### Physical Activity Pyramid

To help you meet your goals for physical activity, try using the physical activity pyramid. The physical activity pyramid was developed by the U.S. Department of Health and Human Services to provide physical activity guidelines. The pyramid helps to distinguish between the different exercises as well as give recommendations for how frequently the exercises should be done on a daily basis.

The recommendations include cardiovascular or aerobic activities to help strengthen the heart and lungs. Moderate intensity exercises can raise the heart rate. Intensity

**EVERY DAY**
**SUPERFOODS**
Chocolate milk (and even beer!) may boost post-workout recovery and rehydration due to their combined protein and carbohydrate content. This effect is evident with one glass after exercise followed by several glasses of water.

---

[16] www.fitness.gov/resources_factsheet.htm

*Nutrition Intuition*

can be determined by the "talk test." Can you still talk and carry on a conversation while performing this exercise? The old saying was "no pain, no gain"; but pain should not be ignored.

### Eating Healthily for Exercise

Adopting good exercise habits often leads to eating healthier. Would you jog to the donut shop? You could burn the calories off but it would not be a good food choice. Eating healthily for exercise includes a lot of the same principles that we have already learned. Balanced meals and small frequent meals are ideal. The intensity of the physical activity will influence the way that our body burns fuel. Carbohydrates and fats are primarily the nutrients that are affected by the intensity of exercise. At lower intensity exercise, more fat is burned. At higher intensity exercise, more carbohydrate is burned. It is estimated that glucose supplies less than half of the energy that is needed when we are sitting or performing light activities. Fat is primarily used during this time. When activities are performed at higher intensity, the oxidation of glucose is increased. Athletes require a higher intake of carbohydrates and may also benefit from decreasing fat intake. Athletes usually require as much as 3000–4000 calories per day depending on the type of activity performed.

### NUTRITION NERD ALERT

A tasty (and healthy) homemade "sports drink" can be made by blending fresh ginger root and unfiltered apple juice. Ginger contains gingerols—natural anti-inflammatory compounds that can reduce joint pain. The unfiltered apple juice may increase production of the neurotransmitter acetylcholine, which improves mental acuity and muscle strength during exercise.

## Energy Metabolism for Physical Demands

Have you ever wondered how many calories you burn doing certain activities? A **metabolic equivalent (MET)** is a physiological measurement to express the energy cost of performing certain physical activities. MET is used to measure the intensity and energy expenditure of activities and is comparable among persons of different weights. For a comprehensive list of MET's see the cancer.gov website at: http://riskfactor.cancer.gov/tools/atus-met/ to look up different MET's for different activities that you do throughout the day.

Have you ever wondered how our food is broken down to provide the energy needed to exercise? Complex systems of chemical reactions take place to break down our macronutrients into energy for our cells. This energy is especially important during exercise. A high-energy compound called adenosine triphosphate (ATP) forms when adenosine diphosphate (ADP) picks up an extra phosphate bond during energy metabolism. ATP is a direct source of energy for the cells. When energy is needed, enzymes break the bonds of ATP to release the energy. In the cells, the ATP is reduced again back to ADP and the process can begin all over again. Protein, carbohydrates, and fat can all be metabolized in the body for ATP production. Each macronutrient is broken down a little differently. For example, proteins require aerobic pathways to

© 2012, Shutterstock, Inc.

generate ATP. **Aerobic** conditions require oxygen. **Glycolysis** is the breakdown of glucose for energy. Glucose can be broken down in anaerobic and aerobic conditions. **Anaerobic** conditions do not require oxygen. When anaerobic pathways are used during glycolysis less ATP is produced.

## Summary

The obesity epidemic is often discussed in the news. The percentage of people who are overweight or obese is rapidly rising. Childhood obesity is also on the rise. The first lady, Michelle Obama, has taken the initiative to create a campaign aimed at decreasing childhood obesity. As obesity increases, so does the risk for many other chronic diseases. It has also been said that obesity is an issue of economics. Some may argue that it is more expensive to eat healthier; others say it is the availability of cheap, calorie dense foods that are causing the problem. Whatever the case may be, this disease is costly to everyone.

A healthy weight can be defined by using the BMI tables. BMI is a measurement expressed as a height to weight ratio. A BMI in a normal range is 18.5–24.9. A BMI that is considered overweight is 25–29.9, and a BMI that is considered obese is over 30. BMI can predict a possibility for developing certain chronic diseases. BMI measurements may not be suitable for all people in the population. Someone who has more muscle than fat will appear overweight or obese on the BMI table. BMI measurements may also not be suitable to be used on children, the elderly, and pregnant women.

Waist circumference is another way to measure your risk for the development of chronic diseases. Women with a waist circumference higher than 35 and men with a waist circumference higher than 40 are at an increased risk for health problems associated with obesity.

Overnutrition and undernutrition are concepts that define excess or inadequate intakes of food. We live in a "toxic food environment" where food is available every day, 24 hours a day. The shift from undernutrition to overnutrition has occurred in less than a generation. The cost of obesity on the U.S. healthcare system is staggering. Other nations are also feeling the effects of obesity and many are not prepared.

Energy in versus energy out is the key to weight maintenance. The secret to weight loss is exercise more and eat less—sound too simple? A table of recommendations for calories is included in the chapter.

Measuring body composition can be done several ways. DEXA is a machine that provides a low-energy X-ray. The subject lays down on a flat surface and the machine scans the patient. This procedure is considered the most accurate way to measure body fat. The pictures that are scanned can show exactly where the fat in the body resides. The DEXA machine is also used to assess bone density.

Bioelectrical impedance is a hand-held machine that sends a low frequency electrical current through the body that estimates the amount of fat in the body. The principle of this procedure is based on the fact that water and electrolytes conduct electricity and fat does not.

Under water weighing requires a specialized tank of water in which the subject is submerged under water.

Skinfold thickness is a measurement commonly used in gym settings. A caliper tool is used to measure the thickness of the skin at different sites on the body. A series of calculations are done to determine the body fat percentage. When done correctly this can also be an accurate measurement.

Components of energy expenditure include the basal metabolic rate, the resting metabolic rate, physical activity, and the thermic effect of food. Several factors can increase or decrease metabolic rates. Factors that increase and decrease the basal metabolic rate are listed in the chapter in Table 11.2.

Theories of obesity attempt to explain the reasons why people are overweight or obese. Obesity is a multifactorial disease. There is not one reason why people become overweight or obese.

Hyperplastic and hypertrophic obesity help to explain the number of fat cells in the body. The more fat cells, the more risk for obesity. The numbers of fat cells in the body are a constant number, meaning that the number does not really change during our lifetime.

The set-point theory says that our body weights are genetically predetermined. The set point acts like a temperature gauge except it regulates our body weight. The body is sensitive to increases or decreases in weight and will attempt to rebalance itself.

Genetics play a major role in obesity. Body shape, size, and metabolic rates can be inherited from your family. Hormones such as ghrelin and leptin are being studied in hopes of solving the mystery behind obesity.

Consequences of obesity include an increased risk for cancer, heart disease, gallbladder disease, fatty liver, GERD, osteoarthritis, gout, breathing problems, and reproductive problems to name just a few. Understanding the difference between visceral fat and subcutaneous fat will help to explain where the fat resides in the body and how that influences our health. Visceral fat is closest to the organs; those who are overweight or obese tend to have more visceral fat which is related to a higher risk for developing chronic diseases. Subcutaneous fat is closer to the skin and is usually the more visible type of fat that causes the dimpling on the surface of the skin.

Just as with being overweight, there is a risk for being underweight. Being underweight is far less common in the United States than being overweight. Societal pressures to be thin often send a message that being thin is more acceptable than being overweight. Being underweight can lead to a poor immune system, problems with stable body temperature, and, in women, problems with menstruation and fertility. In the elderly population, being underweight can lead to weaker immune systems and longer healing times.

Fad diets are a billion dollar industry. People are always looking for the latest and greatest ways to lose weight. Fad diets are usually based on the elimination of certain foods, which could lead to nutrient deficiencies. Products such as supplements, shakes, and special foods are often costly and are not well researched by the manufacturer—if they are researched at all. Consumers should be aware that some supplements can be dangerous and can cause headaches, nausea, vomiting, and sometimes even death. If the claims made by the manufacturers seem too good to be true, then they probably are.

The composition of the diet does not seem to play a big role in weight loss success. The truth is that if there is a calorie deficit, you can lose weight. A 1200 calorie diet that consist of cakes and cookies sounds good on the surface but it will not provide many nutrients.

Low carbohydrate diets have come and gone. Low carbohydrate diets are always being re-invented to offer a new twist. They all offer quick weight loss. The formation of ketones in the body does provide a way to burn fat when carbohydrates are not consumed. The problem is that long-term use of low or zero carbohydrate diets may not be suitable for those with a history of kidney disease. It is also suggested that high protein diets may not be good for bone density which is especially important for women.

What is the secret to successful weight loss? Research has shown that the best way to lose weight is to keep a food journal. Writing down what you eat is a way to keep track of your calories and take responsibility for what you eat. Current technology has made the task of keeping a food journal even easier. There are many online resources that offer food tracking as well as detailed reports on micro and macronutrients that are consumed in the diet. Of course exercise and eating healthy are important too.

Behavior modification is another key to successful weight loss. Change is difficult and we tend to be more comfortable with our bad habits. Adopting good habits takes time. Motivation to change behavior is necessary. If you really want to change something, you have to be willing to try. Losing weight because you want to be healthy is a good reason. Losing weight for someone else or a special event often brings stress and failure. Some people tend to think that if they lose large amounts of weight in a short amount of time they will feel better. The truth is that a 5–10% weight loss can make a big difference in your health. Setting goals is important; knowing what you want to work toward can keep you motivated. Setting realistic goals is the key to success. Unrealistic goals may set you up for failure. Be willing to forgive yourself when you reach setbacks. Reward yourself when small goals are reached; buy yourself something you have been wanting, obviously food should not be the reward. Be aware of triggers, things that may cause a setback for you. Is it a food that you have in the house? Is it an emotional trigger? Recognizing what your triggers are can help you to avoid them or know how to effectively handle them. Feeling full is important; who wants to be hungry while trying to lose weight? Most people do not last more than a few hours to a few days on a diet. Focusing on "feeling full" can help you to not overeat.

It is estimated that 24 million Americans suffer from an eating disorder. There are eating disorders that are diagnosed by a doctor and there are disordered eating behaviors.

An example of a disordered eating behavior would be binge eating. This behavior is characterized by eating large amounts of food in a short amount of time. Often people with binge eat feel guilty or depressed and often eat alone. Another disordered eating behavior is night eating syndrome. It is estimated that people with night eating syndrome consume most of their calories during the evening hours. With night eating syndrome, the person may get up in the middle of the night to eat without realizing they are going to the kitchen and eating. It is kind of like sleepwalking.

Diagnosed eating disorders include anorexia nervosa and bulimia. Anorexia nervosa is characterized by self-imposed starvation. Negative body issues and societal pressures to be thin can be a driving force behind the development of both types of eating disorders. Bulimia is characterized by episodes of binge eating followed by purging. Both eating disorders require multiple health professionals to deal with the many facets of the disease. Family involvement also plays an important role in the healing process.

Despite the many benefits of exercise, most people do not get enough physical activity on a daily basis. There is a difference between movement and exercise. Movement is the physical activity that you have to do to get from one place to another. Exercise is different because it is purposeful and planned. Planned physical activity counts as exercise. Any physical activity that you perform at work is not considered exercise because it is related to your occupation. Different exercises and recommendations are further defined in the chapter.

Adopting good exercise habits often leads to eating healthier. The foods that you choose may depend on the types of exercises you are doing. Higher intensity exercises require a higher intake of carbohydrates. Training for athletic events requires a lot of calories. Fat is the fuel that is burned during lower intensity exercises. Balanced meals and small frequent meals are recommended.

Energy needed to meet physical demands requires a complex system of chemical reactions that take place in the body. A high-energy compound call adenosine triphosphate (ATP) forms when adenosine diphosphate picks up an extra phosphate bond during energy metabolism. Carbohydrate, protein, and fat are metabolized in the body to produce ATP.

# STEPS TO HEALTHY WEIGHT LOSS

Walking is a healthy and easy way to lose weight. Walking does not usually involve expensive equipment or costly gym memberships. The main investment in beginning a walking program will be a little motivation, a pedometer or step counter, and comfortable walking shoes. The Surgeon General developed a program called Shape Up America! This program encourages Americans to walk at least 10,000 steps per day. 10,000 steps are equal to about 5 miles. It is estimated that the average person may only get less than 3,000 steps per day.

© 2012, Shutterstock, Inc.

**Here are some suggestions to get started:**

- Work up to 10,000 steps slowly, wear your pedometer for about 2 weeks to get an idea of how many steps are in your usual normal routine.

- After you get an average of how many steps you take on a usual day, challenge yourself to take an additional 500 steps and see if you can increase your daily amount slowly working your way up to 10,000 steps per day.

There are simple step counters which only count your steps and then there are pedometers which will take into account your stride length for more accurate step counting. It is estimated that 10,000 steps can burn approximately 500 calories. Again this will slightly vary among individuals depending on weight and stride length.

**To put this into perspective, here are some high calorie foods and how many steps you will need to take to work them off:**

- A typical fast food hamburger, fries, and soda—1500 calories—30,000 steps
- 2 large slices of pizza—1000 calories—20,000 steps
- Hot fudge Sunday or piece of cheese cake—500 calories—10,000 steps

Remember that these steps above would need to be taken in addition to your usual amount of steps to burn off the extra calories.

**Here are some ideas to take some extra steps:**

- Take the stairs
- Park your car further away
- Walk on your 15 minute breaks at work or on your lunch
- Walk in between classes

*Before beginning any exercise program, consult with your physician. www.shapeup.org

# Nutrition Throughout the Lifespan

## Learning Objectives

- Learn the importance of good nutrition during pregnancy
- List common nutrition-related concerns in pregnancy
- Describe gestational diabetes and pregnancy-induced hypertension
- Understand the benefits of breastfeeding
- Discuss the benefits of maintaining healthy nutrition throughout the lifespan
- Evaluate nutrition concerns for infants, adolescents, and older adults

## Functional Food Fact  Eggplant

Several hundred years ago, it was believed that eating eggplant caused cancer due to its bitter taste. Today we know that eggplant gets its rich deep purple color from the anthocyanin nasunin, which is a known antioxidant. A diet rich is antioxidants can be a great way to slow the aging process and prevent the possible development of cancer. It is important to eat all of the colors of the rainbow when it comes to fruits and vegetables. Next time you prepare eggplant, leave the skin on!

# Pregnancy and Nutrition

## Preconception Planning

The health of the mother before she gets pregnant is just as important as her health is during the pregnancy. Adverse health consequences can result in the baby when mother's health is compromised. Here are some suggestions for women who are planning to have a baby can do.

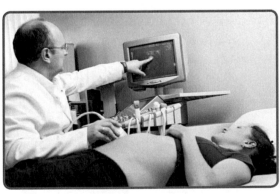

- Lose weight if your BMI is not within the normal range

- Stop smoking

- Stop drinking alcohol

- Include folate rich foods in your diet

- Get plenty of exercise

Research is taking a closer look at health habits and lifestyle factors that affect the fetus. These studies are referred to as in-utero research because researchers can now look closely at the developing fetus. The technology that exists today can give a very clear picture of the developing fetus. Genetic testing and other first trimester screenings can also help to determine the health of the fetus. The health of the father is also important. Drug use, smoking, and alcohol intake can all play a role. A healthy baby who is born today is a reason to celebrate, but where does it all begin?

## From Conception to Birth

It is estimated that half of all pregnancies are unplanned, which means that if a woman is sexually active she should be prepared for pregnancy and take the necessary steps to plan accordingly. The prenatal period is the time from **conception** (when the egg is fertilized) to the time when the baby is delivered. The approximate length of a pregnancy is between 38 and 42 weeks. During the early stages of the development there is rapid cell division. The mass of cells finds a place to rest on the nutrient-rich uterine wall and continues to develop. In about 6 weeks, the mass of cells starts to resemble an embryo and will continue to grow in size and start the development of the organs. After 8 weeks of development, the embryo is now referred to as a fetus. The pregnancy is divided into three stages or trimesters. Although all of the trimesters are important, the first trimester is the time when the fetus is developing at an accelerated rate and exposure to teratogens (substances that can cause birth defects) can have detrimental effects on the fetus. The challenge is that most mothers do not even know that they are pregnant.

### The First Trimester

The pregnancy is divided into three stages or trimesters. The first trimester is referred to as the critical period of development because this is the time that organs are developed. During this first trimester any nutrient deficiencies or other health issues associated with the mother can directly affect the growing fetus. Exposure to toxic chemicals, drugs, and other substances can produce negative outcomes for the fetus and the mother.

### The Second Trimester

The second trimester is the time when the fetus can begin to move. Arms, legs, fingers, and toes are fully formed, and the fetus begins to take on features that resemble a human infant. Although still relatively small and only weighing about an ounce, the mother can begin to feel the movement of the baby.

### The Third Trimester

During this trimester the fetus will continue to grow very rapidly in size. The baby is about 12 inches long and will weigh about 2.5–3 pounds at the beginning of this final trimester. The fetus will nearly double in length and triple in weight by the time the third trimester ends. A normal weight baby will weigh anywhere between 6 and 8 pounds and will be 19–21 inches long.

## Nutrition Matters in Pregnancy

Throughout the pregnancy, the fetus relies on the mother for a steady supply of nutrients. The **placenta** serves as the organ in the pregnancy that connects the mother and the fetus via an umbilical cord. Mother and baby do not share blood, but they do

share nutrients. A healthy diet can ensure proper growth and development of the fetus. The placenta serves as a mechanism for nourishment, but unfortunately it cannot filter out many harmful substances to prevent them from passing to the baby. Many toxic substances that can be passed to the developing fetus include:

- Nicotine from smoking

- Alcohol

- Drugs (prescription or illegal)

- Caffeine

- Harmful chemicals

At about 37 weeks, the developing fetus is physiologically mature enough to survive outside of the womb. If delivery of the baby comes too early, complications may result and the baby may require additional care in a neonatal intensive care unit.

## NUTRITION NERD ALERT

Have an upset stomach? Brown rice (fiber), bananas (potassium), sunflower seeds, papaya (contains papain, an enzyme that helps with heartburn), turmeric (antiseptic), garlic (anti-flatulent), basil (anti-ulcer), and sage (anti-inflammatory) all help to naturally calm your stomach.

## Low-Birth-Weight and Preterm Babies

The weight of a baby at birth can have an overall impact on growth and development. Surviving the first year of life may be determined by the baby's birth weight. Low-birth-weight (LBW) infants weigh less than 5.5 pounds at birth. These infants have been associated with a higher rate of death within the first year of life. Mothers who are under the age of 15 or over the age of 50 are known to have a higher risk of giving birth to LBW infants. Women who smoke are also at risk for giving birth to a LBW

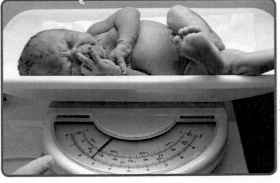

© 2012, Shutterstock, Inc.

infant. Preterm infants are those who are born before the 37th week and may suffer from a variety of health problems.

## Common Nutrition-Related Concerns in Pregnancy

Pregnancy brings a whole host of physiological changes to a woman's body. In the beginning of the pregnancy, she may experience nausea and vomiting; often referred to as "morning sickness." Newly pregnant mothers also complain of tiredness, swollen hands or feet, constipation, and heartburn. In many cases, these symptoms improve after the first trimester. Food cravings may affect the appetite of pregnant women. Pregnant women may crave sweet and savory foods, sometimes wanting to consume them together, such as "pickles and ice cream." Some pregnant women may also crave non-food items in a phenomenon known as pica. **Pica** is the craving for non-food items such as ice, clay, dirt, laundry detergent, starch, chalk, and others. There is not a good scientific explanation as to why pregnant women crave these non-food items.

## Recommendations for a Healthy Pregnancy

Pregnancy is a time when extra calories can be taken in to support fetal growth and development. The appetite of the mother may be affected. Her appetite may vary depending on how she is feeling. Often when nauseated, she will not want to eat too much. When most of the first trimester nausea and vomiting has passed, her appetite will improve. Too much weight gain and not enough weight gain during pregnancy can affect the developing fetus. Calorie needs will vary throughout the pregnancy. In the first trimester, calorie needs are the same as when she was not pregnant. In the second and third trimesters, she 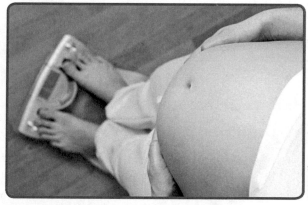 can consume an additional 300 calories per day, which would be equivalent to adding an extra serving of each of the food groups. We want to encourage mothers to take in adequate amounts of calories but not too many. Too much weight gain is not recommended. How much weight should a woman gain with pregnancy? The following recommendations are set by the Institute of Medicine (IOM) for appropriate weight gains during pregnancy. Excessive weight gain during pregnancy can result in complications during labor and delivery. Research today is taking a closer look at weight gain patterns in overweight and obese mothers. The studies are trying to find out if excessive weight gain by mothers is putting babies at risk for being overweight or obese as adolescents or young adults.

**Table 12.1** New Recommendations for Total and Rate of Weight Gain during Pregnancy, by Pre-pregnancy BMI[1]

| Pre-pregnancy BMI | BMI+ $(kg/m_2)$ | Total Weight Gain (lbs) | Rates of Weight Gain 2nd and 3rd Trimester (lbs/week) |
|---|---|---|---|
| Underweight | <18.5 | 28–40 | 1 (1–1.3) |
| Normal weight | 18.5–24.9 | 25–35 | 1 (0.8–1) |
| Overweight | 25.0–29.9 | 15–25 | 0.6 (0.5–0.7) |

## Gestational Diabetes and Pregnancy-Induced Hypertension

### Gestational Diabetes (GDM)

According to the American Diabetes Association and according to new diagnostic criteria, it is estimated that as many as 18% of pregnancies are affected by GDM.[2] GDM is a condition associated with high maternal blood sugar. Elevated blood sugar during pregnancy may have to do with the pregnancy hormones that are present in the woman's body. These hormones that are normally not there when she is not pregnant can contribute to the development of GDM. Family history of diabetes, advanced maternal age, and obesity may also be causes of GDM. High blood sugar in the mother can mean that the baby is getting excess glucose. Excess glucose being

---

[1] http://www.iom.edu/~/media/Files/Report%20Files/2009/Weight-Gain-During-Pregnancy-Reexamining-the-Guidelines/Resource%20Page%20-%20Weight%20Gain%20During%20Pregnancy.pdf
[2] http://www.diabetes.org/diabetes-basics/gestational/what-is-gestational-diabetes.html

passed to the fetus from the mother can result in rapid weight gain. Large babies may weigh over 8.5 pounds and are referred to a macrosomic.

Women are now routinely tested for GDM around the 26th–28th week of pregnancy. A glucose drink is administered and the serum blood sugar is checked to detect GDM. Diet and exercise are usually adequate to treat the condition. In some cases, mothers may require insulin or medications to treat elevated blood sugar.

### Pregnancy-Induced Hypertension (PIH)

Also known as preeclampsia or toxemia, PIH is a serious condition characterized by high blood pressure, edema, and protein in the urine. Severe symptoms include headaches, blurred vision, nausea/vomiting, and shortness of breath. If any of these symptoms occur, the patient is encouraged to go the hospital immediately. PIH is usually treated with bed rest, increased appointments with the physician, decreased sodium intake, and drinking plenty of water. If the condition worsens, the placenta may not get enough blood and nutrients and thus the baby would not get enough nutrients and oxygen from the mother. PIH usually occurs in the last trimester of the pregnancy. If all other treatments fail, the only cure for PIH is to deliver the baby.[3]

## Physical Activity

Physical activity is beneficial throughout the entire pregnancy as long as there are not any contraindications to exercise. Yoga during pregnancy can be a great way to increase flexibility. Physical activity may also benefit pregnant women during labor and delivery as well as help with boosting mothers' moods and energy levels. Here are some guidelines to follow when exercising during pregnancy:[4]

- Never exercise to the point of exhaustion; oxygen may be decreased to the baby

- Wear comfortable clothes and proper footwear

- Take frequent breaks and drink plenty of water

- Do not exercise in hot or humid weather

- Avoid contact sports

- Light weights can be used to tone up; do not lift weights above your head

© 2012, Shutterstock, Inc.

---

[3] http://americanpregnancy.org/pregnancycomplications/pih.htm
[4] http://www.americanpregnancy.org/pregnancyhealth/exerciseguidelines.html

- Do not do exercises that require lying flat on your back

- Stretch at the beginning and the end of the workout

- Eat healthily

## Breastfeeding

### The Lactation Process

The production of breast milk requires the coordination of several hormones. **Prolactin** is the hormone that helps the body to produce milk at the end of the pregnancy. In the beginning of the pregnancy, the body contains high levels of **progesterone** and **estrogen**; these two hormones suppress prolactin. At the end of the pregnancy, a shift in the hormones occurs and prolactin is produced in higher levels in preparation for the birth of the baby. The hormone **oxytocin** functions to allow the "let down reflex." At the "let down," the milk flows into the mammary glands and the infant will be able to begin nursing. There may be several challenges with breastfeeding. The suckling reflex in the infant is required to help with the latching on for feeding. In infants who are born prematurely, this reflex may not be quite developed and the mother may be required to utilize a breast pump to obtain milk for alternative feedings. Lactation specialists are employed by most hospitals and are there to assist the mother with breastfeeding.

© 2012, Shutterstock, Inc.

The first milk that is produced when the infant is born is called colostrum. **Colostrum** is also known as "liquid gold"; this clear yellowish fluid is produced during the first few days after the birth of the baby. This fluid helps to establish the immune system for the baby. Antibodies and rich nutrients provide baby with a healthy start to life. Colostrum changes into mature milk which contains the right amounts of carbohydrate, fat, and protein for the baby. The quality of the breast milk cannot be matched in any formula.

### Healthy Eating When Breastfeeding

Lactation requires more calories than pregnancy. Most experts agree that when breastfeeding, most women need at least 500–700 more calories per day above their usual caloric requirements. Overweight or obese women may require slightly less.

Online resources can assist mothers with eating healthily during pregnancy and breastfeeding. The MyPlate plan is a great online resource that can help moms to plan their meals and eat the right amounts of carbohydrate, protein, and fat. It is important to eat a variety of foods, drink plenty of water, and exercise in moderation.

### Advantages and Benefits of Breastfeeding

Breastfeeding may take some effort at first. Establishing a routine can make breast-feeding more enjoyable for mom and baby. Breastfeeding can save money, provide a food source for the baby in case of an emergency, and help the baby to feel more safe and secure. The close physical contact of the mother to her newborn is very important.

Breastfeeding has been shown to decrease illnesses in babies such as ear infections and diarrhea. Breastfed babies also have a lower incidence of gastrointestinal disorders, respiratory infections, asthma, obesity, and type 2 diabetes. There is also amazing evidence that breastfed babies have higher IQs.[5]

Breastfeeding can benefit the mother's health as well. Women who breastfeed may have a lower risk of type 2 diabetes, breast cancer, ovarian cancer, and postpartum depression.[6]

## Infant Nutrition

Breast milk is best for the infant and exclusive breastfeeding for the first 6 months of life is recommended by most health professionals. Comparisons of breast milk to infant formulas have shown that breast milk is superior in quality. Breast milk is easier for the baby to digest. The proteins in breast milk are smaller and

© 2012, Shutterstock, Inc.

are easier for the infant to break down than formulas and cow's milk. Cow's milk is not recommended for babies under the age of 1 year old.

### Allergies and Intolerances

An **allergic reaction** to a food or other substances will cause the immune system to react. When the presence of foreign substances is detected, the body will respond accordingly. Some allergic responses include:

- Itchy, red, or swollen skin

---

[5] www.womenshealth.gov/breastfeeding/whybreastfeedingisimportant
[6] www.womenshealth.gov/breastfeeding/whybreastfeedingisimportant

- Difficulty breathing, runny nose

- Vomiting, diarrhea, gas, or bloating

Formula fed babies have a higher risk of developing allergies compared to breastfed infants.

**Food intolerances** do not involve the immune system. Intolerance to a food or other substances is usually characterized by the following symptoms:

- Nausea, vomiting, diarrhea

A good example to explain the difference between intolerance and an allergy is to use cow's milk. If someone is allergic to cow's milk, they are allergic to the protein in the milk. If someone is intolerant to cow's milk then they are not able to break down the lactose (the sugar in milk). Whether an allergy or intolerance occurs, most incidences occur without prior warning to the parents. How do you know if you are allergic to something unless you eat it and have a reaction? This can be a frightening event for both the infant and the parents or caregivers.

## Introduction of Solid Foods

Most experts agree that starting solid foods too soon in infants is not recommended and can lead to an increase in allergies and intolerances. Some parents tend to associate the early introduction of solid foods to advances in the child's development. Many new parents are excited to begin introducing new foods to the baby, but caution should be used. The digestive tract and kidneys may not be developed enough to handle some solid foods.

Below are some additional recommendations from the American Academy of Pediatrics on getting started with solid foods:

- Start with iron rich cereals, then vegetables, and then fruit last

- Start new foods one at a time and add new foods every 2–3 days

- Introduce wheat cereals last

- Raisins, nuts, popcorn, and small hard foods are not recommended

- Start with 1–2 small spoonfuls first[7]

Babies have a reflex called an **extrusion reflex**; if the baby is not quite ready for solid foods, they will push the food out of the mouth with their tongue. Some foods that are not recommended for infants under the age of 1 year old include:

---

[7] www.healthychildren.org

- Cow's milk or unpasteurized (raw) milk

- Honey

- Fruit juice, especially in bottles

- Chocolate or nuts

- Foods cut into coin shapes such as hot dogs or carrots

## FOOD IN FOCUS  Anti-Aging Foods

Imagine being able to eat your way to a younger version of yourself. Certain foods may be beneficial to help us grow old gracefully. Here are a few foods and the anti-aging properties they contain.

- Avocados - contain good fat, especially monounsaturated fat. Avocados are also a good source of vitamin E which is a powerful antioxidant.

- Nuts - especially walnuts and Brazil nuts. Add them to salads and yogurt. Although high in calories nuts contain good fat that can help to lower the bad cholesterol in the body.

- Berries - strawberries, blueberries, and raspberries are an excellent source of antioxidants. Add them to cereals or on top of angel food cake for a delicious dessert.

- Water - drinking adequate amounts of water everyday can help to cleanse the body of waste and toxins. Keeping well hydrated can also help to keep your skin looking healthy.

- Chocolate - especially dark chocolate contains more antioxidants than compared to milk chocolate. Research has shown that small amounts of dark chocolate may also help to lower your blood pressure.

- Beans - great source of fiber and protein. It is suggested that replacing at least two meals per week with more vegetarian-based entrees. Decreasing animal protein in the diet can be protective for the heart. More fiber in the diet can help to lower cholesterol.

- Green Tea - contains an antioxidant that has anti-aging properties. Drinking green tea on a daily basis helps to give you a more concentrated dose of antioxidants.

- Red Wine - contains resveratrol which is known to be beneficial for our health. Moderation in drinking alcohol is important. One drink per day for women and two drinks per day for men. A serving size of wine is 5oz.

- Cruciferous Vegetables - contain anti-cancer properties that may help to inhibit tumor growth. Our risk for cancer increases as we get older.

Of course there is no guarantee that you will get younger from just eating these foods alone. Exercise is also important in growing old gracefully.

### Baby Bottle Tooth Decay

It is not recommended to put an infant to bed with a bottle containing milk, formula, juice, or other sweetened beverages. The carbohydrate rich beverages will coat the inside of the infant's mouth with sugar. Bacteria from the sugar can dissolve the enamel on the teeth and can cause cavities.

## Childhood Nutrition

Nutrition during childhood is an important time when taste buds are being formed and food preferences are being established. This is a time for rapid growth and development. Childhood is usually divided into two different age groups. Preschool children aged 2 to 5 years old are one group, and children 6 to 11 years old are the second group. Both groups require balanced diets to support rapid growth and development. Both groups also come with challenges in meeting these nutrient requirements when poor eating habits are taught early. Today more than ever, the concern for overweight or obese children is rapidly increasing and has become a public health crisis. It is estimated that one in every three children ages 2–19 are overweight or obese.[8]

### Obesity among Low-Income Preschool Children

According to the Centers for Disease Control and Prevention, 1 of 3 children is obese or overweight before their fifth birthday, and 1 of 7 low-income, preschool-aged children is obese. American Indian, Alaska Native, and Hispanic children aged 2–4 years old are among those who are at highest risk. Children who are obese are more likely to have high blood pressure, high cholesterol, and type 2 diabetes as adults. Children who are obese at this young age are likely to be obese as adults.[9]

© 2012, Shutterstock, Inc.

### Teaching Good Eating Habits

Children learn food behaviors from their families. Parents and caregivers play a significant role in teaching children about healthy eating habits. When parents or caregivers eat more fruits and vegetables, then so do the children. Parents and caregivers have

---

[8] http://www.letsmove.gov/sites/letsmove.gov/files/TFCO_Challenge_We_Face.pdf
[9] http://www.cdc.gov/obesity/childhood.lowincome.html

many opportunities to teach good nutrition habits early to their children in the home, but food marketing can sometimes make this a difficult challenge. In a 2008 Executive Summary from the Federal Trade Commission, results of a study on marketing of foods to children and adolescents showed a dramatic increase in recent years. Beverage companies, fast food restaurants, packaged foods, cereals, prepared meals, and makers of candy and desserts all showed dramatic increases in the amount of money spent to promote their products to children ages 2–11 and adolescents ages 12–17. Television is the main source of this type of advertising. The more television children watch, the more advertisements for high calorie junk foods they will see. Virtual marketing (such as email and texting) is also gaining popularity. Promotional activities, prizes, and toys are ways that these products gain more popularity with children and adolescents. Children can recognize and ask for these products by name. This type of advertising undermines the efforts of parents and caregivers who try to teach better eating habits.[10]

### Food-Related Concerns

The consumption of certain foods has led to questions and concerns from parents. What about foods that may cause hyperactivity? Are there foods that cause autism? Are the growth hormones used in milk causing early onset of puberty in children, especially girls? These are valid concerns and there is research going on in all of these areas to try to answer these important questions. When parents and caregivers are concerned about food safety and other issues, the best thing they can do is to promote healthy eating habits by setting a good example. Less prepared foods, less fast food, and more whole foods is a great way to begin to do what is best for their children.

### Childhood Obesity

As previously mentioned, childhood obesity has become a nationwide concern. Even First Lady Michelle Obama has gotten involved and is passionate about her campaign, "Let's Move," to motivate U.S. children and families to adopt better exercise and eating habits. Defining obesity in children can be challenging. Telling a parent or caregiver that his/her child is overweight or obese can be a sensitive issue. Most experts agree that that the whole family needs to be involved in order for nutrition education to be effective. Everyone in the family needs to be supportive and commit to following the program for optimal success.

Obesity can be defined by using body mass index (BMI) for both girls and boys aged 2–19 years old. BMI is a number from the calculation of a child's height and weight. After the BMI is determined, the number is plotted on a BMI-age-for-age growth chart as listed below. A percentile ranking indicates where the child's BMI is and how

---

[10] http://www.ftc.gov/os/2008/07/P064504foodmktingreport.pdf

it is defined. This percentile is a comparison among children of the same sex and age. This chart is also listed below. BMI is not a diagnostic tool, meaning that the doctor cannot diagnose any illnesses or diseases based on this number alone. Further tests would have to be done.

## Adolescence and Young Adults

In this stage of life, many choices are being made. Seeking independence from parents to make their own decisions can be a time for adolescents learn good and bad habits. Parents have less influence on food choices made. Social and media influences are also heightened in this stage and peer pressure to eat certain foods can set the stage for unhealthy habits later in life. It is common in this life-

© 2012, Shutterstock, Inc.

stage for fast foods and sugary drinks to be consumed. The onset of puberty in this phase brings changes to the body. Growth spurts can cause weight gain. This is common with the onset of puberty, especially in girls. Boys and girls will usually reach maximum height in this phase of the lifespan and the body matures into adulthood. Physical activity and eating habits formed in this phase of the lifespan often continue well into adulthood and possibly a lifetime. Nutritional concerns for this age group include:

- Obesity

- Early onset of heart disease

- Mineral deficiencies

### Obesity in Adolescents

Obesity rates are growing rapidly among adolescents. According to the Center for Disease Control and Prevention, it is estimated that U.S. children aged 2–19 are overweight or obese. Obesity rates among the different ethnic groups show higher percentages of teens who are overweight or obese. Adolescents who are overweight or obese in this phase of the lifespan are likely to have weight-related health problems for a lifetime. Poor eating habits and lack of physical activity are

**Every Day**
## SUPERFOODS

Broccoli is a winter super food that is easy to grow and find in the grocery store. Steaming broccoli increases the fiber content which helps to lower LDL cholesterol.

mostly to blame. The current recommendations for physical activity are at least 60 minutes per day most days of the week. Homework, extracurricular activities, and other outside commitments sometimes do not allow adequate amounts of time for physical activity. Computer time, television watching, video games, etc. also account for the low amounts of physical activity that are being done on a daily basis.

### Chronic Diseases and Adolescents

Today we are seeing an increase in the number of adolescents who are developing heart disease as well as other chronic diseases such as high cholesterol, hypertension, and type 2 diabetes. Once thought to be adult onset, type 2 diabetes is a serious risk for adolescents who are overweight or obese, especially if they have a family history of diabetes. Heart disease risk and high cholesterol are usually caused by high fat intake, especially saturated fats found in fast foods.

**Table 12.2** BMI for Children

| Weight Status Category | Percentile Range |
|---|---|
| Underweight | Less than the 5th percentile |
| Healthy weight | 5th percentile to less than the 85th percentile |
| Overweight | 85th to less than the 95th percentile |
| Obese | Equal to or greater than the 95th percentile |

## Living Longer, Living Stronger

### Nutrition and Aging

As you have seen throughout this textbook, nutrition can positively and negatively impact our lives. To "grow old gracefully" requires a lifetime commitment to healthy eating and exercise. So much of what we do with our health as children and adults can play a role in what we can expect as we get older. Our aging population is growing. With advances in technology and medicine, people are living longer. The need for

© 2012, Shutterstock, Inc.

more health professionals in this field is growing. Geriatrics is the study of aging and many schools are offering degrees in this field. Being able to care for this population will require special skills and knowledge. According to the U.S. Census Bureau, the fastest growing segment of our aging population is those who are 85 or older.

## Life Expectancy vs. Lifespan

**Life expectancy** is the length of time a person born in a specific year can expect to live. For example, someone who was born in the year 1900 could expect to live to be 47 years old. Today our life expectancy is about 78 years old.[11] As previously mentioned, advances in technology and medicine have increased our life expectancy. **Lifespan** is how long a human being possibly could live. Currently the lifespan of a person born today is estimated to be between 120–130 years old.

### NUTRITION NERD ALERT

We need only 2 minutes every other day of direct mid-day sunlight to get the vitamin D we need on a daily basis. If you live in an area that has "June gloom" or visible pollution, like Los Angeles, you will need about 10–13 minutes of mid-day sun on these gloomy days. Milk is also a great source of vitamin D.

### Growing Old Gracefully

What is the secret to aging gracefully? How do we maintain a good quality of life as we age? These questions have been asked for centuries. The search for the fountain of youth has been told in many poems and fables. The answers are still not clear as to why we age but science may have some suggestions. Today's researchers look at lifestyles and behaviors that may extend our lives. The habits that may help to extend our lives include:

- Sleeping regularly (at least 7–8 hours per day)
- Regular physical activity
- Eating well-balanced meals, not skipping meals
- Not smoking
- Not using alcohol, or using it in moderation
- Maintaining a healthy body weight

---

[11] http://www.cdc.gov/nchs/fastats/lifexpec.htm

*Nutrition Intuition*

This list above is thought to have a positive impact on growing old gracefully. Over the years, these lifestyle choices accumulate. Those who follow these practices may have fewer disabilities and maintain better health. Quality of life is increased. Physical activity is one of the most important habits. Getting regular exercise can help to maintain better balance and mobility as we age.

## Physiological Changes with Aging

The aging process begins the minute we are born. Why we age is not exactly clear. Finding the fountain of youth has long been the desire of many. With aging comes many physiological changes. Listed below are some of those changes:

- Sight

- Hearing

- Digestive (producing less HCl in the stomach)

- Tooth loss

- Loss of lean body mass, gain of fat

- Decreased immune system

- Increased risk for disease

I know getting older does not sound like fun, but remember that we will all be there someday (some of us faster than others). Being sensitive to the needs of our growing aging population is very important. Strong evidence suggests that genetics play a role in our longevity. If you have parents, grandparents, etc. who lived in to their 90s and above, you have a higher chance of living longer too. I believe that you can also live longer by making better choices for your health. Nutrition can improve your quality of life.

© 2012, Shutterstock, Inc.

## Nutrition Concerns with Aging

As we get older our risk for nutritional deficiencies increases. Illnesses can greatly impact our health as we get older. Weight loss during an illness can negatively impact the immune system. Other factors that may have an impact on nutritional concerns are economic factors. Is there enough money to buy food and medications? Is there adequate social and family support? So many factors can impact the health and well being of our seniors. Macronutrients as well as vitamins and minerals may not be adequate in the diet. The following contributing factors may lead to a decrease in food intake:

- Reduced taste and smell

- Difficulty chewing or swallowing

- Tooth loss, ill-fitting dentures

- Lack of income

- Reduced mobility or ability to prepare food

- Depression

Decreases in taste and smell are sometimes related to aging and sometimes related to taking medications. Medications can often alter taste and smell and decrease the appetite. Difficulty chewing or swallowing leads to decreases in food intake. The risk for choking or aspiration is especially increased in those who have had a stroke. Tooth loss or ill-fitting dentures can also lead to decreased food intake. Modifications in food textures and offering softer foods can sometimes help, but these foods may be deficient in some nutrients. A lack of income can determine what kinds of foods or how much food is affordable. Budgeting for food is important but sometimes medical and medication costs outweigh the food costs. Some seniors may have to rely on using food banks, Meals on Wheels, or participating in food programs at local senior centers. Reduced mobility or ability to prepare foods often leads to issues with malnutrition. Depression can occur among seniors, especially those who have chronic diseases, loss of mobility, and loss of a spouse or lack of friends or family. Depression can lead to thoughts of suicide in some older adults and suicide rates are surprisingly high when compared to other age groups.

Many dietary surveys conducted across the United States have shown similarities in micronutrients that are commonly deficient in older adults. Below is a list of common inadequate nutrients:

**EVERY DAY SUPERFOODS**

Proanthocyanidins in cranberries (the catechin-derivative phytochemicals). These phytochemicals may help to keep bacteria from colonizing and causing a bladder or urinary tract infection. They also contain vitamins A and C which help the body to fight infections naturally. This is especially important for older adults.

- Vitamins D, A, C, E, B6, and B12

- Minerals calcium, iron, folate, and zinc

- Low protein intake

## Weight Gain and Weight Loss in Older Adults

Obesity in older adults can lead to more complications associated with chronic diseases. As we age we lose lean body mass and gain fat. Additional weight gain can complicate issues with arthritis, osteoarthritis, and can lead to a higher risk for falls. Weight loss in older adults can also be a health risk. During periods of illness, small amounts of weight loss can lead to a weaker immune system and longer healing times.

## Healthy Eating for Older Adults

A common misconception about eating healthily is that is costs more. Today, most health professionals agree that eating healthier does not have to be expensive. We have discussed the importance of eating a healthy diet throughout the lifespan. Making healthier choices can begin with the following:

- Eat a variety of fruits and vegetables

- Focus on fiber intake

- Choose lean sources of protein

- Limit fat, especially saturated fat

- Enjoy sweets and salty foods in moderation

The amount that older adults can eat varies with the amount of physical activity that is being done on a daily basis. The modified pyramid for older adults below was developed to address nutrient needs and exercise recommendations. The modified pyramid was developed because researchers realize that, as we get older, our nutrient needs change.[12]

## Physical Activity for Older Adults

Staying active could lead to the fountain of youth. You already know the countless benefits of exercise and, as we age, these benefits continue to pay off. Regular exercise as we age can delay the onset of some chronic diseases such as heart disease and diabetes. Regular physical activity can also reduce arthritis pain, anxiety, and depression. The more active you are now, the better your mobility may be as you get older.

---

[12] http://nutrition.tufts.edu/research/modified-mypyramid-older-adults

There are four main types of exercise that are recommended for seniors:

- Endurance activities like dancing, walking, swimming, or riding a bike
- Strengthening exercises that build muscle
- Stretching exercises for flexibility
- Balance exercises to reduce falls

All of the above exercises can help to keep the heart strong and reduce age-related muscle loss. Some research has also found that exercise helps to strengthen our brains too. Learning a new exercise or learning how to dance can make new connections in the brain and improve cognitive function.

## Summary

The health of a woman before she gets pregnant is just as important as during pregnancy. Preconception planning can help to ensure a healthy pregnancy. The truth is that most pregnancies are not planned, and women who may become pregnant should take responsibility to be prepared. The health of the man is also important. In-utero research is finding that the developing fetus is vulnerable at different stages of development. Genetic testing and other first trimester screenings can help the parents to prepare and become aware of problems that may arise with the pregnancy.

The prenatal period is the time from conception to the time the baby is delivered. The approximate length of the pregnancy is between 38–42 weeks. In about 6 weeks, the mass of cells will start to resemble an embryo. After 8 weeks, the embryo is referred to as a fetus. The pregnancy is divided into trimesters or stages. In each trimester, there is rapid growth and development. Exposure to teratogens during any phase of the pregnancy can be dangerous, but this is especially so during the first trimester.

Throughout the pregnancy the developing fetus relies on the mother for a steady supply of blood, oxygen, and nutrients. The placenta serves as the organ in pregnancy that connects the mother to the baby. Many substances can pass the placenta and potentially harm the baby. A healthy diet is very important during the pregnancy. At about 37 weeks, the developing fetus is physiologically mature and is ready to survive outside the womb. If the delivery of the infant comes too soon, there can be complications.

If the woman is suffering from malnutrition or has poor eating habits, she may risk having a low-birth-weight baby. A low-birth-weight (LBW) baby is one who weighs less than 5.5 pounds. A preterm baby is born before 37 weeks. A preterm baby is usually a LBW baby and may be at risk for health complications, especially in the first year of life.

Common nutrition-related concerns during the pregnancy include morning sickness, tiredness, and swollen hands and feet. Some women also suffer from constipation and heartburn. Food cravings for sweet or savory foods can lead to the consumption of odd combinations of foods. Pica is a condition in which women might crave non-food items such as clay, dirt, ice, etc.

Weight gain with pregnancy is important. Too much weight gain as well as too little weight gain can affect the developing fetus. There are not any additional calorie needs during the first trimester. During the second and third trimesters, pregnant women can consume an additional 300 calories per day, which is an additional serving from all the food groups. Recommended weight gains during pregnancy are presented in the chapter.

Gestational diabetes (GDM) and pregnancy-induced hypertension (PIH) are two conditions that have nutrition-related concerns. GDM is a condition that affects as many as 18% of pregnancies. GDM is characterized by elevation of maternal blood glucose possibly related to the various pregnancy hormones present in the body. Excess glucose will pass to the baby and can cause the baby to become too big, among other problems.

Pregnancy-induced hypertension (PIH) is a condition associated with high blood pressure. High blood pressure can cause many health problems for the mother and the baby. PIH is treated with bed rest and sometimes medications. If all other treatments fail, the delivery of the baby is the only cure.

Physical activity during pregnancy is beneficial. Exercise can help with boosting energy levels and mood and may help with an easier labor and delivery. Eating healthily and exercising during pregnancy is a great way to control weight gain. Suggestions for exercise are included in the chapter.

Breastfeeding involves the coordination of several hormones. Prolactin is the hormone that helps the body to produce milk at the end of the pregnancy. Progesterone and estrogen are at higher levels during the pregnancy and they suppress prolactin. The hormone oxytocin assists with the let down reflex and allows the milk to flow into the mammary glands. The first milk that is produced is called colostrum and is full of rich proteins and antibodies to help the baby establish his/her immune system.

Healthy eating during breastfeeding requires more calories than pregnancy. 500–700 calories more per day are needed to support the energy needed for breastfeeding. MyPlate.com is a helpful website that can help breastfeeding moms plan healthy meals.

There are advantages of breastfeeding for both mom and baby. Studies show that breastfed infants have lower incidence of ear infections, less gastrointestinal problems, less allergies, and many more benefits. Breastfed infants may also have higher IQs than those infants who were not breastfed. Benefits of breastfeeding for the mother include a lower risk for type 2 diabetes, breast cancer, ovarian cancer, and postpartum depression.

Breast milk is the best food to feed an infant and most health professionals agree that exclusive breastfeeding for the first 6 months of life can have lifelong benefits to the infant. Comparison of breast milk to formulas has shown that breast milk is superior in quality. However, there are some reasons why some women cannot breast feed, in which case formula is the only option.

At about 6 months of age, most infants will begin to explore new foods. The introduction of solid foods can be fun and exciting and sometimes a little stressful for parents or caregivers. This is also the time that food allergies or intolerances usually occur. A food allergy involves the immune system; reactions can be very mild to very severe. Food intolerances will not activate the immune system but symptoms will occur.

Introduction of solid foods should occur gradually, introducing new foods every few days. The best way to introduce solid foods is to try cereals first, then vegetables, and then fruits last. Once they taste the sugar, there is no going back. There are certain foods that babies under 1 year old should not have, these include cow's milk (unpasteurized), honey, fruit juice in bottles, chocolate or nuts, and foods cut into coin shapes that may pose a choking hazard.

Baby bottle tooth decay occurs when parents or caregivers put the baby to bed with a bottle filled with milk, juice, or other sugary drinks. Baby bottle tooth decay can dissolve the enamel on the teeth and can cause cavities.

Childhood is divided into two sections, the 2–5 year olds and the 6–11 year olds. Both present challenges in teaching healthy eating habits. Rapid growth and development occur during this time and lifelong habits are being formed.

Obesity is prevalent among low-income preschool-aged children. Statistics show that low-income preschoolers are disproportionately affected by obesity due to lack of access to healthy foods. It is estimated that 1 of 7 low-income children are overweight or obese. Additional efforts and resources are needed in this area to educate and provide healthier options for these children.

Teaching healthy eating habits is a big responsibility for parents and caregivers. Television and social media heavily market unhealthy food options to these age groups. Children learn how to ask for certain brand names and can identify many brands at a very young age. This type of advertising can interfere with the efforts made by the parents and caregivers to teach their children good eating habits.

Food-related concerns are questions about the safety of foods and questioning the consumption of certain foods that may contain harmful substances. The research is not quite clear on the outcomes, so for now the best thing that parents can do is to set a good example for their children. Serve your children less fast foods and less processed foods, and focus on using whole foods.

Childhood obesity is a nationwide concern that has received the attention of the first lady Michelle Obama. The Let's Move campaign is attempting to motivate and educate parents, children, and families about the importance of healthy eating and regular physical activity. Definitions for overweight and obese children are explained in the charts contained in the chapter.

In adolescence and young adulthood, many independent food choices are being made. Seeking independence from parents and caregivers and making decisions about food and countless other issues is a time when good and bad habits are formed. Just as with the younger children, heavy marketing of junk foods and sugary beverages also targets this age range. The onset of puberty brings changes to the body. Weight gain, especially in girls, can lead to feelings of insecurity. Dieting is usually attempted by girls in this age range and can lead to disordered eating behaviors or worse can lead to eating disorders. Boys will usually reach maximum height in this phase of development. Boys may have big appetites which can lead to the intake of high calorie foods.

Just as with younger children, obesity rates in adolescents and young adults is climbing. According to the CDC, 17% of children ages 2–19 are overweight or obese. Computer time, television watching, extracurricular activities, and other commitments make it difficult to participate in adequate amounts of physical activity on a daily basis. The increase in obesity brings the onset of chronic diseases at a younger age. Children and adolescents are now developing hypertension, high cholesterol, heart disease, and type 2 diabetes, all diseases that were once thought to happen only to older adults.

The fountain of youth may be found in eating healthy and exercising. Healthy habits are the key to living a healthy long life, and research has shown us that healthy habits can benefit us for many years to come. Our aging population is growing rapidly. Caring for this population will require special skills and knowledge. Advances in technology are allowing people to live longer. What is the use of living longer if you have numerous health problems? The fastest growing segment of the population is those who are 85 or older.

# GIVING YOUR BABY THE VERY BEST NUTRITION

Babies grow so quickly, and their needs constantly change. Here are answers to important questions you may have about your baby's nutrition.

© 2012, Shutterstock, Inc.

## What can I expect my baby to do as he grows?

*From birth to 1 month of age, your baby will*

- Begin to develop the ability to start and stop sucking.
- Wake up and fall asleep easily.

*At about 3 to 4 months of age, your baby will*

- Drool more.
- Put his hand in his mouth a lot.

*At 4 to 6 months of age, your baby will*

- Bring objects to his mouth.
- Begin to eat solid foods, such as iron-fortified infant cereal and pureed or strained fruits and vegetables.
- Explore foods with his mouth.

## What should I feed my baby?

- Breastmilk is the ideal food for babies, and breastfeeding offers many benefits to both mother and baby. Breastfeeding helps mother and baby form a special bond, and it helps the baby resist colds, ear infections, allergies, and other illnesses.
- It is best to breastfeed for the first 6 months of life, but breastfeeding even for just a few months or weeks is beneficial.
- If you think you may not be able to breastfeed (for example, you have conflicts with school or work or a medical condition), or you are worried about not producing enough breastmilk, talk to a health professional, breastfeeding specialist, or breastfeeding support group. They can answer your questions and help you come up with solutions. Your family and friends are also sources of support.
- If you decide to feed your baby infant formula, a health professional can help you choose the right kind and answer your questions about feeding.
- Cow's milk, goat's milk, and soy milk are not recommended until after your baby's first birthday.

## How do I know if I am feeding my baby enough breastmilk?

- Your baby may show she is still hungry by sucking, putting her hands in her mouth, opening and closing her mouth, or looking for the nipple. She may show she is full by falling asleep.
- Your baby will usually have five to eight wet diapers and three or four stools per day by the time she is 5 to 7 days old.
- Your baby will be gaining weight. She should gain 5 to 7 ounces per week and should double her birthweight by 4 to 6 months of age.

## When and how should I introduce solid foods?

- Introduce solid foods when your baby can sit with support and has good head and neck control.
- Offer iron-fortified rice cereal as the first solid food, because it is least likely to cause an allergic reaction, such as a rash. Offer a small amount (for example, 1 or 2 teaspoons) of one new food at a time. Wait 7 days or more to see how your baby tolerates the new food before introducing the next new food.
- Introduce solid foods in this order: iron-fortified infant cereal, fruits and vegetables, and meats.
- Avoid foods that may cause choking, such as hard candy, mini-marshmallows, popcorn, pretzels, chips, spoonfuls of peanut butter, nuts, seeds, large chunks of meat, hot dogs, raw carrots, raisins and other dried fruits, and whole grapes.
- Do not add honey to food, water, or infant formula because it can be a source of spores that cause botulism, which can poison your baby.
- Do not add cereal to bottles, and do not use "baby food nurser kits" (which let solid foods filter through the bottle nipple along with the liquid). Your child may choke on the cereal.

## How do I avoid feeding my baby too much?

- Learn how your baby shows he is hungry, and feed him when he is hungry.
- Feed your baby slowly. Do not enlarge the hole in the bottle nipple to make expressed breastmilk or infant formula come out faster.
- Do not add cereal to the bottle—this may cause your baby to eat more than he needs.
- Comfort your baby by talking to him and by cuddling, rocking, and walking him—not by feeding him. Using food to comfort your baby may teach him to use food as a source of comfort as he gets older.
- Feed your baby until he is full. It takes about 20 minutes for your baby to feel full. Do not force him to finish a bottle or other foods.

## Resources

**American Dietetic Association**
Phone: (800) 366-1655
Web site: http://www.eatright.org

**La Leche League International**
Phone: (800) 525-3243
**Web site: http://www.lalecheleague.org**

**USDA Food and Nutrition Information Center**
Phone: (703) 305-2554
**Web site: http://www.nal.usda.gov/fnic**

This fact sheet contains general Information and is not a substitute for talking with your baby's health professional about your particular concerns about your baby.